D1396856

Journey Song

Journey Song

A Spiritual Legacy
of the
American Indian

Celinda Reynolds Kaelin

Foreword by Ed McGaa, EAGLE MAN

Four Directions Publishing

Credits:

Cover Art: "Black Elk's Vision" by Daryl No Heart

Text and Cover Design: Graphics West, Inc., Colorado Springs, Colorado

Front and Back Illustrations: J. L. "Zeph" Zephier

Chapter Illustrations: Melinda Hazzard

Chapter Quotations: All are excerpted from *Soul of an Indian* written by Ohiyesa (1858–1939) and edited by Kent Nerburn © 1995. Reprinted courtesy of New World Library, Novoto, California.

Library of Congress Cataloging-in-Publication Data

Kaelin, Celinda Reynolds.
   Journey Song: a spiritual legacy of the American Indian/
   Celinda Reynolds Kaelin
      p.   cm.
   Includes index and bibliographical references.
   ISBN 0-9645173-8-8
   1. Spirituality. 2. Nature—Religious aspects. 3. American Indians—
   Religion and mythology. 4. New Age movement.

                                        98-92949
                                        CIP

This First Edition printing by arrangement with Millennia Graphics LLC, Colorado Springs, Colorado.

Contents

Preface

I am not an academic philosopher. I am simply an ordinary human being, but my life and curiosity have led me along a fascinating path of ever-increasing philosophical and spiritual awareness. At the outset of my journey I demanded that any Unified Theory of Reality must embrace the physical world (including current scientific knowledge), the spiritual world, and all of the mysteries throughout the cosmos. Ironically, I found the answer to my quest in traditional American Indian wisdom. The Sioux Indians call the path to wisdom *Okiksapa,* and this is my journey song to share this path. Before I begin my story I would like to give you a thumbnail sketch of the history of our current, modern philosophy.

Western civilization stumbled along for fifteen hundred years after the birth of Christ, guided primarily by religious teachings. Then, in the 1600s, there was a revolution in thinking as human beings began to see the physical world in scientific instead of religious terms. Galileo was severely censured by the Catholic Church for proposing that the earth was not the center of the universe. Pilgrims flocked to begin a New World on the American continent, expressly seeking religious freedom in the form of secular government. And finally, a French mathematician and philosopher, René Descartes, proposed that the universe consisted of two separate realities: the spiritual and the physical (Cartesian Duality). Significantly, there has been no new philosophical system since Descartes despite the incredible scientific advances since the seventeenth century.

Once Einstein proposed and proved his mass energy equivalency theory ($E = MC^2$) in 1905, the distinction between the spiritual and the material began to erode. Then came Quantum Mechanics (1926), which proved beyond a doubt that the physical properties of this world are all illusion. Today we know that all of the universe is pulsating energy with constant subatomic interchanges throughout the cosmos. These scientific advances of the last four hundred years have virtually destroyed Descartes's philosophical notion of the separateness of physical and spiritual. An understanding of our role in the universe can no longer remain stagnated in seventeenth century philosophy while we stand, confused, in the maelstrom of twentieth century technology. Scientists have validated what many cultures, especially the American Indian, have always taught. All is One. The Sioux Indians express this idea with the phrase "MITAKUYE OYASIN (Me-tah-KOOH-ye O-yah-SIN). We are all related."

Great Spirit guided me in developing a philosophical system for this re-awareness that All is One, and I call it unitheism. We are entering the new millennium in the throes of a global environmental crisis, and we must have a new philosophical system to guide us in saving our Mother Earth. It is imperative that we fully understand that there is no separation between us, God/Great Spirit, other human beings, Mother Earth, and the cosmos. This Unified Theory of Reality reflects a cosmic symbiosis at work. Ironically, the very culture that our dominant society tried so hard to eradicate during the past century will provide the spiritual leadership that can now save our planet. This was Black Elk's prophetic vision. This book explains and illustrates unitheism and American Indian Spirituality so that we can learn to live in peace, love, and harmony in the twenty-first century.

Journey song is a phrase that comes from American Indian culture meaning "word map." These first Americans, with few exceptions, had no written language. Consequently, there were no maps to facilitate travel from one section of the country to another. They cleverly compensated by encapsulating directions for travel in verse. These verses lent themselves to easy memorization and so could be readily transferred from one person to another. Journey songs were traded for fur pelts, beads, or other items at Pow Wows or at the white man's Fur Rendezvous. In a similar vein, I have named this book *Journey Song* because it documents the path of my spiritual journey. I offer my philosophical system of unitheism and its expression in American Indian spirituality as a gift. I hope that it will bring you the comfort and guidance you seek.

There is an old American Indian myth concerning the spiritual properties of tobacco that will serve as a metaphor for sharing the *Okiksapa* of this book.

* * *

Many snows ago, there were four brothers who lived in a large village. They were all Shamans [holy men]. One day, Great Spirit taught them the secrets of tobacco. He taught them that the rising smoke mingled with their breath and carried their prayers up to the heavens to Great Spirit. He taught them the ceremonies and the special songs and chants for planting the tobacco and harvesting it. All of these things Great Spirit taught these four brothers. They became proud in their knowledge, however, and didn't want to share it with the people. They wanted to keep all of the power of tobacco to themselves.

In the meantime, an Old Man and Woman left their village as they could no longer be of use. In the Indian way, they decided that their time to live had come to a close. If they stayed in the village, they would not be able to join the hunt, nor help with the work needed to keep their tribe alive. Food and other provisions were scarce. So the two old people left the village and went to wait for death by the banks of a stream.

One night the Old Man and Woman were awakened by strange voices singing beautiful songs. They arose and followed the sounds to the stream. There, Brother Beaver greeted them and took them to the beaver lodge at the bottom of a small pond. The Beaver People welcomed the Old Man and Woman, and spent that night and the next three nights teaching them both all of the secrets of tobacco. When they had been taught all that they needed to know, the Beaver People told them to return to their village and share their knowledge with all of their people. This they did.

In the spring, Great Spirit sent rains that destroyed all of the tobacco crops of the four Shamans. The Old Man and Woman spent that same spring, however, traveling from village to village teaching the sacred ways of tobacco. Their fresh, new seed from the Beaver People was planted in each village and these tobacco crops thrived. Now all of the people were able to send their prayers to Great Spirit as their breath mingled with the tobacco smoke and rose into the skies.

* * *

It is not the American Indian way to proselytize, nor to force one's beliefs or ways upon another. However, as this legend teaches, one **is** obligated to share the truth that has been given by the Great Spirit. The following pages of this book are offered as a gift. I wish to pass on some of the wisdom that life's journey has brought to me. My life has been filled with many tragedies, difficulties, and mistakes; but these have been more than offset by the love offered by my fellow travelers and by the new understanding of Great Spirit (God) and His/Her universe that I acquired along the way.

In the American Indian tradition, there are Seven Directions in this world: East, South, West, North, Father Sky, Mother Earth, and Within Ourselves. I now give you my *Journey Song* for travel in the Seventh Direction.

I wish you peace, love, and harmony. MITAKUYE OYASIN.

Celinda Reynolds Kaelin

Acknowledgments

This book is my gift to all of those who have surrounded me with their love. It is this harmonious energy that brought *Journey Song* into existence. I am simply the scribe who has been honored with recording the lessons that Great Spirit sent me through other two-leggeds and all of Mother Earth's other creatures. I am deeply indebted to all of these teachers.

I am especially blessed with my husband, Harold, who has given me his support and encouragement throughout the long and difficult process of generating this book. I can never thank Ed McGaa, EAGLE MAN, enough for believing in me, and for giving so much of his time and energy toward making this manuscript into a finished message.

My dear friend Jan McKamy is a special spirit who has generously lent her time and talents in copyediting and polishing these final words. I am so fortunate that Great Spirit set our paths to cross.

In addition, I am deeply thankful to Sharon Green and Dan Maio at Graphics West, Inc. for the final copyedit and text design, and to Lee Kilmer for the cover design.

Zeph Zephier's drawings are the perfect embodiment of the union of the spiritual and physical world as they clearly show us the Seventh Direction. Melinda Hazzard's drawings for each chapter focus an energy of beauty and simplicity that augments the energy of the words. I am deeply indebted to both artists for lending their medicine to this work.

It is my wish that these words will help you to see the beauty of Great Spirit's plan, and will lead you to peace, love, and harmony.

Foreword

If we two-leggeds are to save our Mother Earth and ourselves, then we must return to a belief system that provides an understanding that we are part of the whole universe, especially this planet. This solution lies in a new Life Way, as expressed by Native American spirituality.

In the 1800s, an Oglala Sioux holy man, Black Elk, foresaw this change in his powerful vision which he told to John Neihardt in *Black Elk Speaks*. When the Fourth Grandfather (the visionary entity representing the powers of the South) instructed Black Elk, it was about his ability to save life. "Younger Brother, with the powers of the Four Quarters you shall walk, a relative. Behold, the living center of a nation I shall give you, and with it many you shall save." [*Black Elk Speaks*, p. 24] Then, as this Grandfather held his red stick, it branched and sprouted leaves and was filled with singing birds. In the shade beneath it were the circled villages of people and every living thing, happily co-existing. Black Elk understood his vision to mean that "The sacred hoop of my people was one of many hoops that made one circle ... and in the center grew one mighty flowering tree to shelter all the children of one mother and one father. And I saw that it was holy." [*Black Elk Speaks*, p. 36]

In the mid 1970s, a second Oglala holy man, Frank Fools Crow, echoed Black Elk's teaching when he warned that "... these ceremonies do not belong to Indians alone. They can be done by all who have the right attitude, and who are honest and sincere about their beliefs in Wakan Tanka (Great Spirit) and in following his rules." Fools Crow went on to explain to his biographer Thomas E. Mails that "We (the American Indian) are the keepers of certain areas of knowledge, which we are to share for the good of mankind." [*Fools Crow* by Mails, p. 51] A host of other Native American spiritual leaders, including Bill Eagle Feather, Sun Bear, Midnight Song, John Lame Deer, and Ehanamani (Dr. A. C. Ross) agree that these traditional teachings must be shared.

Celinda Reynolds Kaelin's *Journey Song* provides a logical framework for these traditional American Indian spiritual teachings that will appeal to both Natives and non-Natives alike. Kaelin's life journey to this *okiksapa* (wisdom gained by experience) illustrates the process Great Spirit uses in bringing us to an understanding of Oneness. Her *sicun* (spirit guide), Philemon, is the same guide that led the philosopher and mystic, Carl G.

Jung, to rediscover *Black Elk Speaks* in 1962—after it had been out of print for over thirty years.

Most spiritual and religious teachings appeal directly to our emotions, thereby making differences in religious beliefs extremely volatile. Our evolution and survival as two-leggeds, however, was accomplished by thoughtful reflection. Even now, we do not make major decisions about our jobs, our cars, or our homes, without first thinking them through. We must be equally discerning in what we accept as spiritual truth. *Journey Song* sets forth a logic, the philosophy Kaelin calls unitheism, to help us in this work. Unitheism is a tapestry that is woven from numerous threads of truth. With this weaving in hand, we can now evaluate any teaching by viewing it within an overall pattern of truth. We can now see the beauty of Oneness, of Native American spirituality, in Great Spirit's tapestry of All that Is.

No one person, or group of people, can own Truth. Truth comes from Great Spirit and belongs to all people for all time. Native Americans have traveled the Black Road of the dominant society for the past century and a half. Now is the time to return to the Good Red Road of traditional Native American spirituality. Now is the time to show leadership by teaching the truth of Native American traditional Life Way to our brothers and sisters of all colors. MITAKUYE OYASIN.

Ed McGaa, EAGLE MAN, *Oglala Sioux*

About the Cover Artist

DARYL NO HEART, *Oyate Wankapi* (People Look at Him), is a full-blood Lakota/Dakota man, born on the Standing Rock Nation in North and South Dakota. He is a self-taught artist and longtime student of the history, culture, and spirituality of the Lakota/Dakota people. In both his work and daily life he is committed to preserving and sustaining the growth of traditional ways and values and to reviving the integral role the Winter Count society can play for people, culture, and tradition. Daryl No Heart and his wife Sharon live in St. Paul, Minnesota.

Black Elk's Vision

Black Elk, warrior and medicine man of the Oglala Sioux, was born in 1863 on the Little Powder River. During his long life, he saw the passage of his people from nomadic nation, to a warrior nation, to a conquered nation incarcerated on an island of land. When he was nine years old, he was given a great vision foretelling these and other changes in the fate of his People and Mother Earth.

... The next day the camp moved on to where the different bands of our people were coming together, and I rode in a pony drag, for I was very sick. Both my legs and both my arms were swollen badly and my face was all puffed up.

When we had camped again, I was lying in our tepee and my mother and father were sitting beside me. I could see out through the opening, and there two men were coming from the clouds, headfirst like arrows slanting down, and I knew they were the same that I had seen before. Each now carried a long spear, and from the points of these a jagged lightning flashed. They came clear down to the ground this time and stood a little way off and looked at me and said: "Hurry! Come! Your Grandfathers are calling you! ..."

Then the two [arrow] men spoke together and they said: "Behold him, the being with four legs!"

I looked and saw a bay horse standing there, and he began to speak: "Behold me!" he said. "My life history you shall see." Then he wheeled about to where the sun goes down, and said: "Behold them! Their history you shall know."

I looked, and there were twelve black horses yonder all abreast with necklaces of bison hoofs, and they were beautiful, but I was frightened,

*because their manes were lightning and there was thunder in their
nostrils ... Then all the horses went into formation, four abreast ...*

*   The two men with the spears now stood beside me, one on either
hand, and the horses took their places in their quarters, looking inward, four
by four. And the oldest of the Grandfathers [the Grandfather or Power of
the West] spoke with a kind voice and said: "Come right in and do not
fear ... Your Grandfathers all over the world are having a council, and
they have called you here to teach you."* [Black Elk Speaks, pp. 18–21]

In a later segment of his vision, Black Elk was given the herb of understanding, which he planted on earth where it blossomed and grew toward
the heavens; and the rays from its flowers penetrated all darkness. This
vision, and his life, are documented in the best seller *Black Elk Speaks* by
John G. Neihardt.

Dedication

For Harold
and
for all my Red brothers and sisters
who have shared their journey song
for travel in the Seventh Direction.

Admonition of the Creator, Great Spirit, to New Travelers

Somewhere to the south there is a large camp in which beauty and peace abide. There is a council lodge, and inside it sits one they call Grandfather [the Creator]. One day he calls out to a man and woman, and both of them come sit in his lodge.

And he says to them, "You are now going to make a long journey, so do the best you can. Someday in the future you will come back here again. And then you will be asked to tell about how your journey fared. So go now, both of you. But never own more than you need."

Marla N. Powers, *Oglala Women*

We Have Endured

If you talk to the animals they will talk with you and you will know each other. If you do not talk to them, you will not know them, and what you do not know you will fear. What one fears, one destroys.

Unitheism—We Are All One

> *"Let us not forget that even for the most contemporary thinker, who sees a majesty and grandeur in natural law, science cannot explain everything. We all still have to face the ultimate miracle—the origin and principle of life."*
>
> Ohiyesa (Sioux)
> *The Soul of an Indian*

If there is a God who is all-knowing, all-powerful, and all-loving, then why does He/She allow such horrible things to happen on this earth?

Why do thousands of innocent children die terrible deaths each day? Why didn't God intervene to prevent such a monstrous act as the Holocaust? Why did an all-loving, all-powerful God intervene in Biblical times, and then remain passive and detached in historic times? Is evil, then, a permanent and necessary part of life? Where is God? Who is God? And what is God's role in His world? Is God relevant to the daily events of my life? Can I find God only through sanctioned religious practices? Is it possible to have a personal relationship with God, or do I have to have an intermediary? Should I even care whether or not there is a God?

There are so many questions that trouble most people about God—what I have listed here is only a sampling. When I began my search for the answers to these questions, I found that there are only evasive half-answers at best. This was unacceptable to me. So I began to re-examine teachings learned from my American Indian friends. Then I used the principles of modern physics to evaluate these teachings, and they became even more clear and valid. Here at last was truth.

This mingling of ancient American Indian wisdom and modern scientific knowledge gave birth to a philosophical paradigm that I call Unitheism.

This paradigm is based on the hypothesis that everything in the Universe is energy, and that everyone and everything in the Universe is part of this energy. We are all One. The idea of Oneness is ancient. What is new, however, is the logical process that supports the conclusion of Oneness and the logical framework that provides for true answers to life's questions. For me, it was imperative that my philosophy and all known scientific principles be consistent. One could not contradict the other, for that would indicate two separate realities. Life, and my curiosity, have propelled me along a fascinating path that culminated in this philosophy of Unitheism.

When I was young, I was excessively sheltered from the real world around me. My family almost always lived in remote areas and had few neighbors. We were a close-knit unit, and had little contact with the world outside our loving family circle. We suffered many hard times, but each trauma that assailed us only served to bring us closer together. Healing, life-giving love seemed always to be the answer, so I never asked the big questions of life. This all changed for me with the death of my oldest brother, John.

John and I were four years apart, but we were always close friends. There were originally eleven children in our family, but two of them died when they were infants. Of the nine surviving children, six were boys and I was the youngest of three girls. Our family's history was filled with tragic events—loss of one home to flood, loss of a second home to fire, the early death of our mother, and the hardships of a genteel, subsistence poverty.

One of my earliest memories of John was in 1951, when I was four years old. We were then living at our newly built *hacienda* on our farm, the Reynolds Dairy. It was located a few miles north of Old Town Square in Albuquerque, New Mexico. Johnny and I were out on a warm summer night, sitting on the clover-strewn banks of our irrigation ditch. We watched shooting stars in the dark velvet of the desert sky, as John told me an enchanting story of a rabbit who outsmarted a coyote.

I don't know why certain memories such as this stick in one's mind. It is the only recollection I have of that particular home. Dad built the house himself—it was a traditional adobe hacienda, plastered with clay, imbued with the earth tones of the Rio Grande Valley. Each day, exuberant rose-colored sunrises greeted us as we played along the veranda that ran the length of the east side of the hacienda. All of the wooden porch railings, windows, and doors were painted a turquoise blue that matched our clear New Mexico sky. Age-gnarled cottonwoods towered over our roof, sheltering it from the heat of a relentless sun. Waters diverted from the Rio

Grande River coursed through a narrow irrigation ditch with the soothing tones of life-giving moisture.

This idyllic beauty was shattered, however, when Dad suffered a severe heart attack. He was hospitalized for almost a year, and my mother sold our lovely hacienda to pay the hospital bills. It must have been hard for her when we then moved south of Albuquerque.

This new farmhouse was also adobe, but it had only two bedrooms for her six children. Dad soon solved the problem by converting the garage into a dormitory for us kids. After insulating the walls and covering them with wall board, he placed four beds side by side down the length of the room. We children enjoyed the companionship of being so near one another at night. We often filled the darkness with highly embellished stories of monsters, ghosts, and wild animals. At nap time, our favorite sport was turning somersaults from one bed to the next for the full span of beds. My sisters, Pat and Barb, had a room to themselves. They were older than I—almost ten years separated us—so I was allowed the fun of bunking in the dormitory with the boys.

When we weren't busy with chores around the farm, my brothers and I loved playing cowboys and Indians. I almost always preferred to play the part of Indian, and since I was outnumbered by brothers, I was frequently "burned at the stake." That is to say, I was captured and literally tied to the post preparatory to "burning." When Mother called everyone to dinner, I was usually far out in the pasture, firmly bound to a post under the old cottonwood tree. I insisted that I would be able to free myself, and so my brothers simply left me in my captive posture. Of course, my stubbornness almost always netted my three brothers a severe reprimand for "being so mean to their little sister."

Three more little boys were born to my parents while we lived on this farm. The first to arrive were twins, Thomas Roderick and George Jeffrey, or Rod and Jeff. Then, two years later, came the baby of the family, James. Jamie (as we affectionately called him) was the darling of all his older brothers and sisters. He had sparkling blue eyes, blond hair, and was covered with freckles. We boisterously vied with one another for Jamie's attention, and indulged him too much for his own good. Rod and Jeff took the new competition in stride and lost themselves each day in one another's companionship. While they were young they were impossible to tell apart, and our parents delighted in dressing them in identical outfits. Sundays at church were always a great show. We had all been given the obligatory Saturday night bath, and were dressed in our best clothes for the march down the aisle on Sunday morning. This was always done with precise deliberation; the oldest child led the way followed by the remaining siblings in strict birth order. Of course, all decorum was lost when it came time to be seated. Each of us children considered it an enormous treat to sit next to Mom or Dad, so we created many unholy squabbles as we fought for a seat of honor.

Not long after James' birth, the railroad began enhancing the rain/flood diversion ditch near their tracks. These tracks and the ditch were about a quarter of a mile from our farm and a source of great entertainment for us. John and Tim tested my bravery many times by daring me to stand under the old wooden trestle bridge as the train rumbled overhead.

My family's short respite from troubles was shattered late one August night. Torrents of rain pelted our farm, filling the irrigation ditches and spilling over their banks. High above us the dry, hard soil of the Monzano Mountains shed sheet after sheet of the drenching rain down into our valley. Highly vulnerable, the altered drainage ditch melted away below the heavy mountain runoff. Under the cover of night, muddy sheets of water slithered over the railroad tracks and inched toward our silent farm house. I was sound asleep and only remember my father carrying me out to the car in the ankle-deep water. My mother quickly counted heads and found that my next youngest brother, Mark, had slipped into the house and back into bed. Dad went back after him, and we were barely down the road before a four-foot wall of muddy water broke through and destroyed our little adobe house. Fortunately, we were blessed with friends and neighbors who each took a child or two. My little brother Mark and I spent the next year on a dairy farm about four miles south of our ruined home.

We were extraordinarily fortunate that the Nanningas, who were warm and caring, gave us a foster home. They had two sons, Robert (Robbie) and Mark, who were about the same ages as my Mark and I. Robbie and I had been best friends from the time we had met at our friend Jane's fourth birthday party. Mark and I couldn't have had a more loving foster family, and we had a rollicking good time. I was about eight years old and Mark was six. The four of us teased the bulls, helped milk the cows, and chased the large white geese.

My older brothers, John and Tim (who were twelve and ten), weren't quite so fortunate. Dad almost immediately began building a new house on ranch land he owned just west of Albuquerque. He conscripted John and Tim as his entire construction crew. The three of them lived in a one-room hut made of adobe, with no running water and no electricity. Each day the two boys toiled under the merciless sun as they mixed mud and laid the ten-pound adobe bricks on top of one another. Slowly, the shell of a six-bedroom house began to take shape. After two years of intense labor, they eased the twenty-foot long *vegas* for the ceiling into place and nailed a herringbone pattern of boards onto their rounded edges. At last our family could be reunited!

Dad named our new home *Rancho Alegre*—the Happy Ranch. He carefully sawed a number of wooden planks, attached them to one another, and painted the name of our ranch on the rough surface. He hung his sign from a framework of vegas down at the gate where it gaily danced in each sandstorm. We still had no running water or electricity, but it was wonderful to be together as a family once more. We felt that our ranch was appropriately named. Construction progressed slowly, but we soon had a kitchen with real faucets that spewed ice-cold well water when turned on. We no longer had to use the outhouse either. This was most welcome to me, as my brothers always waited for me to shut the door of the privy so that they could torment me. They would howl like coyotes and shake the building, or drop lizards, stink bugs and whatever else they could find through the knothole above the seat.

In self-defense (of course), I chased an offending brother and brought him to the ground with a flying tackle. I then sat on his chest and pounded him soundly until he agreed to leave me alone. My behavior held little promise of my ever turning into a lady—as my mother constantly lamented. I was hopeless. I whistled whenever I got the chance, ran and wrestled on impulse, and even joined my brothers in chewing tobacco. As a concession to my mother's sensibilities, however, I swallowed the fiery tobacco juices for it was well known that "ladies don't spit."

My brothers and I walked about a quarter mile to the bus stop each morning. (Rod maintains that I drove them all crazy as I sang the *Sound of Music* over and over until the bus arrived. Singing is not one of my gifts even though I love to do it. In retrospect, I probably should have sung to the boys instead of tackling them. My back would probably be in better shape today.) We then chatted with our friends for an hour as the bus wound its way across the sand hills and into town to our school. One day as the bus rattled across the mesa and descended toward our ranch, we spotted a huge plume of black smoke. A fire! Since there was only sagebrush and buffalo grass on the mesa, it had to be a building. As the bus pulled to a stop at our gate, flames danced around our new hacienda. Stunned, my brothers and I raced past the cluster of fire trucks and stared open-mouthed at the charred adobe walls. Dad suspected that a chimney fire from the wood stove was to blame. Once again, we were farmed out to friends and neighbors as Mom and Dad attempted to rebuild their lives.

This last blow proved to be too much for my mother. After several months we were all reunited at the partially reconstructed *Rancho Alegre*, but Mom just wasn't the same. She was often in a great deal of pain, and even the brightly colored bouquets of crimson Indian paintbrush and purple asters we picked for her could not cheer her. She would sit quietly for hours with a faraway look in her eyes. Within a year she was dead from an inoperable brain tumor. I had never seen my father cry until her funeral. It all seemed completely unreal to me. I was sure that Mom wouldn't leave us. God could not, would not, take her away. I was about twelve at the time, and I knew that she had been very, very tired. I knew that she needed a rest, and I was glad if she was able to find it, but I was also sure that she would be coming back.

One day at school shortly after the funeral, an elderly nun pulled me aside on my way to class.

"You poor child, I'm so sorry about your mother."

I looked down at my shoes awkwardly. It was difficult to respond to the many well-intentioned expressions of sympathy. I didn't know what to say.

"Your family has certainly had a lot of tragedy! The flood, the fire, now your mom's death. Your family must be very wicked for God to punish you so."

I caught my breath. I couldn't believe what I was hearing. My family was wicked? Most certainly not! I simply stared into the watery blue eyes of the good sister, but said nothing. One did not dare to speak back, for punishment was swift and painful. But indignation welled up within me. My family was not wicked!

It wasn't long after Mom's death before Dad began to seek comfort in his work. He was also plagued by excruciating sinus headaches, and his coffee cup usually contained a few inches of "hooch" as medicine. My sisters, Pat and Barb, were married and had lives of their own by this time. My brothers and I floundered, lost and confused. Then two ladies from the Department of Social Services came to the ranch. A concerned relative had contacted them, and they wanted to place my brothers and me in an orphanage. We couldn't have been more upset if someone had placed a bomb in our midst. We were all best friends; we loved one another; we would **not** be separated again. We were adamant and quite vocal. We were granted a temporary reprieve.

Dad called a family meeting at the kitchen table after the ladies left. We wanted to know how we could avoid being permanently separated. What could we do so that we could stay together? Dad outlined their concerns. Were we fed regularly? Why was our clothing tattered and in need of ironing? Was our house clean and orderly? Were we properly supervised?

Almost all of us were on the honor roll at school and we were never tardy or truant, so the question of supervision was not relevant. Yes, our clothing was deplorable. Our house was still under construction, so the boys and I still spent every spare moment hammering, plastering, or painting; and our clothing showed it. Also, every spare penny was used for building materials and food and there was none left over for a wardrobe. I volunteered to see that all our clothing was washed, patched, and ironed. I would also do the cooking, if the boys would set the table and clean up afterward. It was all agreed. We would be a solid team—all for one, and one for all.

From then on we wore clean, patched, and freshly ironed outfits to school. All our meals were on schedule. Pancakes every morning for breakfast with a syrup made from sugar and a drop of maple flavoring. Peanut butter sandwiches every day for lunch. Deer meat and pinto beans every night for supper. Our house was clean and orderly, even though we still lived in the turmoil of constant construction. We won the battle. We were not separated and sent to an orphanage. We succeeded against overwhelming odds.

My father worked the ranch during the day and painted his fine oil paintings through most of the night. In the evenings he drove into town to try to sell his beautiful landscapes. We survived on a diet of fresh game—deer, rabbit, quail, dove—whatever we could find. My father proclaimed every meal "elegant" no matter how I cooked it. However, he always smothered his food with mouth-burning portions of red or green chile. I was oblivious to his generous use of spicy seasoning and conceited enough to think that I really was a good cook. Of course, the boys were ever ravenous and would have eagerly devoured an old boiled cowboy boot if I had placed one on the table. Dad's art business kept him in town most evenings showing paintings to prospective customers at their homes. Therefore, it fell to Johnny, as the oldest, to act as surrogate father.

During these years, some kind person donated a complete set of Zane Grey's novels to our family. This proved an incredible cache of riches for me, as I loved to read. My father considered reading as recreation, however, so I usually had to hide in the closet or under my blanket at night with a flashlight in order to savor Zane Grey. His wonderful tales of the

Old West were my escape to another world. They also provided me with endless friends and adventures, and I never was lonely again. To this day I feel most comfortable when surrounded with books, my good friends.

I often climbed out my bedroom window at night and set off for my favorite purple sage bush. Sage comes in many varieties, but that on the mesa west of Albuquerque was wonderful. There the sage grows into very large bushes, some up to four or five feet high and nearly as wide. The slender, silver-green branches terminate in delicate, tiny purple flowers in the early spring. Perfume from these flowers is intoxicating and fills the gentle desert nights. Diminutive hillocks of soft desert soil surround the bases of these bushes, creating small islands of sweet-scented refuge in the undulating sands.

Nestling into my favorite sage hillock, I could feel the sun's warmth still trapped there as I inhaled the fragrance around me. Coyotes sang their strange spirit songs, and it seemed that the night and I were one. I have never felt closer to the Great Spirit. Sometimes I stayed under my sage bush until almost daylight, just feeling and thinking. It occurred to me in one of these meditations that even though my life had been quite difficult, still it was very interesting. And this odd thought somehow helped me to cope.

A wonderful dream came to me at about this time. An old man, with flowing white robes and a long white beard, appeared while I slept. He said his name was Philemon, and that he would always be my guide and help me. It was a strangely comforting dream, though I had no idea what it meant at the time.

Hunting wild game with my brothers provided both our food and our recreation. Dad taught each of us how to handle a gun safely almost as soon as we could walk. My eyes were quite good, and I was a sure shot with either my .22 rifle or my 303 British Enfield. Eventually, Johnny chose me as his hunting partner because of my ability to spot game. Prior to this, however, it took some serious lobbying on my part (because I was a girl) to convince my brothers to let me join them. And I wanted to ingratiate my-self as an indispensable asset—to dispel all of their misapprehensions about female frailties. Therefore, I read every book that the library had on the subject before my first season of deer hunting.

Unfortunately, my extensive research led me to regard myself as an expert. Of course, I **had** to tell my brothers the correct way to stalk, to hunt, and to dress their kill. Johnny adroitly conceded my expertise, and kindly **allowed** me to dress out all of his deer. I was so very smug, and so very dumb. It never occurred to me that I had talked myself into a messy, bloody job that no one in her right mind would want. Johnny only told me how much better I did the job than any of the boys.

In addition to their construction duties, John and Tim also worked as cowhands on my aunt's ranch each summer. They left for headquarters at Mount Taylor each spring in time for roundup. After gathering, sorting, branding, castrating, and dehorning cattle for several weeks, they moved on to the line camp. This was a rustic cabin set farther up the mountain and miles away from any semblance of civilization. Line camp duty meant spending hours each day in the saddle, inspecting and mending endless barbed wire fences. Tim maintains that the breathtaking scenery of this Rocky Mountain wilderness was virtually obliterated by the vision of the daily dinner table set with only canned pinto beans, Spam, and a tin plate. When I was finally old enough for ranch employment, I came on as cook for the cowboys. It was fortunate that they were victims of these vile canned goods, or they would never have been induced to eat my cooking.

Before I worked at the ranch, however, the summers were long and lonely. My younger brothers and I were lost without our older brothers. We felt that our team wasn't complete. I tried to compensate for these long summer separations by making our reunions special. John and Tim loved apple pie, so I always tried to have one ready as a "welcome back home." Each year I seemed to have a sixth sense as to when roundup was over and inexplicably baked a fresh apple pie on the very day that they returned home. These summer sabbaticals were difficult for all of us, but both John and Tim earned enough money as cowboys to put themselves through college.

Johnny graduated with honors, and after college he was hired as Chief Administrative Aide to the famous Navy admiral, Hyman Rickover. Rickover is generally credited as being the father of the nuclear submarine. Johnny was one of the crew on Rickover's first nuclear submarine, which sailed around the world on its premiere voyage. When he returned from his cruise, he brought each of his brothers and sisters a gift. He was chagrined when I told him that I already knew that he had brought us back binoculars (for hunting). He couldn't figure out how I knew. But I just knew, as I had always "known" when he would be coming home from roundup.

Johnny was handsome and charming, and enjoyed the social life offered by our nation's capital. He soon married a beautiful woman he had met while working at the Pentagon. They settled into a cozy Washington apartment and were expecting a baby at Christmas time. Then on April 1, lightning struck the small plane that Johnny was piloting. He was killed instantly.

Thousands of miles away, in Anchorage, Alaska, I **knew** the moment that John died. I was happily cleaning my house one moment, and then the next moment I was engulfed in total blackness and felt surrounded by death. I didn't understand what had happened to me until Dad called late that night with the sad news. I was devastated. We had been raised as devout Catholics, but I found no comfort in my religion. My best friend and beloved brother was dead. For years I thought of Johnny almost constantly. I cried whenever I returned to New Mexico. I was sad and empty and in a great deal of spiritual pain. But then—I had a dream one night. Johnny came to me and asked me why I was still crying for him. He said that he was happy—that he was with Mom. He asked me not to be sad anymore. He told me that he would always be with me and would be near whenever I needed him. It was so real. It was Johnny.

After that dream I was comforted. He visited me quite often in dreams after that. About three years later, he forewarned me of the death of my little brother, Mark. In this dream, both John and Mark appeared to me, riding in a copper-colored Jeep. They told me not to be sad, but that Mark was soon going to be with Johnny and was looking forward to the reunion. Mark's death occurred six months later, when his brand new copper-colored Jeep went over a cliff during a snowstorm.

I had a similar visit from Johnny a few years later, just before my brother Jeff's death. And then again just before my Grandfather's and my Father's deaths. Johnny seemed to know that I needed advance notice in order to deal with these tragedies and was somehow able to give me this knowledge and consolation.

The great emptiness that I felt at Johnny's death launched me on the path of a lifelong spiritual journey. The question, "Why?" became the focus of my being. I spent the next twenty years searching for understanding. Great Spirit blessed my life with all of the people, events, and books that I needed to answer my question. I augmented this information with quite a few mistakes, and even repeated a number of them several times before learning their lessons. Great Spirit then carefully combined all of these ingredients with my dreams, and each time I awoke with a greater understanding. At last I knew that Oneness was the key to this life. All that was lacking was a modern term that would somehow correlate this Oneness with existing philosophical systems. There were theism, deism, pantheism, and polytheism.

Why not unitheism?

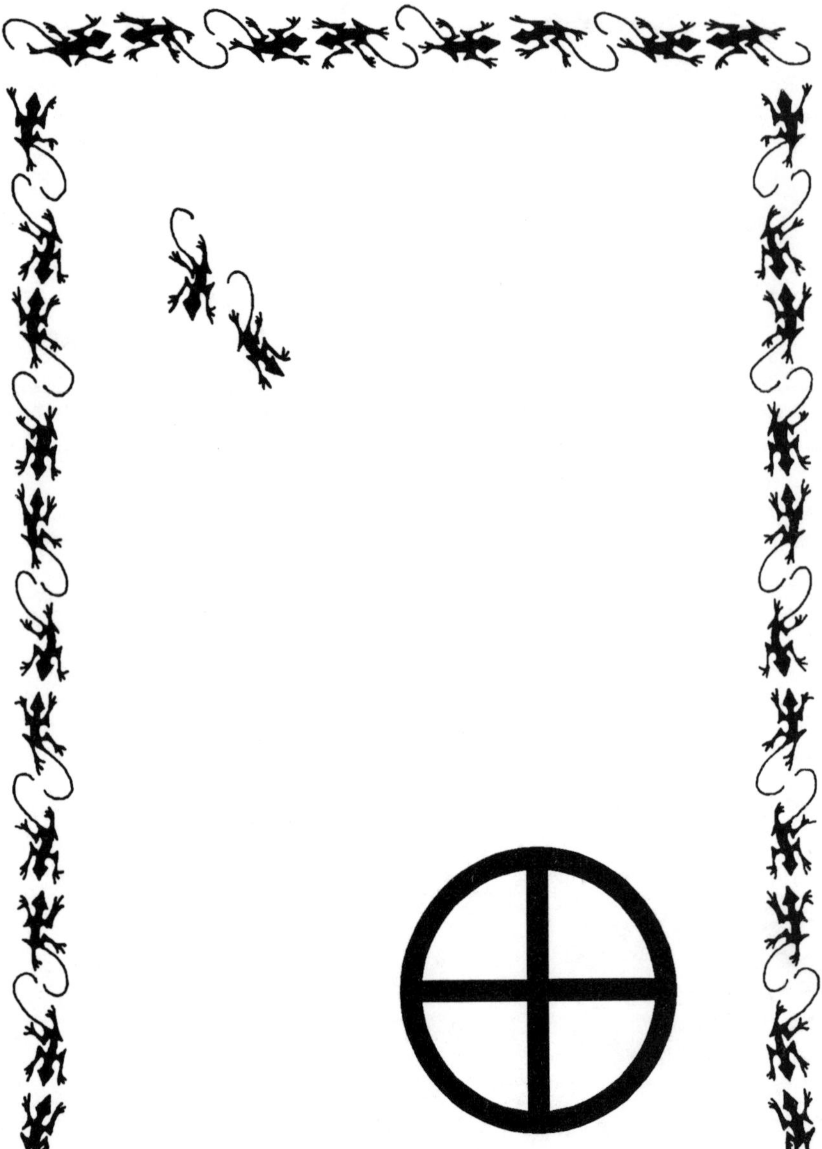

2

Finding the Good Red Road

"Indeed, our contribution to our nation and the world is not to be measured in the material realm. Our greatest contribution has been spiritual and philosophical."

Ohiyesa (Sioux)
The Soul of an Indian

Over the next twenty years following Johnny's death, I dedicated my life to studying religion, philosophy, and the lives of other people. I kept hoping to find some secret formula in the lives of the rich and famous; I read biographies and autobiographies voraciously. Every new person I met fascinated me. Each soul, each fellow traveler, seemed to me to be a new window on a faceless God. Perhaps by studying other people I might find the answers to my questions. Surely someone else had faced similar troubles, had similar doubts, and had finally found peace. In vain, I also searched through a myriad of religious teachings, seeking the wisdom that would fill my spiritual void. My restless mind was not assuaged with platitudes or with vacuous arguments that "faith" was the ultimate answer for all dead-end questions.

Logic is my natural pattern of thought, and I longed for an organized, rational system that would explain this life. Why had my family had so many tragedies? I knew that we weren't wicked, but why would a loving God keep sending us so many trials if not as punishment? Where did my precognitive dreams come from? Why did I usually "know" what Johnny was thinking? With time, I finally began to unravel some answers. My conclusions could be wrong. However, the logical structure presented by unitheism seems to address virtually every aspect of life and spirituality without exception. Only Great Spirit can know the complete truth, and I have sought His/Her guidance on each step which details this journey song. I am, however, only a two-legged, mortal being.

During my twenty-five-year professional career, I increasingly found myself sharing what I had learned with others. Consequently, I was able to bring them a measure of comfort. It is at their urging that I now sit down to write this book and share my journey song.

It seems to me that all of the great truths in life are very simple. Whenever an argument becomes excessively complex, the truth is obscured. Dissimulating is a favorite tactic for people who are not truthful or who are not sure of the truth. For this reason, I tried to keep the verse of my journey song brief and simple while still expressing the logical tenets of unitheism. Then again, if my journey song were too complex, it wouldn't be possible to apply it to the problems of daily life.

Before I share the stanzas of Journey Song, however, we need to discuss the "G" word. I approach this subject somewhat gingerly, because I have found so many people fill with anger and hostility at the mere mention of the word "god." It is sadly ironic that the very name which should bring comfort instead triggers profound anger and anxiety.

Unfortunately, humans have always sought to control other humans in one way or another, and God has simply become another weapon toward this end. For most people, the word "God" has become synonymous with hurt and pain. As a basis for further consideration, then, perhaps we can agree that there is something in our cosmos that the American Indian calls the Great Mysterious. We have so many phenomena in this world, unexplained by religion or science, that reflect this Great Mysterious. Precognitive dreams—such as the dreams I experienced. Ghosts and spirits. Mental telepathy. Spontaneous healing. Astral travel. UFOs. The mysterious workings of the Ouija Board. Astrology. Numerology. Psychokinetic energy. Auras. Life of the soul after death. As you can see, human beings by no means have explored nor explained all that one experiences in this life.

I propose to give you a philosophical system that will embrace all of these phenomena. Unitheism is much like a stained glass window, made of oddly assorted shapes—some round, square, triangular, and so on. Each unexplained phenomena may be picked up, examined, and then neatly fitted into the unitheism "window" where it all begins to make an exquisite pattern of reality.

Religion is generally a system of beliefs which is used to control others by ensuring that they adhere to the same beliefs and practices. Philosophy, however, is secular. That is, it is above and beyond religion and religious practices. Philosophy provides a perspective of the universe that helps human beings to understand our place and purpose in the universe. It addresses the causes and effects, the laws, which underlie reality. A philosophical system, or paradigm, is a global perspective of human beings' place in the universe. If a philosophical system is valid, it will address the mundane questions of everyday life as well as the esoteric questions of human existence.

Walt Whitman said it best in his *Leaves of Grass*.

> Wisdom cannot be passed from one having it to another
>   not having it,
> Wisdom is of the soul, is not susceptible of proof, is its
>   own proof,
> Applies to all stages and objects and qualities and
>   is content,
> Is the certainty of the reality and immortality of things,
>   and the excellence of things:
> Something there is in the float of the sight of things that
>   provokes it out of the soul.
> Now I re-examine philosophies and religions,
> They may prove well in lecture-rooms, yet not prove at
>   all under
> The spacious clouds and along the landscape and
>   flowing currents.

Unitheism is a philosophical paradigm which I propose for your daily use. At its heart is the Great Mysterious. In order to help us with this dialog, I will call this Great Mysterious the Great Spirit. I have chosen the words Great Spirit for two reasons. First, I find that most people are very comfortable with this name as opposed to the name God which, as I have shown, carries an excess of emotional and psychological baggage. Second, I have found that American Indian cosmology, embodied by the term Great Spirit, is a valid and accurate expression of unitheism.

Since we are hopefully agreed on the existence of this Great Mysterious, we must next come to terms with the attributes of the Great Spirit. Who or what is the Great Spirit? If we define the attributes of the Great Spirit in conflicting terms, then the semantics of Great Spirit can cause us a vast amount of confusion. Many religions refer to God or gods when they actually only intend to speak of an advanced spiritual life-form. In order to truly be the Great Spirit, however, an entity must possess certain attributes unique only to this Ultimate Being. Among these attributes are:

Omnipotence, Omniscience, Omnipresence, Infinity, Absolute Truth, and Absolute Good.

Omnipotence (all powerful). Obviously, for an entity to be *the Great Spirit*, He/She must be omnipotent. If an entity is not omnipotent, then there is always the possibility that another, more powerful being exists. If there is even the possibility of another, more powerful being, then the lesser being could be subjugated and would fail to fulfill the role of Supreme Being, or Great Spirit. Therefore, Great Spirit is omnipotent.

Omniscience (all knowing). In order for Great Spirit to be omnipotent, He/She would also have to be omniscient, or all-knowing. If Great Spirit were not all-knowing, there is the logical possibility that somewhere in the vast universe, an event could transpire without Great Spirit's knowledge. If an event could transpire without Great Spirit's knowledge, then He/She would not be omnipotent or all powerful. You will also notice that I refer to Great Spirit without gender. Gender is an animalistic attribute, and should not be logically applied to a Supreme Being. To possess an animalistic attribute would connote that such a being participated in an animal nature with all of its limitations.

Omnipresent (simultaneously present everywhere!). Great Spirit must also logically be omnipresent. Great Spirit must be everywhere. If there is even one small corner of the universe that exists without Great Spirit, then Great Spirit cannot logically be omniscient nor omnipotent, since an event could transpire outside of His/Her control or knowledge. We have already seen in the previous paragraphs that this cannot be logically so if the entity is truly the Supreme Being.

Infinite. Great Spirit must be infinite—endless, subject to no limitation. If Great Spirit can be contained, if Great Spirit can come to an end, then He/She would not be omnipotent and therefore not the Supreme Being. If Great Spirit is finite, then He/She is subject to the same limitations as all other finite beings in the universe. Therefore, for Great Spirit to be *the Supreme Being*, He/She must be infinite.

Is the existence of an infinite Great Spirit consonant with scientific knowledge? I think that modern physics provides us with an excellent explanation of Great Spirit's infinity. In *A Brief History of Time*, Stephen Hawking explains the Big Bang theory of the creation of the universe.[1] According to the Big Bang theory, about twenty thousand million years ago the distance between neighboring galaxies in the universe was zero. Therefore, the density of the universe and the curvature of space-time would have been infinite at this point in time.

Within the thermodynamic arrow of time entropy (disorder) increases, thereby allowing the universe to expand. As the universe continues to expand, this disorder also increases. Many scientists believe that this expansion and attendant disorder will ultimately result in another singularity, and the entire universe will again collapse into a hyper-dense black hole. At this point, the universe will have come full circle. This is the paradox of infinity.[2] The beginning is the end, and the end is the beginning. In the preceding paragraphs, I have illustrated that the Great Spirit is omnipresent in the universe and therefore subject to its fate so He/She is, by definition, infinite.

These concepts of omnipresence and infinity are key to much of what follows in this book. In the beginning the universe was encapsulated in a tiny point of infinite density. This point exploded, flinging its mass outward, creating our universe from this first energy which became the essence of all things. Chinese Taoist philosophers call this omnipresent energy Chi or Tai Chi. American Indian tradition teaches that this is Medicine. I have used this idea of First Energy in naming the resulting philosophical paradigm, "Unitheism." The term unitheism connotes the concept that Great Spirit is omnipresent. Spirit, First Energy, is within **all** things.

Absolute Truth. One of the more immediate attributes of Great Spirit is that of Absolute Truth. Since Great Spirit is infinite, truth also has an eternal, harmonious vibration. All lies are the antithesis of truth, and both cannot exist simultaneously. Since truth is harmony, then we can logically conclude that lies (the opposite of truth) are dissonance. Therefore, as any musician can tell you, dissonant vibrations have an extremely short life.

Einstein's theory of relativity tells us that mass (or physical matter) is simply a form of energy. Quantum theory tells us that all mass is comprised of bundles of energy in differing configurations.[3] These bundles of energy are constantly changing. They are dynamic; they are vibrating. Therefore, from the smallest subatomic particle to the largest galaxies far away, the entire universe is continually in a state of vibration. However, dissonant vibrations always, eventually cease to exist. Lies, which are dissonant vibrations, simply will cease to exist. Since Great Spirit is infinite, He/She is also truth because only truth has a harmonious, infinite vibration.

Only Great Spirit is infinite, and only Great Spirit is absolute truth. It is impossible for any one finite individual to possess absolute truth or knowledge. To do so would make that person the Great Spirit, and this is logically impossible. There can be only one Great Spirit. Instead, each individual is a prism of Great Spirit's truth. Great Spirit manifests Himself/Herself through all of His/Her universe and through all people. There are, however, certain people who have attained a higher vibration of their mass and their spirit. This higher vibration is more harmonious with Great Spirit's infinite vibration. The prism provided by these individuals will contain a greater spectrum of the truth without holding complete, infinite truth in itself.

Absolute Good. The godly attribute of Absolute Good is somewhat similar to the attribute of Absolute Truth. Evil is the antithesis of good; and evil, therefore, creates a dissonant vibration. Again, dissonant vibrations are always very short-lived, which makes them finite. Great Spirit is infinite, and only those vibrations that are infinite can be of the Great Spirit. Within the context of Absolute Good, we can also include the attributes of justice, mercy, and love. Of these attributes, love is perhaps the most important to us two-leggeds.

This understanding of the attributes of Great Spirit is integral to further discourse on a viable philosophy of life. As I have shown, Great Spirit is Omnipotent, Omniscient, Omnipresent, Infinite, Absolute Truth, and Absolute Good. I have attempted to simplify this compilation by focusing only on the essence of these attributes rather than entering into a complex philosophical debate. This dialog must also be kept simple so that it can easily be understood. Only then will it become a useful tool in our daily lives. I feel it essential to establish the nature of Great Spirit, as it is quite surprising how diverse the concepts of His/Her nature can be.

Many religions teach of a God somehow separate from the world—a transcendent deity. This view holds that an entity, God, exists apart from the universe. They teach that, at some time in the past, this God used a type of magic to create this world and the beings who dwell here. Once the act of creation was complete, He rarely deigned to notice our existence. Occasionally, He will *zap!* us poor mortals in order to teach us a thing or two. This Mysterious Dilettante is even divorced from the laws of science which govern His universe. He is also divorced from most philosophies, and plays no part in the psychological or spiritual health of human beings. It is no small wonder that humans are so alienated from such a being. This God presents no logical connection between godhead, science, religion, philosophy and psychology. This God is not a relevant part of anyone's life. Who could take Him seriously?

In contrast, unitheism presents the idea that Great Spirit is an integral part of every minute of every day. As the Sioux Indians say, MITAKUYE OYASIN! We are all One. We are all related. Great Spirit is everywhere and

Spirit fills all things. Science, philosophy, religion, psychology: All are simply various means to discovering more of the truth of Great Spirit and are manifestations of His/Her energy.

Let me emphasize again that Great Spirit is Omnipresent, for this is the key concept of unitheism. Great Spirit is present in all things, even in the most minute, subatomic particles of which all things are made. Modern science has set the foundation for verifying Great Spirit's Omnipresence with the discovery that all matter is simply vibrating energy—First Energy. Each step forward that science takes simply reveals further knowledge of Great Spirit. Stephen Hawking explains God's revelation through science: "The whole history of science has been the gradual realization that events do not happen in an arbitrary manner, but that they reflect a certain underlying order ... ."[4]

Human beings are not exempt from the laws of science. We are made of the same subatomic particles in which Great Spirit is present. Most philosophies agree that human beings are made of four components—body, mind, emotions, and spirit. Logically, each of these components vibrates at a different frequency because each manifests itself differently. Human beings are possessed of free will which governs thoughts, actions, wishes and desires—all of the components of our being.

Because Great Spirit is Omnipresent, even within us two-leggeds, it is logically possible for humans to achieve infinite life with Great Spirit. In order to achieve the same infinite vibration as Great Spirit, however, we can have no trace of lies or evil within us. As we have seen, lies and evil are finite attributes, and as such will not have an infinite vibration. It is, therefore, imperative that we exercise our free will to eradicate lies and evil within ourselves. We must also live in the harmonious state of love. In this way we will achieve an eternal life with Great Spirit. In other words, spiritual growth is a mandate for human beings. "The ultimate goal of life remains the spiritual growth of the individual ... ."[5]

Another of the illogical views of human nature is that Great Spirit can control our actions. If this were true, human beings would be mere puppets for that silly god that sits apart from the world and simply dallies with it whenever it amuses him. This line of thought would also indicate that the great acts of evil committed by humans throughout history were actually the work of god's puppets. This is an illogical line of thought, for we have already seen that Evil is antithetical to Great Spirit.

Evil cannot logically exist as an attribute of Great Spirit because of its dissonant vibration. Humans are rational beings, in control of our actions. When we make certain choices, exercising our free will, we create either harmonious energy or dissonant energy. We either will participate in an eternal life with Great Spirit or we will cease to exist. It is our choice. As I said earlier, the primary purpose of this life is spiritual growth. We must become more godly. We must eradicate all dissonant energy (evil, lies, hatred, etc.) from our lives. We must live in a state of love for Mother Earth and all her creatures.

There are a number of correlations to the hypothesis that dissonant energy will simply cease to exist. The first illustration which I have used was that of the sound waves in music and the differing fates of harmony and dissonance. Capra further illustrates this principle in *The Tao of Physics* when he speaks of the sum of two light waves: "… in those places where two crests coincide, we shall have more light than the sum of the two; where a crest and a trough coincide, we shall have less."[6]

This principle has just recently been most dramatically illustrated with the scientific development of "anti-sound." With the aid of computer analysis, scientists have been able to chart the wave patterns of noxious sounds—a jackhammer, for example. Using this computerized analysis, they have then programmed the computer to produce a counter-wave of sound. These simultaneous waves of sound and anti-sound virtually negate any sound that is emitted by the jackhammer. This is because the dissonant sounds of the jackhammer crash against its anti-sound, and both simply cease to exist.

These examples provide an excellent correlation to the energy waves created by good and evil. They also serve to illustrate why good deeds, why Right Acting must always accompany Right Thinking.

If our deeds are not in harmony with our thoughts, then the energy waves of each crash against the other and both are negated. Please see Figure 2.1 for a visual illustration of this concept. It is alarming to see the number of fundamentalist religions around the world which teach that their adherents must simply say "I believe in thus and such" in order to experience eternal life.

Our thinking must be in harmony with our acting or the energy vibrations will cancel one another. The appeal of the faith approach is that it requires no work and no commitment. It is a lazy way to a supposed salvation. This is not surprising, however, in the context of our society's appetite for instant gratification. In contrast, it is logical to assume that a person who is spiritually alive will also be an ethical person. Aristotle reaffirms this premise by teaching that "… human good turns out to be activity of soul in accordance with virtue … ."[7]

Effect of Consonant and Dissonant Waves Upon Each Other

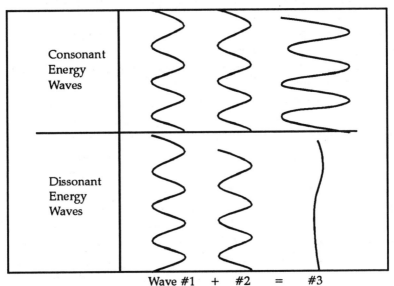

Wave #1   +   #2   =   #3

Figure 2-1

M. Scott Peck, in his book *The Road Less Traveled*, provides a wonderful tapestry of lives which illustrates the importance of spiritual growth. He notes that "... in chronic mental illness we stop growing, we become stuck. And without healing, the human spirit begins to shrivel."[8]

Virtually all of the great religions have stressed the importance of this spiritual growth. Many provide a great deal of guidance for this growth, such as Buddhism's Threefold Training (Trisiksa). Threefold Training teaches that virtuous conduct will result in higher morality; that intense concentration, through meditation, will result in higher thought; and finally, that in transcending our bodies we receive enlightenment and higher insight.

In Catholicism, participation in the sacraments (baptism, marriage, confirmation, communion, confession, holy orders and the last rites) is the path for spiritual growth and salvation.

The Mormon Church, or Church of Jesus Christ of the Latter Day Saints, offers a similar prescription for spiritual growth. Its teachings reach an even more detailed level, however, prescribing the activities of a good husband, father, wife and mother.

Islam, which is taught through the Koran, emphasizes five "pillars" which must govern human beings' relationships with God. Among these are prayer, fasting, almsgiving, and pilgrimage. Islamic Law goes one step further than most religions. It not only requires its adherents to do good and reject what is "reprehensible," but it also requires them to see to it that their fellow Muslims also act correctly.

American Indian spirituality teaches that spiritual growth comes through living in harmony with all things—two-leggeds, four-leggeds, wingeds, and all of Mother Earth. American Indian spirituality also teaches that spiritual growth is enhanced through certain sacred rituals such as the Sweat Lodge, the Vision Quest, and the Peace Pipe Ceremony. Spiritual guidance, in the form of visions and dreams, is sought during and after these ceremonies.

American Indians also observe the natural world around them for lessons in spiritual growth. Great Spirit created all of nature; and nature, therefore, reflects Great Spirit's will. This natural world is filled with the spirit of its Creator and provides a bible for those who take the time to study its laws. For instance, two robins in the simple act of building their nest can provide many lessons for two-leggeds. Their nest is always round, a reminder of the sacred hoop. This circle, Great Spirit's promise of eternity, is present throughout nature. American Indians pattern their circular tepees from this teaching, and each home becomes a reminder and a promise from Great Spirit. Both the male and female robin participate in building their nest and in feeding and rearing their young. In this way, the robins also provide a lesson for two-leggeds on both the equality of the sexes and the functioning of nuclear families.

As you can see, the American Indian experiences each minute of each day and every occurrence within nature as a revelation and a teaching of Great Spirit. Spirituality and spiritual growth are the basis for following the Good Red Road of the American Indian.

MITAKUYE OYASIN. We are all One. This is the essence of the philosophy of unitheism. There is only one Great Spirit, and Great Spirit is everywhere and in all things.

Chapter Notes

1. S. Hawking, *A Brief History of Time*, Toronto: Bantam, 1988, p. 46.
2. C. Kaelin, *Unitheism: The Path to Cosmic Symbiosis*, unpublished manuscript, p. 17.
3. F. Capra, *The Tao of Physics*, New York: Bantam, 1988, p. 188.
4. S. Hawking, op. cit., p. 122.

5. M. Peck, *The Road Less Traveled,* New York: Simon and Schuster, 1978, p. 168.

6. F. Capra, op. cit., pp. 33–35.

7. Aristotle, *On Man in the Universe,* New York: Black, 1943, pp. 134–243.

8. M. Peck, op. cit., p. 17.

Spiritual Growth: Traveling the Good Red Road

> *"More than this, even in those white men who professed relig-ion we found much inconsistency of conduct. They spoke much of spiritual things, while seeking only the material."*
>
> Ohiyesa (Sioux)
> *The Soul of an Indian*

A yearning for spiritual growth is an innate hunger within virtually all human beings. When discussing the attributes of Great Spirit earlier, I established the hypothesis that Great Spirit is Omnipresent. It is Great Spirit's very presence in man that spawns this innate hunger for spiritual growth. Harmonious energies attract and hold other harmonious energies, acting like magnets. When this hunger for spiritual growth is thwarted—through conscious choice (free will) of words, thoughts, or actions—then evil is said to exist. Carl Jung considered evil to be real, and that even something good could become evil if one were to become a zealot or to succumb to it:

> Evil has become a determinant reality ... . Touching evil brings with it the grave peril of succumbing to it. We must, therefore, no longer succumb to anything at all, not even to good. A so-called good to which we succumb loses its ethical character.[1]

Colorado's Ute Indians have a charming legend that teaches the dangers of succumbing. It goes something like this:

*   *   *

*One day coyote walked down to the creek for a drink of water.
Mingled with the cheerful voice of the dancing waters were other voices
of people talking and laughing. When coyote peered through the red
willows he could see Chickadee people throwing something up into the
air. Coyote watched them for a minute and then asked, "What are you
laughing at?"*

*The Chickadees were busy tossing their eyes into the air. Finally
they paused and explained.*

*"We take our eyes out and throw them up in the air, and then
berries fall down and we eat them. But our eyes make a funny noise
when they come back in our heads, and it makes us laugh."*

Coyote thought that this looked like fun, and he was very hungry.

"I would like to do that too. Will you show me?"

*So the Chickadees fixed his eyes so that he could take them out and
toss them into the air. They warned him, however, never to throw his
eyes up when he was in a grove of yellow willows.*

*Coyote spoke the magic word when he threw his eyes up, and then
his hands were magically filled with delicious berries. He then spoke the
word again and his eyes came back into his head. Coyote enjoyed the
tasty berries, and he liked the way his eyes felt when they came back into
his head.*

*Coyote traveled with the Chickadee people for a while, then he
became bored.*

*"You go your way, and I will go mine." And so the friends parted
company.*

*Coyote poked along, throwing his eyes up into the air over and over
again. He came to a grove of yellow willows but ignored the Chickadees'
warning. He threw his eyes up and then called the magic word. But his
eyes would not return to his head. Everything was now totally dark.
Coyote called and called, but his eyes never came back.*

*   *   *

Excess of every type holds the danger that, like coyote, we will succumb to the object of our excess—whether it is power, control, or religion.
Zealots, especially religious zealots, are an impediment to their own spiritual growth. They become stuck and are not free to proceed along the path
of learning offered within each individual's life. Scott Peck's book illustrates the various forms of mental illness or dysfunction which afflict those
individuals who avoid this inner thirst for spiritual growth.

Also, many religions teach that there will be a cycle of rebirth until the human soul achieves spiritual growth or a harmony with God's will or vibrations. Buddhism teaches that this rebirth will continue until spiritual growth has been achieved:

> As long as there is this 'thirst' to be and to become, the cycle of continuity goes on. It can stop only when its driving force, this 'thirst,' is cut off through wisdom which sees Reality, Truth, and Nirvana.[2]

At the center of most New Age religious thought is the theory of karma. This theory proposes that all of a person's actions in each successive lifetime will determine his fate in the following lifetime. The theory of karma is logically consonant with known theories of physics (matter and energy interchanging form) and with most religious teachings. Karma implies reincarnation (rebirth into another body), although the Hindu religion also believes it to mean transmigration (rebirth into animals).

Nonetheless, transmigration does not seem to be as logical a theory for humans due to the different vibrations that we attain because of our rational being. Animals do not have our free will to choose between good and evil, a necessity for spiritual growth. It would seem reasonable, however, that a spirit simply could choose to become an animal in order to help others by giving his body for food or by providing some other service. But only Great Spirit knows the full truth.

In the American Indian tradition, all things have spirit. Trees, flowers, water, stones, animals—all are imbued with spirit. Animals have a special role in their relationship to man, similar to that of guardian angels in the Christian tradition. Certain animals are generally affiliated with different familial clans and are called totems.

Running Deer, an Iroquois, explained how this relationship works. His totem is the wolf, and he belongs to the clan of the wolf. One day as he was driving down an icy road in a blinding snowstorm, a wolf suddenly appeared in his headlights. He swerved to avoid the wolf, and pressed heavily on the brakes. As he came to a stop and looked through the falling snow, he realized that the wolf had stopped him just before he ran into a car stalled on the road ahead.

On another occasion, he awakened during the night to sounds of a wolf howling. Vaguely uneasy, he sat in bed and tried to collect his thoughts. Just then the phone rang, and his brother sadly told him that their mother had just died.

When my husband and I first moved here to our ranch in Colorado, we received an unusual welcome. Sometime during our first night at the ranch a wolf began to howl. It first howled under our bedroom window on the west. Next, it went to the north side of the house and howled, then to the east, and finally the south. I knew then that we had made the right decision on where to live. Prayer to the four directions is American Indian tradition. To have this prayer sung by the gray wolf was an especial honor.

American Indian cosmology teaches that gray wolf carries a special message from the Great Spirit. Gray wolves closely followed the buffalo herds, feeding themselves on the sick and the old animals. By its very presence the gray wolf led hunters to the buffalo herds, ensuring new life for the people. For this reason, the gray wolf is known as the medicine wolf.

It is interesting that our society has become so enamored of the gray wolf. Recently, our government spent millions of dollars to reintroduce this species to the forests of the West. I feel that this fascination with the gray wolf indicates a hunger among all our people for a new spiritual life. It is a good omen, especially because it springs from the American Indian psyche. Astrologers teach that our earth is entering the Age of Aquarius—an era of cosmic energy that will be marked by a new understanding of the brotherhood of all human beings and our oneness with the universe. Perhaps this fixation on the gray wolf is a harbinger of MITAKUYE OYASIN, Oneness, the Age of Aquarius.[3]

Not long after our visit from the wolf, golden eagles and peregrine falcons became my special guardians here at the ranch. They arrived in great numbers when I began work on this book. They tell me when I have spiritual work to do with someone. Certain guests will have their visit blessed by the presence of golden eagles or peregrine falcons (spotted eagles). In the American Indian tradition, eagles and falcons represent spiritual knowledge. They are able to fly closer to the Great Spirit than any other bird. Also, they are able to observe everything that transpires on the earth below them from their vantage point high in the skies and this gives them special knowledge.

Recently, when I was seriously ill, I received a special message from Great Spirit carried by a peregrine falcon. I had just finished meditating one morning when a sudden movement just outside the kitchen window caught my eye. At that moment, a falcon swooped down and caught a tiny sparrow in mid-flight just a few feet in front of me. Somehow the sparrow escaped the falcon's death blow and sought a brief refuge in the blue spruce next to the window. She then attempted a desperate flight out over the east pasture. I heard the falcon cry out from high overhead as he executed a power dive down onto the hapless sparrow. I turned away just as the falcon completed this second midair strike. I couldn't bear to watch the final outcome. This was quite clearly a teaching from Great Spirit, as it was highly unusual and had happened where I could so easily view it. But what was the lesson? This incident was very unsettling, and I asked Great Spirit for enlightenment.

Understanding came during my next meditation—this falcon was teaching me a lesson. Like the sparrow, I could escape death from my illness (this time), if I chose. However, just as the falcon ultimately caught the sparrow after her narrow escape, so death would ultimately catch me. The choice to stay or to go was mine, this time. Obviously, I chose to stay, mainly because I wanted to finish this book in order to share its message with my children and with anyone else who is searching for comfort and understanding.

When we carefully observe the natural world around us, there is much that we can learn. Great Spirit readily teaches us through all things including plants, animals, stones, the wind, and the stars. The possibilities are all around us in everything that Great Spirit has created, and all reflect His/Her constant presence and love. In modern, urban society our household pets are substitutes for the wild totems that aid American Indians. Doesn't your cat or dog seem especially attentive whenever you are sad or ill? Oftentimes, a new phase in our spiritual life will be preceded by the death or the loss of a beloved pet. Although this loss brings us great pain, it can also help us to understand that our guardian spirit, our pet, has finished its work in this particular phase of our life.

Plants are also wonderful teachers, as I will show in the lesson I was taught by a field of wild sage. Several years ago, my husband Harold plowed up a large section of the east pasture. We intended to build a riding and roping arena in the newly leveled area. When I later fell prey to pneumonia, we put the project on hold. Soon our future-arena was filled with fragrant, silvery-green mountain sage. It was a pleasure to look upon and to smell, but it meant that all of Harold's hard work was undone. Then, in a dream one night, I was told that if I would boil the sage and inhale its steam it would help to make me well. When I gathered the sage, I remembered to thank it for giving its life.

By thanking the spirit of the plant in this way we can maintain the vitality, the harmonious energy, of that spirit. It does not shrink from us or withdraw. We are then able to forge a link between the medicine (Great Spirit's energy) in the plant and the harmonious energy generated by our words and actions. This same principle applies to the food that we eat, whether it is plant or animal. Both consciously give their lives in order to feed us, and we will receive the maximum benefit from the plants and animals that we eat if we simply remember to thank each spirit for its sacrifice.

American Indian medicine men and women have recounted many stories of how the plants themselves tell how they are to be used in order to bring about healing. This knowledge sometimes comes as a flash of intuition, by the signature (leaf and root patterns) of the plant itself, or through dreams and visions. This method of healing simply reveals a harmony of energies between the healer and the plant. It is not magic, but simply a different form of communication. Each of us has a gift to give to the world, and the manifestation of this gift depends on the vibrations of our being.

Radio signals operate in a similar manner and are a good analogy for psychic phenomena. They manifest themselves at different frequencies and can only be received when our radio is tuned to that particular frequency. The air around us is filled with these signals. They exist whether or not our radio is turned on or tuned in to their frequency. Simply because we are not listening does not mean that these sounds don't exist.

Science has not yet documented most psychic phenomena, but that does not mean that they do not occur or are any less real than a radio signal.

In summary, the *raison d'etre* for human beings is our spiritual growth. With this growth, the energy vibrations, the totality of our being, will come into harmony with the energy and being of the Great Spirit. This harmonious union with Great Spirit will ensure that human beings also experience an eternal life, because Great Spirit is infinite.

I remember a time when I was about five or six years old. My family put a great deal of effort into attending church every Sunday, and I always felt a great richness and fulfillment in the ritual. It seemed to me that the priest was in direct communication with the Great Spirit as he raised his hands in prayer. I was intrigued and inspired by their private communications, and I thought that communicating with the Great Spirit, and sharing with other human beings in such a way, was the most wonderful type of work to which anyone could aspire.

I vowed that I, too, would become a priest and share the teachings of Great Spirit with all people. I assembled a costume, and for a very long time re-enacted the ritual of Mass and gave my brothers a communion made of small slices of bread. I was crushed when I later learned that women were not allowed to be priests. Remarkably, this innate hunger to share an understanding of the Great Spirit was never crushed, and my early years were spent as an avid student of Catholicism. Later, as I hungered for more than Catholicism offered, the quest itself became spiritually enriching. I possessed a certainty that there was more to this life than the material. As a result of this inner quest, my life has always been rich and full despite many tragedies.

Recently, a young woman wrote to Dear Abby contemplating suicide. This young woman had a wonderful life with every advantage. She was beautiful, intelligent, and doing well in college. Nonetheless, she was plagued with a sense of emptiness and hopelessness and had constant thoughts of suicide. She felt that her life was meaningless. Sadly, no one had taught her that spiritual life is the only real life. It appeared that this young woman did not know that this life is simply a journey for our soul in the Seventh Direction.

It seems to be the nature of human beings to ignore our spiritual life until we are pushed to the brink of despair. Only then do we wake up to the true meaning of life. Ironically, I have often felt that I was fortunate to have had such a traumatic childhood, for I was forced to begin my spiritual journey at a young age. Hopefully this young woman's thoughts of suicide will help to start her on a lifelong path of spiritual growth.

> Tell me not, in mournful numbers,
> Life is but an empty dream!
> For the soul is dead that slumbers,
> And things are not what they seem.
> —Henry Wadsworth Longfellow

If the question, "Why?" is answered by "spiritual growth and union with the Great Spirit," then the next question that logically arises is, "What is spiritual growth and how is it achieved?"

Spiritual growth is a refinement of the total self—body, mind, and spirit—toward a vibration that is in harmony with the vibration of the Great Spirit. A vibration that is consonant with the energy of Great Spirit will naturally embrace (or offer no conflict with) the attributes of Great Spirit. If we have any vibrations of body, mind or spirit that are dissonant with the rest of our vibrations, then many of our positive vibrations will be negated. In order to achieve harmony within ourselves and with Great Spirit we must live it completely—body, mind and spirit.

Every human being can realize a life of beauty and harmony by embracing a guiding philosophy of life. But, like a lost traveler, we risk missing our destination unless we carefully plot a course with the help of a map. *Journey Song* is offered as a road map for your spiritual journey. American Indians call this "traveling on the Good Red Road."

A guiding philosophy of life is the basic structure upon which our religious beliefs, our value system, and our actions are predicated. As an example, if I were an atheist, then I would probably not embrace the Catholic faith and live by its teachings. Or—if I believed that human life had no intrinsic value, then I might be inclined to murder, and even consume, my enemies. Hitler wholeheartedly embraced the philosophy of Nietzsche, and used it to rationalize his policy of genocide in his attempt to establish an ideal master race. Our philosophy of life is a powerful influence on how we actually live our lives.

In my search for meaning in this life, I studied virtually every religion that I came across. Inevitably, when I reached a logical impasse, the teachings of that religion mandated that such and such a teaching be accepted on faith alone. I always found this answer to be untenable, for faith is defined by Webster's as "belief that does not rest on logical proof or material evidence."

As a child, I had accepted the tooth fairy on faith, and then found it to be nothing but charming rubbish as I grew older and more knowledgeable. I also accepted the Easter Bunny and Santa Claus on faith, only later to learn that they were also charming but empty. These childhood myths rely upon the gullibility of children and are credible only because of childish faith.

I have always been suspicious of any argument which ends with a premise that must be accepted on faith. It seems to me that if such an argument must be accepted on faith, then perhaps there is no real answer, only another mythical tooth fairy lurking in the outer reaches of reason. In order to illustrate the relationship of faith, belief, and knowledge, I have placed faith/belief at the beginning of a continuum with knowledge at the other end. Refer to Figure 3.1.

Belief / Faith   Experience   Information   Knowledge

Figure 3-1

We can begin with faith that a certain belief is true. We then measure this faith against the events of our lives and accept it or reject it based upon its relevance or validation in relationship to these events. For instance, we may believe that God is Love until an innocent child dies in a brutal manner. At this point, most of us will question a loving and all-powerful God's failure to intervene and save the child. However, if we believe that every human being has participated with Great Spirit in planning the events of our lives (before we are born), then an innocent child's death will be seen in that context and will validate that belief.

Or let us look at a different example, such as a man who believes himself to be a faithful husband. This remains only a belief, however, until he has squarely faced temptation and overcome it. Only when he has been irresistibly attracted to another woman and is presented with an opportunity to act upon this attraction, but doesn't, is he faithful. With this new information and experience in hand, he now has the knowledge of truly being a faithful husband. He began with a belief and transformed it into knowledge through experience.

Our next step in growing from faith to knowledge is to gather as much information as possible until we have knowledge that supports and confirms our original belief. With such confirmation, the end result is "knowing" and is no longer merely "believing." Unitheism itself provides a good example of this concept.

Our experience on this North American continent for the past four hundred years has shown that we are not such capable stewards of the earth as our red brothers. Consequently, our **experience** has taught us that these extensive environmental and spiritual problems demand a new philosophy, a philosophy of Oneness. This is the only spiritual path that will ensure life for our planet and the life on it. The ancient traditions, the **beliefs**, of almost all American Indians have taught that our red brothers and sisters will be our spiritual leaders in the next millennium. Current scientific **precepts** (information) are embodied in these American Indian teachings, and provide their validation. In summary, American Indian **beliefs**, verified by our **experience** and buttressed by scientific **information**, culminate in the **knowledge** that the Red Road will lead human beings safely into the future. We are all One. MITAKUYE OYASIN.

Knowledge of the Great Spirit takes a lifetime of work, and it will still be incomplete. We can grow steadily in spirit, both through life experience and gathering information, but we will never have absolute knowledge, for that is an attribute of Great Spirit alone. As we strive to grow in spirit, it is imperative that we understand that knowledge is only acquired with effort and, once acquired, it must become a part of us. Spiritual growth is not attained by going to church on Sunday or by reading pages in a book. It is not a special image that one wears only once each week. Body, mind, and spirit—they must be totally integrated. Going to church or reading a book can be tools in attaining spiritual growth, but a total integration of all words, thoughts, and actions is absolutely necessary in order to reach spiritual maturity.

Chapter Notes

1. C. Jung, *Memories, Dreams, Reflections,* New York: Random, 1973, p. 329.
2. R. Gard, ed., *Buddhism,* New York: Braziller, 1961, p. 116.
3. J. M. Woolfolk, *The Only Astrology Book You'll Ever Need,* Lanham, Maryland: Scarborough House, 1990, p. 328.

4

Tools for Spiritual Growth

"It has always been our belief that the love of possessions is a weakness to be overcome. Its appeal is to the material part, and if allowed its way it will in time disturb the spiritual balance for which we all strive."

Ohiyesa (Sioux)
The Soul of an Indian

Philosophy of life is the framework for spiritual growth. Our religious, or ceremonial, practices are the tools with which we nurture and effect this growth. There is a proliferation of religions around the world, and each one usually proclaims to be the "One and Only True" or "God's Words." How does one know which is the correct religion? This is a question which can only be answered on an individual basis. Philosophically, any religion which leads one to act in harmony with Great Spirit's will and Great Spirit's ways is correct. The objective of our life is reunion with Great Spirit.

However, we need to exercise caution when searching for a religion or other ceremony to use as a tool for spiritual growth. Unfortunately, most religions are focused on a need to control. If we succumb to this aspect of religion, then our spiritual growth can actually be stunted rather than enabled.

It is interesting to study the original theology or philosophy upon which any religion is based and then to try to reconcile its current teachings with this basis. Most often there is little if any correlation. Theology (or religious philosophy) and religion are disparate entities. As I noted earlier, religion generally seems to have degenerated into a system of coercion and control. Those within the hierarchy of most established religions seem intent on ensuring that everyone thinks exactly as they do.

Enforcing this homogeneity is a logical response to our human instinct as a herd animal, where conformity is highly valued. Simply look around you the next time that you visit a shopping mall or the next time that you go to a dinner party. There will be a great deal of homogeneity in the way that people are dressed, and those who fail to conform will be ostracized.

This need for conformity is based on fear. Our primary response to this world is one of fear. In primeval times we were afraid of wild beasts, the forces of nature, and any strange human. Psychologists teach us that the response to this fear is fight or flight. As humans grew more intelligent and civilization progressed, we learned that we could assuage our fears by controlling our environment and our fellow human beings. In a civilized society it is unacceptable, and often impossible, for humans to fight or run away from whomever we fear.

For this reason, then, rational humans augmented this instinct for "fight or flight" with "control." This need to control is exemplified by the regime of Communist China. Their government views any type of independent thought as a threat. They literally fear the thinking of the Chinese people. Consequently, all aspects of an individual's life are closely controlled—what is read, what is heard, what is done, and what is said.

On a more personal basis, Letty Cottin Pogrebin details the interpersonal dynamics of control in her book, *Family Politics—Love and Power on an Intimate Frontier.* Pogrebin illustrates the different motivation and forms of this control in family relationships.[1] It is this need for control that spawns emotional, mental, and physical abuse. A spouse or parent will attempt to control the actions of a mate or child by threats, beatings, and other means of intimidation. There is a strong need to destroy self-esteem, by any means, in order to keep one's mate or child dependent and under control. Murder is sometimes employed as the ultimate form of control.

Unfortunately, religions are not exempt from the same fears that assail governments and individuals; and the result is, again, a strong need to control. One of the best illustrations of the disparity between a non-controlling philosophy and its religious application is Taoism. The Chinese philosopher, Lao Tzu was very clear about the issue of control in the *Tao de Ching:*

> Giving birth and nourishing,
> Having without possessing,
> Acting with no expectations,
> Leading and not trying to control;
> This is the supreme virtue.[2]

It is interesting to contrast these words with the practices of Tao religion. Each village must hire Taoist priests at least every six years to perform the important rite of cosmic renewal. This is an expensive, week-long affair, with stringent rituals and prayers. Modern Taoism also has strict rules for daily life that even include the placement of each piece of furniture in one's home. I can't help but think that the gentle Lao Tzu would be greatly surprised to see how his philosophy has been transmuted into a religion of so many rules and regulations.

Another interesting transmutation of philosophy is Christianity. Jesus (Christ) was a simple carpenter who taught that we must love God and we must love our neighbor. Within the last two thousand years, however, his simple philosophy has devolved into a vast empire of thousands of religious sects. Hundreds of wars have been fought and millions of people killed, because of the religious beliefs spawned by different interpretations of Christ's words of love.

Abortion, one of the most divisive political issues facing the United States in the last half of this century, has become the focus of religious conflict. Yet in spite of the heated rhetoric it has spawned on the value of human life, 30,000 to 40,000 children around the world die from hunger every day. Why haven't the people so opposed to abortion expended an equal amount of energy on saving these starving children? If these children received the same passionate focus, then perhaps these expressions of concern over human life would carry more validity. Without this focus, the actions of these anti-abortion groups seem to be primarily concerned with controlling women's bodies. This creates a virtually irreconcilable conflict with the many women who believe that human life does not begin until the soul enters the body, and that this does not happen without the mutual agreement of mother and child. Both of these opposing viewpoints stem from religious conviction, and only Great Spirit can know which is truth.

When we embrace a personally viable philosophy of life (which leads to godliness), then we can effectively utilize religion without succumbing to it entirely. With this philosophy we may also utilize a religion even though we have reservations about some aspect of its teachings. Different religions are like different languages of the soul. All language is used for communication, although no one language is used throughout the world. This difference in tongues reflects the rich cultural diversity of our earth. Diversity, like an artist's contrast in color and texture, is beauty. It is a reflection of Mother Earth herself as created by Great Spirit.

In general, civilization does not condemn one ethnic group simply because they speak another language. Instead, human beings understand and respect each culture's right to its language. Therefore, force has rarely been used to coerce everyone into speaking one language. It is a great tragedy that religion, which purports to bring godliness and spiritual growth, lacks the same tolerance exhibited by secular society.

Different religions also address the differing levels of spiritual growth of individuals. This is analogous to the different grades of school that are (supposedly) commensurate with the individual's level of intellectual development. Obviously, a first grader will be unable to comprehend the more complex lessons of a twelfth grader. Some religions are able to span the whole range of spiritual development and embrace and nurture a widely diverse group of followers.

It is a grave mistake to think that all people are on the same level of spiritual development. Many make this mistake, and then are disappointed or angry at the actions of those who are only in the infancy of their spiritual growth. How can we be angry with a child who only cries because he does not know how to speak? Understanding the great disparity and diversity of spiritual development is a very necessary step in living compassionately. And compassion is one of the integral truths for a successful spiritual journey.

I have among my various friends many who are fundamentalist Christians. (I will not use any person's real name in these anecdotes in order to ensure privacy.) Notable among these fundamentalists are two individuals at opposite ends of the spectrum of spiritual growth. Merle is quite active in his church and quite visible in his participation. He is a hard worker and a good provider for his family. He is also a talented raconteur. Unfortunately, most of his amusing stories are total fabrications. He is not able, consciously, to discern truth from lies. He is also physically and emotionally abusive to his children, who all bear the scars of his abuse. Merle's religion is not something that is integrated into his daily life, and seems to be engaged for only a few hours on Sundays.

At the opposite end of this spectrum is a dear friend of mine, Rob. Rob and his wife are both ordained ministers and are also fundamentalist Christians. They are involved in the community and are an inspiration to all of their friends. They love and nurture one another and their children, and the family is a joy to be around. Rob works in a nondescript job, never pushing his religion nor flaunting his credentials. While both Merle and Rob are fundamentalists, Merle might be said to be in the kindergarten of his spiritual development, while Rob is working on his master's degree.

This type of spiritual diversity is not unique to fundamentalist Christians. I am also acquainted with a beautiful and gifted Buddhist girl, Marla. She comes from a good family and has had every privilege. In spite of all of her advantages, however, she is addicted to drugs. Buddhism is quite specific that its adherents should not use any mind-altering substance, including alcohol. But this does not deter Marla. She is a practicing Buddhist and seems to have little trouble reconciling her life style with her religious beliefs.

At the other end of this spectrum is an exceptional woman named Eunice, also a practicing Buddhist. Her life, however, is a model of Buddhist teachings. She will harm no living thing and is therefore a strict vegetarian. She lives a very simple but beautiful life. Her home is located in the remote forests of the Rocky Mountains and utilizes only solar energy. She and her husband are actively involved in the community but do not call attention to themselves. They live a life of simple beauty while a palpable aura of peace and gentleness surrounds them both.

As for Catholicism, I have two other friends, a priest and a nun, who illustrate the wide divergence of spiritual growth within that religion. Father Bill's only ambition in life was to become a Catholic priest. He began his seminary studies as a teenager and was later ordained at a young age. He is an extremely intelligent man who, unfortunately, has succumbed to the myth of his superior intellect. He is unable even to listen to another point of view. Yet he is one of this country's foremost theological scholars. Unfortunately, Father Bill also has a serious drinking problem.

When Father Bill experienced a conflict with members of his parish, he was uncompromising. He felt that none of his parishioners possessed the knowledge that he had acquired—he alone was right. He felt himself far superior to everyone. This conflict exacerbated his drinking problem, and this finally drove the whole situation to an unhappy climax. Father Bill was dismissed from his parish, and is now in an alcoholic rehabilitation program. In sharp contrast to the unhappy life of Father Bill, is the perspective of my dear friend, Sister Margie.

Sister Margie was born in Ireland, and when she turned seventeen she was swept away by dreams of becoming a missionary. She joined a convent but was disappointed when she was sent to America instead of Africa. Her girlish dreams of working beside someone like Albert Schweitzer in "darkest Africa" would never be realized. When she found herself working on the American Indian reservations instead, she did her best to adjust and find a different joy. Her job at the missions was to teach music. Lonely Indian children at the Catholic boarding schools found Sister Margie to be a sympathetic friend and a cheerful mentor. Her life of continual, loving service is somewhat different from what she anticipated, but it is a testimony to her spirituality.

Even some American Indians seem to have trouble following the Good Red Road. An example of this is one of the more memorable characters from my childhood, a Navajo Indian named Nash. He was the foreman for the Navajos who worked on my aunt's ranch. It was the general practice among ranchers in the area to employ one foreman for the regular cowboys and a special foreman for the Native Americans who worked only during spring and fall roundup. As I mentioned earlier, my older brothers worked as cowboys at Aunt Lou C's ranch each summer in order to buy groceries for the family and also to save for their college tuition. I, too, spent many summers at the ranch as camp cook and in this way became acquainted with Nash.

Nash was an attractive and kindly man and we all felt close to him for, like us, he also had a large family—thirteen children. He taught us many of the Navajo legends and ways and was especially helpful to us during hunting season. Aunt Lou C and Uncle Lee looked the other way whenever Nash hunted deer to feed his children. Because of his year-round hunting activity, Nash knew where and when to find the best mule deer. Our family virtually lived on wild game, and deer meat was an essential staple in our diet. Nash knew this, and during hunting season he would magically appear at our camp to help my brothers and I plan our strategy.

We spent those raw November evenings bundled against the cold, crouching as close to the campfire as possible, both to warm ourselves and to catch every word of Nash's stories and advice. Our camaraderie was further enhanced when Nash pulled a small flask from his pocket and shared its fiery contents. Johnny, Tim, Mark, and I took a swig of the orange-flavored gin that traced a warm path into our half-empty stomachs. Nash made us feel that we were his equals, even though I was only about twelve, Tim was fourteen, Mark was ten, and my oldest brother, John, was sixteen.

Years later, we were devastated when we learned that Nash and his wife were run over by one of the cattle trucks. It seems that he and his wife had been in town drinking, and on the long walk back to the ranch they lay down on the road in front of the truck. It was such a terrible end for our dear friend. I was haunted for years with the "why?" of it all.

At the other end of the spectrum of American Indian religious thought is my esteemed friend, Running Deer. He is a Seneca medicine man, and a highly respected resident of our area. Running Deer is married to a warm and loving lady who is also a psychic. The two of them are quite active in their community and are leaders in their intertribal government. Both are now in their eighties but have not slowed their pace much in spite of their advancing years. Running Deer is also a devout Christian, and his life provides an example of the blending of native religious beliefs and Christianity. He and his wife are a joy to be around and exude an aura of peace and contentment. His religious beliefs and American Indian culture have proven an asset for the community at large. Running Deer does not seem to have suffered from any of the cross-cultural trauma that plagued Nash.

It is important to remember that vibrant spiritual life is not unique to any one religious sect. There are ample saints and sinners within all organized belief systems. Any religion that leads to the Great Spirit is valid, but this requires humans to be tolerant and understanding. This tolerance and understanding must extend to the knowledge that not all human beings are at the same level of spiritual development—we each have our own special path. It is a journey that we all must make. Some of us are only beginning our journey in the Seventh Direction. Others have already reached their destination and have returned to help the rest of us find the way. As I illustrated earlier, the logical mandate for all of us two-leggeds is to achieve harmony with the Great Spirit. I have found that the best tools for my own journey are embodied by traditional American Indian spirituality.

These traditional American Indian practices, however, should not be confused with the Native American Church. This relatively new church was officially incorporated and recognized in the United States in 1918.[3] Peyote, a wild cactus, is the focal sacrament for this religion. In addition to using peyote, the participants also incorporate the Sweat Lodge, the Pipe Ceremony, and other traditional practices. Peyote was originally employed by Aztec priests until their Spanish conquerors forbade its use. It didn't surface again as a ceremonial drug until the Mexican Indians gained their independence from Spain in 1821. Afterward, use of this hallucinogenic cactus gradually spread northward along the indigenous trade routes and onto America's plains in the 1880s.

Traditional American Indian spirituality does not employ any hallucinogens. Its ceremonies and traditions are cataloged and explained in Ed Eagle Man McGaa's book, *Mother Earth Spirituality*. This spirituality embraces seven major ceremonies practiced by our red brothers and sisters in striving for harmony with Great Spirit. These ceremonies include the Sweat Lodge, the Vision Quest, the Sun Dance, the Spirit Calling, the Peace Pipe, the Making of Relatives, and the Giveaway Ceremony. It is important to note the positive purposes of each of these ceremonies, including an emphasis on spiritual growth and participation in the Oneness of all creation. Eagle Man, a Lakota Sioux Indian, encourages all people to experience these Mother Earth ceremonies, and then to go "your own path, strengthened in a deeper respect and understanding for our Mother Earth and the perceptive natural view, which was followed down through time by the successful caretakers who served well their stewardship of this western hemisphere of Mother Earth."[4]

Arguably, the most important of all these ceremonies is the Peace Pipe Ceremony. It is also the one which is most familiar to the non-Indian, probably because Hollywood featured it in virtually every western film. Unfortunately, these movies captured only the most colorful aspects and completely ignored the deeper, spiritual significance of the ceremony. American Indians believe that the Peace Pipe ceremony is one that was taught to them by the mythical White Buffalo Calf Woman many generations ago. This ceremony usually precedes all other ceremonies and functions to bring all participants into harmony with the Great Spirit and His/Her cosmos.

Before I had my own peace pipe, I was able to access the energy or power of the ceremony by using a special crystal (or *Wotai*) instead. Even though I now have a ceremonial pipe, I nonetheless continue to use my wotai out of deference to those of my red brothers and sisters who are offended when the peace pipe is used by non-Indians. Both the wotai and the peace pipe are simply tools that are intended to aid spiritual growth. Therefore, any tool that can be used to accomplish the job is the right tool.

One of the most memorable ceremonies that I performed with my wotai was for a friend I'll call "Dave." In the early 1990s, he invested all of his savings to build a fishing resort on the western slope of Pikes Peak. Aspens and pines lined the banks of a small but lively creek that coursed through the campgrounds. He constructed several dams along this stream and then stocked the newly created pools with rainbow trout. Dave worked hard to develop this fishing retreat, but each spring the rains came, burst through the concrete spillways and flooded the campgrounds and access roads.

After the third year of this misfortune, I offered to do a Peace Pipe Ceremony to bring the construction on his property into harmony with Mother Earth. By this time Dave was ready to try anything and agreed to my unconventional solution, although with some skepticism. One chilly spring morning, I hiked along the banks of his creek, fastening appropriately colored flowers and bird feathers to the pines in order to define the area for the ceremony. I then used my wotai to conduct a traditional Peace Pipe Ceremony, focusing the energies on the newly marked area. Early the next day the mountains were deluged by a terrible thunderstorm. My friend's dikes held not only the flood waters but also a special gift. A large smoky quartz crystal glistened on top of the dam the morning after the rains stopped. For the next three mornings various other crystals presented themselves at the same place. The Peace Pipe Ceremony created a harmony between Mother Earth and the dramatic changes that my friend had carved onto her face. In this ceremony, I asked that Great Spirit bless the site so that all who visited this resort would be touched by the beauty of Mother Earth and return to their homes with a new resolve to defend her.

This ceremony was successful because the blessing that I asked for was in harmony with the attributes, the basic energy, of Great Spirit. I did not create the changes on Dave's property; Great Spirit did. I was simply a tool for focusing the infinite energies of Great Spirit, much as a lens can create a powerful laser beam from simple light. If I had asked for money or prosperity, for example, my ceremony would not have been effective because these energies are not in harmony with the attributes of Great Spirit.

In the Sweat Lodge Ceremony the focus is on cleansing and healing. A Sweat Lodge is traditionally made of saplings placed in a circle, then arched and bound together in order to make a dome-shaped structure. This dome is then covered with a tarp or blankets and the ground inside is strewn with aromatic grass and sage. Stones are heated in a fire outside the lodge, then placed in a pit in the center. Participants begin with a Peace Pipe Ceremony, then enter the lodge for the sweat. This sweat consists of a series of prayers to the Great Spirit, with special invocations to the spirits of each of the four directions. As the red-hot stones glow and release steam when doused with ladles of water, the participants offer their prayers. Colors and visions are revealed. This ceremony, like the Peace Pipe, seems to create a harmonious energy between the participants and Great Spirit.

This harmonious energy is the power of American Indian ceremony. This is Oneness, MITAKUYE OYASIN. The great Sioux medicine man, Black Elk, eloquently explained this Oneness, saying, "It is the story of all life that is holy and is good to tell, and of us two-leggeds sharing in it with the four-leggeds and the wings of the air and all green things; for these are children of one mother and their father is one spirit."[5]

American Indians have always understood this Oneness, and their ceremonies emphasize a creation of these harmonious energies between man and nature. Our red brothers and sisters do not strive to conquer nature, nor to control either nature or other two-leggeds. Each person is left free, through ceremony, to develop personal harmony with the Great Spirit. There is no other person between an individual and Great Spirit. No traditional American Indian ceremony is rigidly structured or controlled. Individual interpretation, beyond the basic form, is valued and encouraged because it is clearly understood that Great Spirit works through every human being.

When Europeans first set foot on the shores of America, they encountered a virgin wilderness teeming with wildlife and Great Spirit's gifts. Rivers and lakes ran clear and blue with no trace of pollution. America's Indians and their ancestors had been stewards of the land for over 20,000 years, and its vigorous health was testimony to the wisdom of their philosophy of Oneness. Sadly, European invasion brought about the near extinction of the native peoples as well as the extinction of thousands of plants and animals in a little over 500 years. This massive destruction is testimony to the folly of our philosophy of Cartesian Duality, the separateness of the physical and the spiritual.

Our universe is from Great Spirit and of Great Spirit. Our entire universe is simply pulsating energy. Even the most minute segment in the furthest galaxy throbs with Great Spirit's energy. As I illustrated earlier, the sum of two consonant waves of energy is exponential. One energy wave augmented by a second wave in consonance has the force of at least a thousand waves, not just two.

When we place ourselves in consonance with nature and with Great Spirit, miracles are possible. When we can sustain this harmony, our lives and our world will change dramatically. Much as the jet streams swirl and dance across the face of Mother Earth, the energy streams of the Great Spirit also swirl and dance along the arrow of time. When we are in harmony with these energies, we will travel an exciting and peaceful path toward our reunion with the Great Spirit.

However, if we are out of harmony, we will be left behind, dazed and confused as the winds of this energy sweep through our lives. All of us experience this energy throughout our lives in tragedies and triumphs, in joys and sorrows. The choice of how we respond is ours alone.

I did not begin to write this book until the swirl and force of Great Spirit's energy carried me to the point where I had to write. Many of my friends and loved ones had urged me to write this book for years. Still I resisted, feeling that I wasn't qualified to propose a new philosophy or to write about it. Then I had to have surgery and was in a great deal of pain during my recovery. In fact this pain was so intense that I couldn't read or even watch television. I was totally immobilized. At that time I didn't realize that my pain was simply an instrument to help me along my spiritual path.

During this period my mind was a whirlwind of activity for it was not constrained by the pains of my body. Desperate for an outlet for these energies, I began to compose this book in my head. It was at least a year later, though, when events changed my life so dramatically that I was finally able to begin setting this book down on paper. My husband retired; I took an early retirement; and we bought our ranch in a remote valley in the Colorado Rockies. It was there that I was awakened by the howling of the gray wolf that I mentioned earlier.

When I began *Journey Song,* several golden eagles circled the pasture each day as I wrote. As the book neared completion, there were thirteen golden eagles circling the pasture each day. When I completed my manuscript, I still wasn't quite satisfied. Something was lacking. Then I read Ed Eagle Man McGaa's *Mother Earth Spirituality* and knew that *Journey Song* was not complete without embracing American Indian spirituality. My earlier work had led me to understand the great truth of these teachings. However, most of my Indian friends and teachers had cautioned that these teachings were not to be shared.

On the other hand, Eagle Man proposed an entirely different attitude toward disclosing the secrets of American Indian spirituality. Eagle Man wrote that all of the great medicine men taught that this spirituality must be shared with non-Indians. Eagle Man felt that without these teachings, without this outlook, human beings would not be able to save Mother Earth. About this time I remembered the legend of the four Shamans who refused to share the sacred powers of tobacco (the story related in the Preface). I was exhilarated and finally felt as free as my golden eagles to spiral upward toward *Wakan Tanka* (Great Spirit).

When I revised *Journey Song* to incorporate these American Indian teachings, the thirteen golden eagles were replaced by thirteen peregrine falcons circling the ranch each day. The peregrine falcon, or spotted eagle, is considered one of the greatest spiritual guides in American Indian cosmology. Peregrine falcons can fly higher, and therefore nearer the Great Spirit, than any other bird.

Ironically, each publisher that expressed an interest in my manuscript insisted that I remove all the American Indian "stuff." This proposal seemed preposterous to me. These teachings are the very heart—the essence—of unitheism. This is the only idiom that correctly expresses this philosophy of Oneness. These teachings have sustained America's native peoples for thousands of years, and they provide the only philosophical track record that also sustains this earth.

Jack Weatherford speaks to this issue in his book *Indian Givers*.

> ... we have overlooked the contributions that [Indians of the Americas] made to the world. They mined the gold and silver that made capitalism possible. Working in the mines and mints and in the plantations with the African slaves, they started the industrial revolution that then spread to Europe and on around the world. They supplied the cotton, rubber, dyes, and related chemicals that fed this new system of production. They domesticated and developed the hundreds of varieties of corn, potatoes, cassava, and peanuts that now feed much of the world. They discovered the curative powers of quinine, the anesthetizing ability of coca, and the potency of a thousand other drugs, which made possible modern medicine and pharmacology. The drugs together with their improved agriculture made possible the population explosion of the last several centuries. They developed and refined a form of democracy that has been haphazardly and inadequately adopted in many parts of the world. They were the true colonizers of America who cut the trails through the jungles and deserts, made the roads, and built the cities upon which modern America is based. ...
>
> The world has yet to utilize fully the gifts of the American Indians. Hundreds of plants [used by the American Indian] such as amaranth and quinoa are hardly even known, much less fully utilized. Who knows how many more plants might be out there waiting to serve humans? We still do not understand the complex mathematical systems of the Mayas and the sophisticated geometric science of the Aztecs. Who knows what completely different systems of computation and calculation now lie buried in the adobe of Arizona or beneath the rocks of Inkallajta? The civilizations of Mexico and Guatemala developed a more accurate calendar than the one used in Europe, but it took decades of work for us to understand its superiority. Who knows what additional knowledge they had about the stars, the planets, the comets, and who knows how much knowledge still lies locked in the stone monuments yet to be discovered ... .[6]

I would add one more question to Weatherford's litany. "Who knows what invaluable lessons in philosophy the American Indian has to offer?" I feel that *Journey Song* answers this question, and I in turn offer it for all those who are seeking true spirituality and an understanding of "Why?" MITAKUYE OYASIN. We are all One—the four-leggeds, the two-leggeds, the stones, the trees, and the winged ones. This is unitheism. Unitheism mandates Cosmic Symbiosis. Whatever happens to the least of these creatures also happens to us.

My journey song is quite simple. It consists of only six easy verses. I have written it in verse, in the manner of the American Indians, in order that it may be easily remembered.

Journey Song

Trust Great Spirit, Trust Great Spirit.

MITAKUYE OYASIN!

Love the Truth and by it live.

MITAKUYE OYASIN!

Walk life's path with Simplicity.

MITAKUYE OYASIN!

Bathe yourself and others with Patience.

MITAKUYE OYASIN!

Carry only Compassion in your heart.

MITAKUYE OYASIN!

Seek Knowledge of our Creator and enhance your spirit.

MITAKUYE OYASIN!

The remainder of this book focuses on each of the sentences of this journey song, with a general discussion of each and an argument as to its relevance and importance. As I explained earlier, it is vital that any philosophy we adopt become fully assimilated and integrated into our daily lives. If it is not assimilated and integrated, then our actions will be in conflict with our philosophy. This is hypocrisy. It will also lead to failure, for a philosophy that is not integrated will fail to provide comfort. In addition, dissonant energies created by the conflict between our thoughts and our actions will tend to leave us restless and unhappy. *Journey Song* presents a path that will bring you peace, harmony and love. I find, however, that following this path takes daily discipline.

I began the procedure of integrating these teachings by taking one sentence and repeating it throughout the day for several months. I started with the most difficult one for me, Trust in the Great Spirit. Worry has always been my constant companion. When I was younger I constantly walked around with the burden of the world on my shoulders. I had to remind myself a million times a day that Great Spirit was in control of the world and it is not my burden.

Now, whenever I catch myself worrying, I repeat the phrase "Trust Great Spirit" and I am able to set my worries aside. I would recommend this approach for all of the verses—focus on one sentence daily, for an extended period of time, until it has been assimilated. Don't be discouraged if it takes awhile to develop this new philosophical outlook. For, unfortunately, we humans do not learn in a linear fashion. Our learning is more like "one step forward and two steps back." With *Journey Song* as a basis, I am confident that you too will soon find a life filled with peace, love, and harmony.

Chapter Notes

1. L. Pogrebin, *Family Politics,* New York: McGraw-Hill, 1983, pp. 86–115.
2. Lao Tzu, *Tao Te Ching,* New York: Harper & Row, 1988, ch. 10.
3. J. Weatherford, *Indian Givers: How the Indians of the Americas Transformed the World,* New York: Ballantine Books, 1988, pp. 208–210.
4. E. McGaa, *Mother Earth Spirituality,* New York: Harper San Francisco, 1990, ch. 6.
5. J. Neihardt, *Black Elk Speaks,* New York: Washington Square Press, 1959, p. 1.
6. J. Weatherford, op. cit., pp. 252–254.

Trust the Great Spirit

"... In our original belief we were content to believe that the spirit which the Great Mystery breathed into us returns to the Creator who gave it, and that after it is freed from the body it is everywhere and pervades all nature ... Thus, death holds no terrors for us."

Ohiyesa (Sioux)
The Soul of an Indian

W e have begun a spiritual journey. People want to go back to find that missing link, that hole in their being. They want to fill it with all the possibilities of what we can be."[1] With these simple words, Carole Anne Heart Looking Horse, a Sioux Indian, voices the malaise of all human beings.

Before we can begin to fill this hole, we must first examine how we view God, the Supreme Being, and our relationship to Him/Her. In Chapter 2, I discussed and defined the attributes of God, and settled upon using "Great Spirit" instead of "God" as the designated expression. The attributes ascribed to Great Spirit include (but are not limited to) Omniscient, Omnipotent, Omnipresent, Infinite, Absolute Truth, and Absolute Good. I will first expand on the definition of Omnipresent in order to clarify its relevance to our individual lives.

In the 1920s, three famous scientists—Werner Heisenberg, Erwin Schrodinger, and Paul Dirac—developed a revolutionary new theory of physics called Quantum Mechanics, based on the uncertainty principle.

In this theory particles no longer had separate, well-defined positions and velocities that could not be observed. Instead, they had a quantum state, which was a combination of position and velocity.[2]

Quantum mechanics was an important step forward for scientists in fully understanding the nature of matter. As they attempted to define the most basic subatomic building blocks of the universe, they instead found that these particles could not be measured because the very act of observing or measuring changed the particles. They also discovered that these particles were not discrete, concrete entities but were packages of energy that they labeled "quanta." This is the basis of Einstein's famous mass-equivalency formula, $E = MC^2$.

Quantum mechanics and the mass-energy equivalency theory are also important and exciting steps forward philosophically. Our universe does not consist of separate and distinct parts existing independently of each other. Instead, there is an "inseparable quantum interconnectedness of the whole universe."[3] Philosophically, then, the implications of quantum theory mandate that there be a symbiotic relationship among all quanta (all energy) throughout the universe. Symbiosis is a wonderful word defined in Webster's dictionary as "the relationship of two or more different organisms in a close association that may be, but is not necessarily, of benefit to each." I view symbiosis as a magical word simply because of all the possibilities it implies. You are a part of me, and I am a part of you. We are both a part of the stones, trees, flowers, and animals. We are all a part of the earth, and the earth is part of the Universe. Great Spirit is everywhere, Omnipresent. MITAKUYE OYASIN. We are all Related!

Quantum mechanics and symbiosis are rather abstract ideas that would at first seem to have no relevance to our daily lives. I have a simple and very interesting experiment, however, that can help to illustrate their relevance at this very moment.

You will need two friends and a number of pieces of colored paper or cloth. I generally use colored napkins, either linen or paper will do. You will need paper or cloth representations of the colors blue, pink, green, white, yellow, and orange. Now, stand with your arms raised level with your shoulders on each side.

Have one of your friends stand behind you and then push downward on both of your arms with as much strength as he or she can muster. Make a mental note of your strength in resisting the downward pressure. Now, have your second friend hold each of the differing colors of paper or cloth about eight inches in front of your eyes so that it dominates your field of vision.

Try this strength test on your arms again as you are exposed to each of the different colors. The results are *very* interesting. Most people will have no strength in their arms when they are exposed to the color pink. (I have one friend, however, who only registered a no-strength response when exposed to the color white.)

How can the mere presence of a certain color deprive us of our strength? Quantum Mechanics! If the mere presence of a color can change us physically,[4] in such a dramatic way, then how many other quanta in the universe are impacting us without our knowledge. The mathematical/ metaphysical theories of astrology have maintained the significance of this interaction for thousands of years. There is nothing mystical nor magical about these astrological interactions. They are simply manifestations of quantum mechanics.[5]

I have found a great many people feel that the sum of their lives is the result of their own indomitable willpower. They feel that their every success, their every accomplishment, is a matter of individual pride. Ironically, any misfortune that comes their way is attributed to fate or to God. Somewhat along these same lines is a new theory on health that maintains that our subconscious is responsible for all of the illness in our lives. If we can somehow eradicate the psychological problem, then we will also eradicate the physical problem. I could be wrong, but there is ample logical evidence that both of these suppositions are incomplete or incorrect. Take, for example, my own astrological chart.

Based upon the time and place of my birth in Albuquerque, New Mexico, on April 7, 1947 at 1:27 P.M., virtually anyone can consult an astrology book and develop my natal (birth) chart. A birth chart begins by listing the astrological sign (the ascendant) present at the moment of birth on the eastern horizon. Most astrologers assign this as the first of twelve houses representing different areas of an individual's life such as domestic life, health, or partnerships and marriage. The zodiac is an imaginary belt that circles the earth and contains the orbits of all our solar system's planets (except Pluto). The sun and moon are also counted with the planets in the zodiac. Ancient astrologers arranged the stars and planets in patterns called constellations and named them for mythological animals. The very term "zodiac" comes from the Greek word *zodiakos* which means "circle of animals."[6]

Each of the planets is thought to be imbued with a certain type of energy, and the position and combination of planets at the time of birth are thought to impart these energies to the newborn child. Carl Jung surmised that, "We are born at a given moment, in a given place, and like vintage years of wine, we have the qualities of the year and of the season in which we are born."[7]

The twelve houses of my birth chart, representing the twelve signs of the zodiac, contain the planets as listed in Figure 5-1. Note that a given sign and its house can hold either no planet or several planets.

Natal Chart for Celinda Reynolds Kaelin		
Planet	*In the Zodiac Sign*	*In the House*
Sun	Leo	First
Moon	Scorpio	Fourth
Mercury	Pisces	Eighth
Venus	Pisces	Eighth
Mars	Pisces	Eighth
Jupiter	Scorpio	Fourth
Saturn	Leo	First
Uranus	Gemini	Eleventh
Neptune	Libra	Third
Pluto	Leo	First
Ascendant	Leo	First

Figure 5-1

Based upon this natal chart, virtually anyone can consult an astrology book and decipher the major events of my life. The early loss of my mother is there, the untimely death of my three brothers, the absence of a stable place to call home, the dramatic change of my occupation at midlife. This chart shows that my character was shaped by the early events of my life and even shows that the energies are present that will compel me to write this book and have it published. It also clearly indicates all of the health problems that I have experienced.

How, then, can I possibly assume all of the credit, or the blame, for the defining events in my life? Great Spirit is all-loving, and harmony or re-union of our being with Great Spirit is the natural goal of this life. Great Spirit is Omnipresent. I was part of Great Spirit prior to my birth, just as sugar is part of the sugar cane before it is refined and remains a part of the cane even after it is refined. From this analogy we can understand how Great Spirit collaborated with my spirit prior to my birth in order to provide me with all of the energy fields, internal and external, that I would need for my spiritual growth. This is the sum total of an astrological chart. It in no way implies predestination, because my free will can transform any event into an occasion for spiritual growth or decline. The choice is mine to use the packets of energy in my life pattern for harmony or for disharmony.

I feel that one day a full scientific study will be made of these phenomena, and astrology will then be accorded its proper place within the scientific community. It is a wonderful tool for self-acceptance and understanding. This same reasoning also follows for the various theories of numerology, which, my research has shown, reflect and categorize types of energy. Currently both astrology and numerology are viewed by much of the scientific and religious communities as magic or demonic.

However, if numerology and astrology are simply manifestations of quantum theory—as they logically seem to be—how can they be magic or hocus-pocus? It would seem to me that they warrant serious scientific investigation. As for being demonic, how could this be so if Great Spirit is Omnipresent? Doesn't quantum theory validate Great Spirit's Omnipresence? Astrology and numerology are simply manifestations of the Divine Order of His/Her universe, and of the First Energy that is present everywhere.

American Indian spirituality has a long tradition of seeing quantum mechanics and symbiosis at work in the world and in our daily lives. Within this rich tradition, all things—living and non-living—are imbued with spirit. This spirit comes from, and is a part of, the Great Spirit. All is One—unitheism. Stones have spirit, trees have spirit, and animals have spirit, as well as human beings.

A prayer of thanksgiving is offered to the spirit of the animal to be eaten at each meal. The hunter knows that it is not merely his prowess that has provided the food. A sentient, sacrificial act on the part of the animal has resulted in him offering himself to be slain for food. Trees and plants have spirit and, prior to harvesting, are thanked for offering their lives.

American Indians are filled with an immanent awareness of the symbiotic relationship of all things. Even the most mundane acts of daily life acknowledge this brotherhood. This relationship is an integral part of their vocabulary. Animals are addressed as Brother Deer or Brother Squirrel. The Spirits of the Wind are thanked for a refreshing breeze, as are Father Sky and Mother Earth. Everything is related. MITAKUYE OYASIN.

Craig Carpenter, a Mohawk Indian, provides an eloquent explanation of this lifestyle.

> I am supposed to uphold the Indian message to try to promote their [American Indian] teachings. ... Because ceremonies are involved with everything Indians do—from gathering food to waking up and taking a bath—there's always a song or a prayer that goes along with it. I encourage people to consider Thomas Banyacya's [a Hopi leader] four words: "Stop, consider, change, and correct." Stop what you are doing. Consider the effects of what you are doing. Is it upholding life on this land? Or is it

destructive to the life on this land? If it is destructive, then change your value system and your actions. We are not supposed to be subduing the earth, treading it underfoot, vanquishing the earth and all its life. We are supposed to be taking care of this land and the life upon it.[8]

Symbiosis is a life way for the American Indian; a conscious, moment-by-moment way of life. Unfortunately, when Europeans encountered this spirituality, they had no philosophical framework for its interpretation. They used their Judeo-Christian value system for categorizing what they encountered. Consequently, American Indian spirituality was (and still is) labeled pantheistic (worship of nature) or polytheistic (worship of multiple deities). These labels and perceptions are gravely in error, however. American Indian spirituality is unitheistic, not pantheistic nor polytheistic. American Indian spirituality acknowledges the Oneness of the Universe and only one Creator.

Einstein had no such American Indian spirituality to bring him comfort or understanding. He was greatly troubled by the implications of quantum mechanics, even though his theory of relativity was instrumental in giving birth to the theory of quantum mechanics. This theory introduces a certain unpredictability and randomness into science, simply because it proves that a specific result of a measurement cannot be stated unequivocally. This troubled Einstein, for he felt that "God does not play dice."[9] Einstein was correct about God's not being a gambler. Quantum mechanics is simply a manifestation of the scientific order rather than the serendipity of God's universe. The energies of the universe move in quanta or packets, with probabilities of result A, B or C. This does not mean that they are out of control anymore than that the energy packets which make up our body are serendipitous amalgamations and out of control. Quantum mechanics proves an omnipresent intelligence.

Scientific laws and theories are manifestations of Great Spirit's ordering of the universe. These laws and theories are not in conflict with Great Spirit's order. Science cannot logically be in conflict with Great Spirit's order because this would make science a separate, conflicting deity. Einstein's own general theory of relativity adds another dimension to this discussion: Great Spirit's Omniscience.

Einstein's first intuition concerning the general theory of relativity came when he was about sixteen years old. At that time it was already known that light travels at a speed of 186,000 miles per second. This intrigued Einstein. He speculated on how light would appear if one were able to travel in tandem with light. He theorized that it would appear as an oscillating "particle." With this new insight, Einstein then developed his theory of relativity on a very basic premise—that space and time are simply relative to the observer.[10]

If the observer is at an infinite distance, as Great Spirit would be, then all events would appear to occur in an instant. Since Great Spirit is infinite, He/She would therefore have infinite knowledge—and all events would occur instantaneously and simultaneously.

To the participants (us) of space and time, the events of life are measured by minutes, hours, days, and so on. The energies of the universe (of Great Spirit) come in quanta, with an uncertainty of outcome measured only by our temporal standards. This quantum theory of Great Spirit is vitally important when addressing the issue of free will in the context of Great Spirit's omniscience. Through our free will we are able to respond in a number of ways to the quanta of energies that swirl through our daily lives. There are any number of possible outcomes available to us.

As we ponder and then act, we exercise our free will. Even though we do not know the outcome in advance, the Great Spirit does. In His/Her infinity, all events are simultaneous. We, however, are "traveling alongside the train." And from our perspective, the train of events in this life is slow moving. Certain individuals are able to resonate at a frequency with Great Spirit that permits momentary insight into future and past events of which they would normally have no knowledge. We term this clairvoyant or psychic knowledge. This resonance is generally intermittent and not a constant state of being. It accounts for my precognitive dreams and the visions or understandings that I have while I am meditating. It is interesting to note that the ego must be shut down before this resonance occurs. When our ego is engaged, we will not be in harmony with Great Spirit.

Science has had difficulty documenting this phenomena and has met with mixed results. Logically, this erratic manifestation is due to the problem of disabling the ego at will. How can a scientist possibly measure whether or not an individual's ego is engaged while being tested? As in quantum mechanics, the very act of testing may change the results by engaging the ego. The lack of scientific validation does not mean that there are no bona fide clairvoyants or psychics. It simply indicates that the methods of testing are inadequate.

When our responses to the quanta of energy in our lives are in harmony with Great Spirit, we will experience peace, harmony and complete love.

Prayer and meditation are tools for discerning the quantum movement of Great Spirit's energy patterns in our lives. When we impose our will on people and events, we only experience frustration and dissonance. No matter how hard we might try, we do not control the people and events in our lives. This is an illusion and it is a dissonant vibration.

It seems that most of the anger people feel toward God is due to the painful events of life. Life holds a great deal of pain for everyone sooner or later. No one is exempt. Only the details and the levels of the pain differ. In the context of unitheism, however, God is not at fault. Because we are a part of Great Spirit, we participate in Great Spirit's infinity. Together we planned the events of our lives prior to birth. We timed our birth into this world so that the planets would impart the energies that we would need in order to grow spiritually. We planned our lives so that the circumstances of living would facilitate this growth. This life is simply a transient state of being until our reunion with Great Spirit. Unfortunately, human beings are lazy. As long as life is comfortable, we usually ignore the need to grow spiritually. Our complacency and lethargy can only be shattered with pain, which then prods us onto the path of spiritual growth.

Life is given to us as a tool for bringing our energies into greater harmony with the Great Spirit. We choose the events in life that will be presented to us in order to effect our spiritual growth. This is done before we are born into our physical bodies. We literally set the stage. Now the choices are ours. If we choose dissonance over an extended period of time, we will simply cease to exist. If we choose harmony, if we walk the Good Red Road, we will have infinite life.

There are a number of aids that one can use in determining how to walk the Good Red Road. One of the most useful that I've found is to examine the talk that goes on inside one's head. When one hears the words "shoulda," or "coulda," or "woulda," **ignore the message**. This is usually our ego speaking. "You shoulda introduced yourself to the chairman; your career woulda been made." Or, "You woulda been great if you'd just had an opportunity." These words are destructive. Ignore them. Erase them from your consciousness whenever they appear.

If, however, a voice inside your head speaks in the imperative, this is usually your spiritual guide—your higher self. "Go to the meeting today" is a message in your head saying that you should, indeed, attend the meeting. "Speak to the lady on your right" is a message telling you that there is spiritual work to be done with this person.

I would offer this caution. These same imperative messages can also be destructive and dissonant if one is living in a dissonant state. For example, if one is heavily engaged in anger, hate, jealousy, or any other dissonant energy then that person is susceptible to further dissonant energies.

Dissonant energy attracts dissonant energy. Harmonious energy attracts harmonious energy.

Each person is on his or her own path of spiritual growth. The quanta of Great Spirit's energies needed to effect this growth are available to each individual. Imposing our own will and causing a dissonance in another person's life, or within nature, is contrary to Great Spirit's will and therefore is evil.

> In harmony with the Tao,
> the sky is clear and spacious,
> the earth is solid and full,
> all creatures flourish together,
> content with the way they are,
> endlessly repeating themselves,
> endlessly renewed.
>
> When man interferes with the Tao,
> the sky becomes filthy,
> the earth becomes depleted,
> the equilibrium crumbles,
> creatures become extinct.[11]

This leads me to make a further argument for working at spiritual growth throughout our lifetime. Psychologists Joseph Luft and Harry Ingham developed an interesting model for analyzing the dynamics of interactions between self and others. This model, shown in Figure 5-2, is labeled the Johari window (by using half of each first name). It illustrates that the nature of relationships is defined by the extent that one knows himself/herself and the same extent that one understands or knows the other.[12] As an example, the less one knows about oneself and the less one knows about the other (labeled the "undiscovered self"), the greater the extent of conflict between the two. At the other extreme, the greater the knowledge one has of oneself and of the other (labeled the "open self"), the greater the absence of interpersonal conflict and the greater the trust.

The Johari window provides a graphic illustration of the dynamics of our relationship to Great Spirit. The less work that we have done on knowing ourselves (growing spiritually), the less we will be able to trust in Great Spirit and order our actions according to His/Her will. Conversely, the less work we have done in coming to know and trust Great Spirit, the less we will be able to know ourselves. Therefore, we will experience greater conflict with Great Spirit's will. We must *work* at spiritual growth.

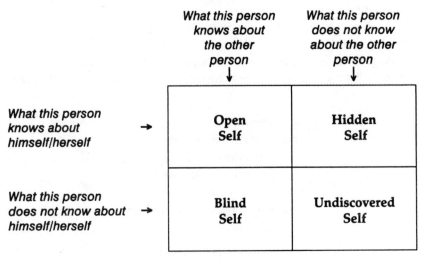

Figure 5-1

Chapter Notes

1. S. Johnson, *The Book of Elders: The Life Stories & Wisdom of Great American Indians,* New York: HarperCollins, 1994, p. 31.
2. S. Hawking, op. cit., p. 55.
3. F. Capra, op. cit., p. 124.
4. M. Wilcox, *Blue and Yellow Don't Make Green,* Cincinnati: ——— 1989, ch. 4.
5. N. Campion, *The Practical Astrologer,* New York: Abrams, 1987, pp. 6, 7.
6. J. M. Woolfolk, op. cit., p. 309.
7. Ibid., p. IX.
8. S. Johnson, op. cit., p. 105.
9. S. Hawking, op. cit., p. 56.
10. F. Capra, op. cit., pp. 151–159.
11. Lao Tzu, op. cit., ch. 39.
12. F. Luthans, *Organizational Behavior,* New York: McGraw Hill, 1981, pp. 377, 378.

Love the Great Spirit

"... But, in a broader sense, our whole life is prayer because every act of our life is, in a very real sense, a religious act."

Ohiyesa (Sioux)
The Soul of an Indian

Our next step on the path of spiritual growth is that of truly loving Great Spirit. American Indians "know how to be with life," addressing their every action with song or prayer to Great Spirit. It is a life way of love for Great Spirit.

> There's a new awakening for our people, and it's growing fast. I find comfort each and every day that all that I do is going to bring changes and hope and new visions. Not only for my own people, but for people of the world, because people of the world are also suffering. You know, they are their own victims. So they are looking for answers with us, because we know how to be with life, all life-forces upon Mother Earth.[1]

We must know and trust Great Spirit in order to love Him/Her. When we come to know someone, and therefore come to trust someone, then we can truly love that someone. To say that we love someone, if we don't trust them, is empty rhetoric. Likewise, to say that we love Great Spirit, when our lives reflect a lack of trust in Great Spirit, is empty rhetoric.

In setting out on this path to Love we must first remember that our words and our actions have to be consonant or they will cancel one another. When I think of this conflict between words and actions, I am reminded of a charming friend of mine whom I'll call Frank.

Frank is an attractive, divorced, and successful businessman. He is also in his fifties, which makes him quite a catch for all the divorcées and widows in his same age group. Frank has a great need to be loved, but his divorce left him embittered and afraid of any long-term commitment. Nonetheless, he has developed a unique solution to his dilemma.

Frank must have at least twenty "friends" (as he euphemistically labels his sexual partners). He is kind and solicitous to all of these women, and has told each of them about all of his other friends. However, his actions are so sincere and so caring that each woman chooses to believe he loves her exclusively. Although he has avoided telling anyone "I love you," his actions speak only of love.

In the meantime, Frank reaps all of the benefits of a much-loved man. All of his friends are vying to be the one-and-only, and competition is fierce. Frank rarely buys anyone dinner, and instead enjoys mouth-watering home-cooked meals with a different friend every night. There is never a shortage of invitations to concerts or to the theater. Frank is openly proud of the many women in love with him, and is quick to clarify that he has never led them on. His bedside table looks like a trophy shelf, lined with photographs of beautiful women, each inscribed "To Frank, with love." Clearly, all of these women are confused because Frank's words and actions contradict each other.

Along the same vein, but not quite so amusing, are a number of unscrupulous, evangelical, television preachers who gained notoriety in the 1980s. These men enjoyed incredible success, bringing the "Word of God" to everyone within range of a television set. Along with their inspiring words of hope and love, however, was a plaintive plea for donations. Millions of dollars poured into their pockets from well-intentioned people who believed their emotionally-charged sermons.

Unfortunately, these unscrupulous men used this money for dissolute lifestyles, not for the betterment of humanity. Millions of good-faith donations were squandered on luxurious homes, cars, jewels, and deviant sexual activities. These men preach Love of God, but live lives filled with love of self. Their words and their actions are completely dissonant.

New Age seekers, enamored with American Indian spirituality, provide a new arena of opportunity for charlatans posing as shamans. True medicine men and medicine women are acclaimed as such because of skills and talents given them by the Great Spirit. They do not name themselves Medicine Woman or Man; their friends and community do this for them based upon their healing and spiritual powers. They will readily admit that what they accomplish is actually done by the Great Spirit. True medicine men and women take no credit for their powers. There is no school that can certify one as a medicine man or woman. These gifts come from Great Spirit and cannot be bought for any amount of money.

Rose Auger, a Cree medicine woman, has healed numerous people across Canada and the United States. She provides a glimpse of her life in *The Book of Elders*.

> ... I would never have the kind of [healing] gifts I do today if I had not pursued this [traditional] learning, or how to practice self-sacrifice and live exactly as I am told. If I was told to go and fast for so many days in the mountains, that's exactly what I did. If I was told to go work with people, I did exactly that. I lived as holy as I could because I carried a great gift, and I was taken care of ...
>
> Sometimes I have to sell things in order to keep going, but I am never without help, any place, any time. That's how it used to be, and that's how we need to be now. Greed is useless because you can't take nothing with you, and to be truly serving of the Creator and the gift that is yours to help people, you have to be humble.
>
> To be humble is to be giving, and to remember that it isn't you who did the curing, that it's those spirits working with you. You are a vessel, just a vehicle and a human being.[2]

The great religions of the world all teach that we must love Great Spirit. We have seen that this love and the mandate to trust are inseparable. Our words and actions must be consonant. If I say that I love, but my actions are only of self-love, or if I say that I trust, but spend my life trying to control my friends and my surroundings, then there is no truth in what I say. There is no consonant vibration, and the dissonance created by the energy from one cancels the other. We are the sum of what we think and feel and do.

Rose Auger attributes the serenity of her life to her love and trust of the Great Spirit.

> Even now, if I have any problems, there's always help. I have such great faith, I'll go anywhere without fear. It is so fulfilling to live by the motivation of your spirit. That's what people lack today, and that's what has to be established. To begin listening to their own inner selves, their own spirit, or for us, our guardian spirit. That's why this traditional life is not hard, because if you listen, you'll know how to have a full life. That's what all peoples need to develop, because all peoples know subconsciously what is right and what is wrong.[3]

Failure to love Great Spirit, and therefore place trust in Him/Her, is reflected in our lives in many ways. Our most basic failure as a two-legged is when we succumb to fear and then respond with fight, flight, or control.

Alvin Toffler, author of the best seller *Powershift*, expounds on three sources of social control: violence, wealth, and knowledge—all products of our fears. "What's more, all three can be used at almost every level of social life, from the intimacy of home to the political arena."[4] Toffler goes on to give examples of this use of control in the concentric circles of society—home, work, society, and government.

> In the private sphere, a parent can slap a child (use force), cut an allowance or bribe with a dollar (use money or its equivalent), or—most effective of all—mold a child's values so the child *wishes* to obey. In politics, a government can imprison or torture a dissident, financially punish its critics and pay off its supporter, and it can manipulate truth to create consent.[5]

This need for control is an extremely heavy burden and causes great stress within the individual because we *do know* that we are not Great Spirit. Alcoholism is one of the symptoms of this stress and is a pervasive illness within our society. One of the first steps Alcoholics Anonymous utilizes in helping the alcoholic to recover is *to have the alcoholic acknowledge that Great Spirit, or some supreme being, has control of their life*. This same acknowledgment (of Great Spirit in control) is an integral part of the recovery process for most social illnesses from drug addiction to spouse and child abuse.

It is interesting to note that alcoholism did not ravage American Indian populations until their European conquerors actively sought to suppress American Indian spirituality. The introduction of alcohol alone would not have been so devastating had it not been accompanied by this religious suppression. As the successes of Alcoholics Anonymous have shown, trust in Great Spirit is implicit in the recovery process.

Traditional American Indian spirituality is a life way of trust in Great Spirit. The most serious threat to the survival of American Indians is not alcoholism. It is the forced eradication of their spirituality, their life way, and the attempt to supplant it with a totally alien Christianity. In fact, the United States Congress made all American Indian ceremonies illegal beginning in 1890. American Indians could not legally practice their way of life until the Freedom of Religion Act of 1978.

Another of the rampant social problems in America is the conflict endemic in second marriages where children are concerned. This conflict also reflects a lack of trust in Great Spirit. The child does not feel secure in the love of the new stepparent, and therefore does not trust their motives or actions. In addition, the child usually resents the presence of the stepparent as an interloper and longs to have the "real" mother and father reunited.

Exacerbating the situation even further, the new stepparent generally interprets the meaning of parenting as controlling rather than nurturing.

As Toffler illustrated, the stage for conflict is set. The true stories (not true names, however) that follow show the tragic consequences of this fight for control.

Clyde and Mary, both divorced, met and married when Mary's two children were still just toddlers. At the time Clyde worked for the State Highway Department. Several years later, having completed thirty years of service, he retired and moved his family to a remote region of the Rocky Mountains where he could indulge his passion for fishing. The most difficult decision that now faces Clyde each day is choosing a fishing spot. However, Clyde's pension is not quite enough income for a family of four to survive on, so Mary works as a maid at a local dude ranch. Clyde had a drinking problem prior to his retirement, but now the long days without real purpose have transformed Clyde into an ogre. His drinking is totally out of control.

Mary's two sons, now teenagers, are virtual prisoners in this idyllic mountain hideaway. Clyde controls their every move. They may only read certain books; their school friends may not visit; only certain phone calls are allowed and then are monitored and timed. Physical violence as punishment for any supposed infraction of these numerous rules is a daily occurrence.

Both of the boys had hoped for a career in the military as a means of escape, but Clyde would not allow it. After a particularly nasty late-night incident when Clyde threatened to cut the younger boy's throat, both boys ran away from home. They have now turned to gangs and drugs in an attempt to belong and to escape the harsh reality of their lives. Mary only makes a few hundred dollars each month (not enough to support herself) and therefore remains an economic prisoner of Clyde.

Andrea comes from a different type of family and yet she met the same tragic end as Clyde's boys. Andrea's parents are religious fundamentalists. Hard work and little play are the basis of their ethic, which also dictates that they not spare the rod for fear of spoiling the child. Andrea is a beautiful girl, the eldest of eleven children, all born at home. She is expected to provide all of the homemaking and to care for all of the other children, in addition to doing her schoolwork.

Because of these duties, Andrea missed more school than the attendance policy will allow and was suspended from school in the fall of her senior year. Then her parents forced her to stay at home and care for the younger children full time. Andrea, too, lost all hope for the future. She ran away from home, fell in with the wrong crowd, and now spends her days in a drug-induced haze. A bright and beautiful girl, also lost.

The last of the stories that I will tell you concerning the excessive use of force to control is that of Regis and his stepfather, Bill. Nancy remarried when Regis was just a toddler. Her new husband, Bill, already had two children from a previous marriage. He also had a history of physically and verbally abusing them, but Nancy was in love and didn't care.

Bill is quite active in his community church and makes a show of his religious convictions. To meet Bill without knowing of his family problems, one would think that he was a pillar of the community. When Bill began to abuse Regis, however, Nancy put her foot down insisting that he choose either counseling or a divorce. In accordance with Nancy's ultimatum, Bill is now in therapy, trying to overcome his obsessive need to control those around him. He understands his problem in an abstract way, but cannot (or will not) recognize it within the context of his actions.

Regis has had every material advantage but the constant abuse has virtually destroyed his self-esteem. In a recent clash of wills, Bill levied a barrage of verbal and physical abuse on Regis and he ran away from home. In his desperation he took Bill's credit card, and Bill filed criminal charges. Regis is a charming, attractive, intelligent young man, and now he too seems lost to society.

According to Toffler, the second tool for controlling society and our environment—money—is almost as destructive as the use of violence, the first source. The experience of a fellow that I knew (I'll call him Jack) is one of the best illustrations of the dangers of succumbing to the power of money.

Jack is an atheist. He is gifted with a genius I.Q. and is a card-carrying member of Mensa, the club for geniuses. He believes that his superior intellect enables him to think through any problem and arrive at the very best of all possible solutions.

Jack has only contempt for all other humans of lesser intellect. As a young man, he became alienated from his mother and father since he felt that they were stupid. He refuses to ever have children for fear that they might be dumb. Sadly, Jack feels that his superior intellect requires him to control all of the people and events within the parameters of his life.

One of Jack's tools for accomplishing this objective is to have adequate cash. He is a highly paid government contractor but, in spite of this, he will go to any lengths to accumulate more money. He participates in illegal stock trades, lies on his income taxes, and cheats his friends in business deals. All of this is justified in his mind, however, since he thinks his moral mandate is to have enough cash to implement his superior judgments.

Predictably, Jack is an alcoholic. Drinking is his only escape from the heavy burden of constant vigilance over the people and affairs in his life. He is only able to enjoy sex when he is paying for it, because that ensures him complete control. His timorous wife is the proverbial doormat because of the constant barrage of mental, physical, and emotional abuse. Eventually, Jack self-destructed. His drinking gradually diminished his mental capabilities, and he was caught selling "Top Secret" information to a foreign power. His hunger for enough money to adequately control life ultimately destroyed his career and his personal relationships.

This craving for money is one of the great seducers of our society. Our heroes are inevitably the individuals who have accumulated the most wealth, regardless of the type of lives they lead. Our United States is one of the most affluent nations in the world. In spite of this, however, we have one of the highest infant mortality rates and one of the highest crime rates in the world. Among the leading causes of death for our young people is suicide. Clearly, money and violence are not the answers to building a great civilization.

Our society must again instill a value system wherein the center of our lives is Great Spirit—where we trust in Great Spirit. Only then will the destructive forces of our fears be neutralized.

Interestingly, the ability to place trust in Great Spirit and live within the harmony of Great Spirit bears little correlation to the religious activities of an individual. If this were the case, there would be no alcoholic priests, rabbis, or ministers. Often, religion (or a presumed intimate knowledge of God) is simply used as another, more acceptable means of power or control. A tragic example of this was the murder of a Colorado Springs woman by her husband's lover.

Jennifer Reali, the young woman who confessed to the murder, told prosecutors and psychiatrists about her motivation to kill Dianne Hood. "The driving force was that she (Reali) had become convinced by him (Hood) that it was God's will to eliminate the woman from her misery and that it was her job to do it."[6] The victim, Dianne Hood, was suffering from lupus, a debilitating disease. Brian Hood, her husband, allegedly convinced Reali that his wife was in pain and that it was "God's will" that she die.

> He brought Reali a guide to the Bible, "God's Word," with passages from the Bible he had highlighted "for her daily review." And she did review them daily, Morall [the psychologist] said.

One particular passage caught Reali's eye, Morall said. It was about King David's elimination of his mistress' husband by sending him off to war. David then married Bethsheba with God's approval.

Another passage she took to heart seemed to say she should be right in taking Hood's advice, Morall said. The passage reads that man is the "image and glory of God and woman was the image and glory of man," Morall said.

Mr. Hood told her she could not make a mistake, because "God would interfere and stop her if it was a mistake," the doctor said.[7]

The case of Jennifer Reali and Brian Hood is tragically interesting. It illustrates the way that many people are misusing religious teachings—the Bible, for example—as a means to control others. It is almost impossible to enter into a philosophical discussion with people who adhere to fundamentalist religious teachings. A palpable fear is engendered by any such discussion, and anger is the most common response.

Unfortunately, some Christians of this type will often unleash a barrage of Bible quotes, angrily hurling them at anyone who offers a different opinion. These quotes are assiduously memorized and provide an effective deterrent to any meaningful dialogue. Rules of engagement for such a discussion demand retaliating Bible quotes only. These conversations are usually devoid of true feelings or spirituality, but this tactic is nonetheless effective in discouraging independent thought.

Knowledge as a source of control is the third of Toffler's social tools that we humans use to assure a false sense of control within our lives. However, this type of control poses a serious threat to a free exchange of ideas. Without full knowledge of one another, gained through full and frank discussion, we are subject to the fourth quadrant of the Johari Window—total lack of trust in one another. This is an unhealthy and even dangerous form of social interaction.

As a means toward false control of our lives, money, force, and knowledge (real or perceived) can be effective for short periods of time. Over the longer term, however, they break down and become destructive. This is inevitable, as they create an energy which is dissonant to the energy of Great Spirit's will. This type of energy, when used knowingly and willfully, is what society calls evil.

Governments that practice these kinds of control are generally labeled Evil Empires. Adolf Hitler, Idi Amin, Saddam Hussein, Joseph Stalin—all exerted iron-fisted control over their people—what they read, what they thought, how they worshipped. In line with Toffler's theory, this control was implemented by force (the SS Troops and similar groups of thugs), by knowledge (extensive use of spying and informants), and by money (limited access to a select inner circle). These same control techniques are endemic in every type of tyranny.

How, then, does one live his or her life so that it is in harmony with Great Spirit's will? "The basic oneness of the universe is ... one of the most important revelations of modern physics."[8] This is also one of the most important revelations of modern philosophy. Great Spirit is Omnipresent throughout the Oneness of the Universe, and every manifestation is a part of His/Her cosmic pattern, complete with its own micro-energy charge that flows from the same cosmic pattern.

An individual who lives in harmony with Great Spirit's will has no need of forcing his or her will on anyone or anything around him/her. Such an individual will simply adapt his/her course of action so that it is harmonious with the cosmic pattern in question and, thereby, in harmony with Great Spirit's will. "The Master doesn't try to be powerful; thus he is truly powerful."[9] There is nothing more powerful than acting in harmony with Great Spirit's will!

One of my favorite stories in the Taoist teachings is from the *Huai Nan Tzu*.

> A poor farmer's horse ran off into the country of the barbarians. All his neighbors offered their condolences, but his father said, "How do you know that this isn't good fortune?" After a few months the horse returned with a barbarian horse of excellent stock. All his neighbors offered their congratulations, but his father said, "How do you know that this isn't a disaster?" The two horses bred, and the family became rich in fine horses. The farmer's son spent much of his time riding them; one day he fell off and broke his hipbone. All his neighbors offered the farmer their condolences, but his father said, "How do you know that this isn't good fortune?" Another year passed, and the barbarians invaded the frontier. All the able-bodied young men were conscripted, and nine-tenths of them died in the war. Thus good fortune can be disaster and vice versa. Who can tell how events will be transformed?[10]

This story is a classic insofar as it shows the wisdom of accepting Great Spirit's will and not forcing the events of our lives. Had the farmer intervened in any of the events and imposed his will, his son's life might not have been spared in the end. This story also reminds me of an old Irish poem that my grandmother brought with her when she immigrated to the United States in the 1880s. I don't know the title or the author, but I still remember the verse.

I seek in prayerful words, dear friend,
My heart's true wish to send you,
That you may know that far and near
My loving thoughts attend you.

I cannot find a dearer word,
Nor fonder to caress you,
Nor song nor poem that I have heard
Is sweeter than "God bless you!"

God bless thee! And so I wish thee
All of brightness life possesses.
For how can sorrow bring you harm
If 'tis God's way to bless us.

And so through all thy days
May darkness harm thee never
But this alone, "God bless thee dear"
Then art thou safe forever.

—Unknown

Both the story of the farmer's horse and Grandmother's poem illustrate the ways in which one can trust in Great Spirit. Proverbs tell us to: "Trust in the Lord with all thine heart; and lean not unto thine own understanding. In all thy ways acknowledge Him, and He shall direct thy paths."[11] Sitting Bull advised his followers to attempt a course of action only until thwarted by several failures. Then, when it became clear that there was no medicine (harmonious energy) in that path, it should be abandoned.

Teachings of placing trust in Great Spirit are central to most Eastern and Western religions. They are perhaps the most unifying and similar of all religious teachings. Another important extension of this philosophy of not forcing the people and events of our lives is that of religious tolerance.

There are many valid paths to the Great Spirit. We are all prisms of Great Spirit's truth, with no one person in full possession of this Truth. Our ability to live such a philosophy of tolerance and submission to Great Spirit's will can have a profound effect on the world in which we live. Each person can make a difference. I have attempted to illustrate the exponential effect of consonant energy waves in earlier chapters. Always, the effect of two harmonious waves is much greater, exponentially greater, than the mere sum of the two waves.

Our world is composed of concentric circles of these waves beginning with the individual, then to the family, the community, society, government, nations and, ultimately, the universe. The rippling effect of one person acting in harmony with Great Spirit's will has the potential to reverberate throughout the universe! Love can literally transform our cosmos. Also, don't forget that the clashing of "good" and "evil" energy waves is necessary in order to obliterate evil. The harmonious convergence of good energy waves is also synchronous with Great Spirit's energy, and the cumulative effect is limitless.

I think that one of the most powerful and persuasive examples of the convergence of harmonious energy waves is the incredible experiment conducted by Nikola Tesla.

> Tesla constructed a device no larger than an alarm clock, so constructed that frequency of vibrations could be altered at will. He set the vibrator in "tune" with the [steel] link. For a long time nothing happened—vibrations of link and machine did not chance to coincide, but at last they did and the great steel link began to tremble, increased its trembling until it dilated and contracted like a beating heart—and finally broke.[12]

The steel link that Tesla broke by enhancing its vibrations was approximately two feet long and two feet thick and made of the best quality steel. In addition to breaking this steel beam, Tesla's experiment also set off a small earthquake in the area of his laboratory, thoroughly frightening him and all of his neighbors. In related experiments, he calculated that the earth's vibration had a periodicity of about one hour and forty-nine minutes. He further theorized that one could literally break the world in two by similarly enhancing its normal vibrations.

If Tesla was able to enhance the natural vibrations within a steel beam to such an extent that he was able to break the beam, think how much more powerful the enhancement of Great Spirit's energies within ourselves could be. When we live our lives filled with love, the possibilities are limitless!

Before I go any further with this line of thought, I would like to digress for a moment in order to clarify the presence of Great Spirit's energies.

Traditional Western religions somehow transmit the idea that God/Great Spirit is separate from the world, a transcendent deity. As I explained earlier, this concept was expounded by Descartes in the form of Cartesian Dualism—the idea that there are two radically different kinds of substance, the physical and the spiritual. This line of thought further separated God/Great Spirit from the world in the minds of human beings. However, American Indians and Eastern religions have taught an opposing concept, that Great Spirit is an integral part of all His/Her creation. In a somewhat similar vein, Buddhists teach that reality is nothing but an extension of the mind of Buddha.

As I argued in the first chapter, it is much more logical to establish Great Spirit as an immanent reality that is Omnipresent. "... lo, I am with you always, even unto the end of the world."[13] In the Book of Joshua, we have God telling Joshua and his people, "Do not fear nor be dismayed, for the Lord, your God, is with you wherever you go."[14]

Christians in the seventeenth century defied the Catholic Church when they accepted the scientific truth that the world was round and not flat. Now, our knowledge of scientific fact mandates that we change our concept of Great Spirit from transcendent to immanent. Great Spirit is everywhere, and we are all one with the universe. This is the truth that will successfully carry human beings into the twenty-first century. This knowledge will allow us to live lives filled with love for Great Spirit and for all two-leggeds, four-leggeds, winged ones, plant people, and Mother Earth.

Chapter Notes

1. Sandy Johnson, *The Book of Elders: The Life Stories & Wisdom of Great American Indians,* New York: HarperCollins, 1994, p.144.
2. Ibid., p. 140.
3. Ibid., p. 138.
4. A. Toffler, *Powershift,* New York: Bantam, 1990, p. 13.
5. Ibid., pp. 13, 14.
6. *The Gazette Telegraph,* May 1, 1991.
7. Ibid., May 1, 1991.
8. F. Capra, op. cit., p. 117.
9. Lao Tzu, op. cit., ch. 38.
10. Ibid., pp. 106, 107.
11. Proverbs, 3:5–6.
12. I. Hunt & W. Draper, *Lightning in His Hand—The Life Story of Nikola Tesla,* Denver: Sage Books, 1964, p. 101.
13. Matthew, 28:20b
14. Joshua, 1:9

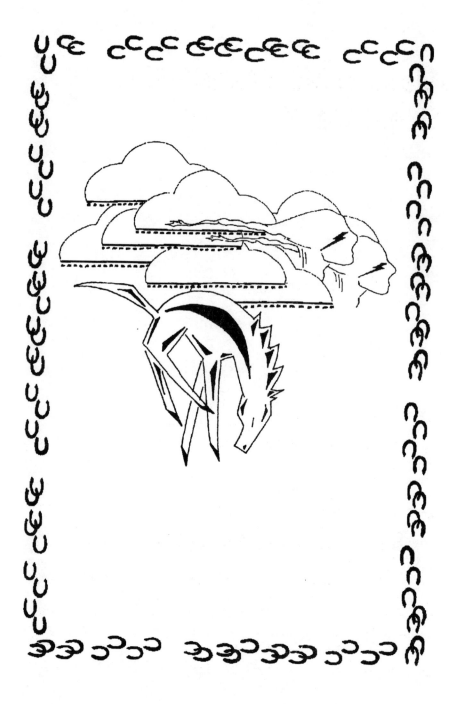

7

Making Medicine with Great Spirit

"If you ask, 'What is silence?' we will answer, 'It is the Great Mystery. The holy silence is God's voice.'
"If you ask, 'What are the fruits of silence?' we will answer, 'They are self-control, true courage or endurance, patience, dignity, and reverence. Silence is the cornerstone of character.' "

Ohiyesa (Sioux)
The Soul of an Indian

Essential to the concept of an immanent Great Spirit, Omnipresent in the world, is the concept of a spiritual energy called Teh in Taoist terminology, Holy Spirit in Christian terminology, and Medicine in the American Indian tradition. This is the energy of Great Spirit that orders and controls the universe. "God does not play dice." Einstein vehemently argued that the order of the world around us provides ample evidence of an intelligent design, of Great Spirit's medicine.

But how can there be a logical ordering when scientific data seems to indicate that the patterns of atoms, the quanta of energy, which makes stars or plants or humans are a result of serendipity? If our physical world is truly the result of serendipity, then why and how are these patterns repeated billions of times with complete accuracy? Theories of statistical probability indicate that accidental assembly is highly improbable. Anyone can look at the homogeneity of the human race, or of any species, and grasp the fact that these results are not accidental. I am only a two-legged, but it seems clear to me that science simply has not yet discovered how Great Spirit uses His/Her medicine to arrange creation.

Perhaps one of the strongest clues in defense of the manner in which the energy of Great Spirit pervades and orders the universe lies within Kirlian photography. Experimenters in Kirlian photography have documented something called the phantom leaf effect.

> Experimenters prepare a Kirlian photo plate and then obtain a leaf from a tree, which has a part of it torn off. The damaged leaf is placed on the film and the high-tension source turned on. What appears on the picture is an image of the field of the whole leaf.[1]

Instead of a transcendent Great Spirit, separate and apart from the universe, maybe the Buddhist, Taoist, and American Indian teachings are more valid. Perhaps all of reality is simply like a Kirlian photograph—the pattern exists by way of the Holy Spirit/Teh/Great Spirit's Medicine and matter simply fills in the pattern. Doesn't Kirlian photography reflect the Buddhist teaching that all of reality is actually a manifestation of the mind of Buddha?

This concept of an immanent, omnipresent Great Spirit is critical to a successful philosophy of life. This concept plays a key role because human beings must let go of fear in order to fully love and trust in Great Spirit. However, letting go of fear is impossible if Great Spirit is not involved/concerned with the minute details of our life. If Great Spirit is an entity separate and apart from the universe and only involved on an occasional basis, then it logically follows that we two-leggeds must govern every detail that falls within our span of control. This line of thought is not correct. I am only a two-legged, and I could be wrong, but it is not logical to think of Great Spirit as a separate reality. As I illustrated earlier, Omnipresence is an integral attribute of Great Spirit. Great Spirit's energies are all-pervading and all-important, and are interwoven in the fabric of our being and the texture of our lives. All is One.

The more rapidly the world changes (as it has been doing in this complex age of technology), the more frightened humans become because so many events are beyond our control. Conversely, the more that events are beyond control, the more frightened we humans become. Our fears create a vicious cycle. Human beings generally seek a release from these fears through at least one of three panaceas: drugs, alcohol, and religious convictions. However, the only true remedy is a philosophical system that firmly places Great Spirit in control of our lives while still acknowledging our free will.

These three panaceas are manifest in our society by the growing drug and alcohol problems and the resurgence of fundamentalist religions. This pervasive fear also explains the hunger for New Age spirituality.

As I argued earlier, trust in Great Spirit is the most effective antidote to the fears that permeate the fabric of our lives. This comes from knowing that Great Spirit is present and involved in our lives. There is a Cosmic Plan—our spiritual growth and our ultimate reunion with Great Spirit. In order to effect this plan, however, our lives must be in harmony with Great Spirit's will. Energy waves from our thoughts and words and deeds must be consonant with Great Spirit's energy. We have the free will to choose, but our choices must be in harmony with Great Spirit's attributes of truth and love if we hope to achieve oneness and infinity.

Trust in Great Spirit can be realized within our daily lives when we give up control and controlling. All of our actions must be motivated by love, not fear. In order to follow the Good Red Road, in order to find consonance with Great Spirit's energy, we can use prayer and meditation.

Generally speaking, prayer is used for acknowledging Great Spirit as the Supreme Being, thanking Great Spirit for blessings received or, most commonly, presenting Great Spirit with a shopping list of "gimme" or "I need."

The problem with the shopping list approach to prayer is that human beings don't have access to the Big Picture. There's a wonderful country and western song called "Thank God for Unanswered Prayers." In the song the man tells of his teenage love and the desperate prayers that he prayed for them to be together. His prayers weren't answered; he didn't win her love. However, years later he meets the true love of his life and is thankful that he developed no lasting attachment to this teen love.

I have a close friend who told me a story similar to the one in the song. My friend said that his first, passionate love did not end as he hoped. Instead, he was sent into combat in a foreign land and she married someone else. At the end of the war my friend put himself through college where he received an advanced degree with honors. His life was filled with one fascinating adventure after another. He maintains, however, that his greatest adventure was discovering Great Spirit. In this new spiritual awareness, my friend found inner peace. He told me that he saw his first love many years later. She asked him if he still had regrets that they had not married, and my friend replied with great sincerity: "Now I have the wisdom to see that the pain of losing you started me on my path of spiritual growth. I wouldn't trade my adventures and all that I learned from them, despite my early years of sorrow and a broken heart. If we had married, especially as young and unprepared as we were, I doubt that I would have received the knowledge that I have now."

Nonetheless, prayer can be appropriate when we need help to reach an objective that is in harmony with the attributes of Great Spirit. American Indians teach that these prayers to Great Spirit should be preceded by the words "… it is for a good cause." It is also a good idea to begin such prayers by giving thanks for the many ways that Great Spirit has blessed our lives. Giving thanks helps us keep our humility and remember the vital role that Great Spirit plays in our lives. American Indian prayer usually begins by acknowledging the spiritual energies of each of the directions and thanking them and Great Spirit for their gifts to us two-leggeds.

I generally begin my prayers by facing west, but the only rule in this type of prayer is that there are no rules. I structure my prayer in the manner that Black Elk taught and have found that to be very effective. When facing west, I thank the Great Spirit's energies there for the life-giving rains and the winds that carry those rains. I also thank the spirits of my relations and ancestors, for I know that they are working to help me.

As I next turn to the north to thank Great Spirit's energies, I am grateful for the snows from the north and their blanket of moisture that slowly seeps into the soil replenishing the earth's underground water reserves. I am also grateful for the truth that comes from Great Spirit which is symbolized by the white purity of snow.

In the east, I remember that each day the sun rises I am given another opportunity to learn something new. I thank Great Spirit for the knowledge that each new day brings.

As I turn to thank Great Spirit's energies in the south, I am mindful that the life-giving winter sun rises and sets in the southern sky. I am thankful for its warming rays that give life to all things and for the spiritual growth that each new day brings.

Finally I turn to Mother Earth and thank Great Spirit's energies there for nourishing all plants, animals, and people in her bosom, and for nurturing our bodies in life and embracing our bodies in death. I always end with thanksgiving to Father Sky and Great Spirit for all of the gifts of life, for the endless love and beauty that surrounds us, and for his constant and omnipresent love.

Giving thanks in this manner serves as a reminder of our place in the universe, and the omnipresence and love of Great Spirit. Giving thanks helps to keep us humble and helps us avoid the hazards of our own egos. Prayer in this manner also allows us to exercise our free will toward truth and love and still acknowledge our dependence on Great Spirit. Such prayers, however, keep us cognizant that we do not know Great Spirit's overall plan.

On the other hand, if our prayers are for money and prosperity, we should probably just save our breath. Great Spirit did not create money; humans did; and it was not created out of love. Great Spirit is not a billionaire loan officer. This is not to say, however, that Great Spirit will not use money as an occasional tool. Great Spirit can and will use anything in this world as a tool for our spiritual growth.

In contrast to typical prayer, meditation allows us to empty ourselves of all wants and desires and become vessels filled with Great Spirit's will. When we are filled with Great Spirit's will, we are in harmony with the universe and will feel peace, love, and harmony. We will no longer feel stress or dissonant energy. This is the "quest" of the American Indian Vision Quest.

In prayer we might be tempted to ask for that wonderful new sports car, that high-paying job, or a special person's love. In meditation, however, we simply leave ourselves open for **direction** toward the right job or car or love. The Cosmic Plan of Great Spirit will direct us toward those people, things, and events in our lives that will be most conducive to our spiritual growth. When we impose our wants and desires, we lose the opportunity for this spiritual growth.

Meditation is also a powerful tool for helping other people. When we meditate and focus love on another individual, we become like a prism that directs a beam of light. When a person in distress is surrounded by this energy field of love, all things are possible. Again, this focuses even more of Great Spirit's love on that individual. We can pray for someone's health, but perhaps the path of their spiritual growth begins with an illness or disability. Only Great Spirit knows what is best. We may be engaging in a prayer that will be frustrated because it reflects only our wants and desires and not what is best for our spirituality. When we meditate and surround someone with love, that person's energies and spirit will be enhanced by that love toward spiritual growth in whatever form or direction is best for them.

I remember receiving this type of energy at one of the lowest points in my life. I had come to a personal crisis that seemed beyond my spiritual strength. I thought that my heart would break, and I simply could take no more pain. As I lay in bed that morning and began to meditate, I was soon surrounded with a beautiful rose-colored light. I felt such intense love at that moment that I began to weep. It was a powerful moment of grace. I knew, then, that I was truly loved and that I was not alone; and from this I found new strength.

My experience with a Vision Quest is another example of the way that Great Spirit works within us. In American Indian spirituality, the Vision Quest is an extremely important ceremony. In it, one releases the need for control and experiences the oneness of the universe. Eagle Man suggested that it would be very good for me to go on a Vision Quest and include the experience in this book. However, what I expected from my Quest was very different from what I actually experienced.

A Vision Quest is similar to a retreat, except that in the American Indian way one retreats to commune with nature and the Great Spirit. The purpose of the Vision Quest is self-improvement. I was specifically seeking guidance for my journey in the Seventh Direction—spiritual growth. I began preparing for my Vision Quest by scouting the mountains around our ranch for a suitable location. I wanted a high, remote hilltop with a view of Pikes Peak in the east and of the Puma Hills in the west.

On a warm autumn afternoon, my husband, Harold, and I set out on our horses, Brownie and Tess, to find this Vision spot. Just as we turned onto the gravel road at the end of our drive, I heard an eagle's call. Immediately over our heads flew five peregrine falcons, with one of them engaged in a showy, aerobatics display. I smiled, for the presence of the falcons was a good sign from the Great Spirit. I knew that our Brother Falcon would lead us to the place for my Quest. We followed the falcon to a nearby hilltop where he landed on a ponderosa pine just above our heads. This pine marked the edge of a high, rocky clearing with magnificent views of the Peak and all of the surrounding mountaintops.

As we rode out onto this promontory the falcon stayed with us, finally perching on the dead branches of a tree that had been struck by lightning. This was clearly the spot for my Vision Quest.

A few days later, I prepared for my Vision with a Sweat Lodge Ceremony. Billowing flocks of mountain bluebirds swelled across the pasture in the warm autumn air. Dark gray thunderclouds loomed all around our valley, but the sweat lodge was bathed in shafts of golden sunlight. I knew that the timing was right, and I was eagerly looking forward to my Vision Quest. While I was gathering sage for the Sweat Lodge Ceremony, I found a very curious stone. It was crimson-colored except for a small section of white quartz. It contained the image of a man and a woman standing close together, with the man enveloping the woman in an Indian blanket. Their faces seemed etched in the white quartz. I knew that this was a Wotai which must be used during the Sweat Lodge. I didn't understand its significance until after my Vision Quest.

After the Sweat Lodge, as I began my climb up the mountain, I again saw Brother Falcon circling just above the ponderosa pines alongside my path. Suddenly he swooped down, flying right over my head, then turned back toward Harold and the Sweat Lodge. I thought it was a strange omen and wondered if it meant that I was to go back and give up the Vision Quest. I ignored these thoughts, however, and pressed on toward my mountaintop.

When I reached the area under the lightning-marked tree, a black Abert's squirrel scolded me while I set out colored markers delineating my Vision spot. I was puzzled, but went ahead and spread my sleeping bag on a bed of sage, then sat on it, and began my meditation. I anxiously looked up at the dark clouds that had circled the valley all afternoon. They were now being driven south by the winds and were passing too quickly to drop any moisture.

It is amazing how perceptive you become on a Vision Quest. Even the most insignificant things seem to carry a message. My attention was soon drawn to a line of ants traveling along a nearby granite boulder. They were all returning to their anthill empty-handed. This was curious behavior. Next, the winds suddenly changed direction, now coming from the east. A gale gathered all of the dark clouds that had passed earlier and brought them back directly overhead.

I was certain that if the Great Spirit intended that I remain on the mountaintop for two days, then this would be just a brief shower. I zippered my jacket and climbed into my sleeping bag to wait out the storm. Darkness fell, rain pelted me, and barking dogs in the valley below announced a bear on the prowl. I surprised myself, for I was not afraid of the bear's fierce growl. Earlier in the year, a bear had made a sustained attempt to claw his way into the horse barn. I was fearful then, and carried the rifle out each morning when I went to feed. Now, my only thoughts of this bear were that he was a part of the beauty of the Great Spirit's creation. It is a good feeling to know that the bear and the trees and the clouds are related to us. We are all One.

I prayed for guidance, as it was beginning to seem that I was going to have to abandon my quest. The rain now came down in torrents, and I received my answer when two icy cold rivulets coursed their way into my sleeping bag. My lungs are weak, and I could not risk another bout of pneumonia. Disappointed, I gathered my things and trudged the mile back to the ranch through the dark and the rain. I was soaked to the bone and covered with mud, but glad for the smell of woodsmoke as I neared the ranch house.

Our library was nice and cozy from the fire in the woodstove, but Harold was lying on the couch with a raging fever. I made us both a steaming mug of herbal tea, then gave him a Tai Chi touch therapy and put him to bed. He ran a temperature most of the night. I had never seen him so ill. As I lay in bed that night, I felt that I finally understood the falcon, the scolding squirrel, and the empty-handed ants. Later, I asked my friend Eagle Man for his opinion about my aborted Vision Quest.

"When you have learned not to fear Mother Earth or her creatures, and to appreciate the signs that Mother Earth and her creatures reveal to you, then you have had a good Vision Quest."

I am extremely thankful that the Great Spirit canceled my Vision Quest and sent me back home when Harold needed me. I laugh at myself for being so oblivious to all of the signs from nature, but I also thank Great Spirit for my unanswered prayer.

Just as the winds and rains and creatures of the forest worked in concert with the Great Spirit to cancel my Vision Quest and send me home to my sick husband, so do our bodies work in concert with our souls to facilitate spiritual growth. All of these phenomena are manifestations of unitheism, of Cosmic Symbiosis. All is One. MITAKUYE OYASIN!

There is no Cartesian Duality, no separation of body and spirit—our physical and spiritual realities are integrated in such a manner as to help us maximize our spiritual growth. Webster's dictionary defines emotion as "a psychic and physical reaction subjectively experienced as strong feeling and physiologically involving changes that prepare the body."

Emotions are also a tool, emanating from the body, and present in order to help us with our spiritual growth. The most basic of emotions, fear, is one of the prime motivators for spiritual growth. The spirit lives and grows through the body. Helen Keller tells of the great void of darkness and nothingness in which she lived prior to discovering her senses and the world around her. Where was her spirit, her soul, before she learned to communicate? The history of two-leggeds is filled with stories of the redeeming power of love, the most potent emotion.

Emotions are a tool and must be used as such. One does not worship a hammer; one does not indiscriminately use a power drill. Neither should we allow an emotion, such as anger, to control our lives by venting it indiscriminately. If we feel anger, it is a symptom of something deeper, just as fever is a symptom of an illness. Ignoring the fever will not cure the underlying infection any more than ignoring our anger will cure the problem that spawned the anger.

I would like to share a heartwarming story that illustrates the constructive use of anger. One of my friends (I'll call her Melissa) is a beautiful and intelligent young woman who carried a thorn in her spirit from childhood. Melissa's father is a cold and distant man, frozen by fear and unable to engage in the normal give-and-take of an intimate relationship. Melissa worshipped her father when she was a little girl but was never able to bridge the frigid gap within him. Her parents separated when Melissa was four, and she grew up in a single parent home.

Melissa felt unloved by her father, and her mother's love alone could not suffice. Her pain finally erupted in anger when she was a teenager. Where she had previously been a model student, she began to drink heavily and hang around with the wrong crowd. Fortunately, she was arrested for drunk driving, fined, and required to enroll in Alcoholics Anonymous. Through the required AA counseling sessions, Melissa was at last able to confront her anger and disappointment over the lack of her father's love. The first step of AA's Twelve Step Program also forced her to acknowledge that Great Spirit was in control of her life. In this way she began her spiritual journey in earnest. Her anger, expressed by her drinking, was a tool that forced her to reevaluate her life and to begin the work on her spiritual growth. Great Spirit had a plan for her life—if the police had not arrested her for DUI, the whole chain of events that led her to work on her spiritual life would not have transpired. Drinking and driving are a tragic mixture that can easily take an innocent life. Melissa was fortunate that she was caught the first time it happened, before anyone else was hurt.

Any tool can be used either to build a house or to destroy a house. The same is true of emotions; they can either be used to build our spirit or to tear it down. Constructive or destructive, the choice is ours.

Another woman that I know (I'll call her Susan) was able to use her jealousy as a tool for spiritual growth. Susan's mother died when Susan was ten years old. Susan wasn't old enough to understand death; she thought her mother had left her by choice. A child's greatest fear, that of abandonment, was a reality for Susan. Thinking that she was the cause of her abandonment, Susan felt that she had to be perfect in every way in order to avoid being abandoned again.

She married very young and completely submerged her personality and her needs. She was so anxious to please her husband that she became false. She was false in that she suppressed every need and desire of Susan. She felt that she had to be the perfect wife or her husband also would abandon her.

Susan feared that she was unlovable and that her husband would leave her for almost any other woman. As usually happens in such cases, her husband did leave her for another woman. Susan repeated this pattern in several subsequent relationships, intensely loving a man until he did finally leave her for someone else. Eventually, Susan was forced to confront her jealousy. Why was she jealous? Why was she so afraid of being abandoned?

Susan's emotions triggered her growth. She came to see that she was a lovable person without having to deny who she was. She was worthy of love. Her first step was to trust in Great Spirit and to love Great Spirit by loving herself. She could not control others no matter how jealous she became. Once Susan began to relax and trust her life to Great Spirit, her life changed. She met a warm and sensitive man, and they have now been happily married for fifteen years.

Melissa's and Susan's stories show how we can constructively use our emotions to move ourselves forward on the path in the Seventh Direction. Our emotions are simply tools that we have been given in order to begin our journey toward spiritual growth. We are always given all of the tools that we will need in this life, but the choice on how to use them is ours alone.

There are numerous ways to make medicine with the Great Spirit, and all are exciting and beautiful in their simplicity. *There is no need for an intermediary between us and Great Spirit.* No person or thing separates us, for We are all One. Prayer and meditation are simply a means of focusing our energy in a harmonious connection, making miracles possible. After all, miracles are nothing more than a revelation of Great Spirit in a physical manner that astonishes us. This is strong medicine.

There is also gentle medicine in a falcon that appears from nowhere and circles our heads, or a meadowlark that sings outside a church window as if translating the day's sermon. Or sunlight breaking through the clouds at an auspicious moment, or a policeman ticketing a drunk driver. Or a stranger speaking a comforting word just when we need it most. Or a lover abandoning us for someone else. When we are open to the signs, we will see that medicine is everywhere. We are surrounded by the beauty of Great Spirit's love.

Chapter Notes

1. M. Shallis, *The Electric Connection*, New York: New Amsterdam, 1988, p. 128.

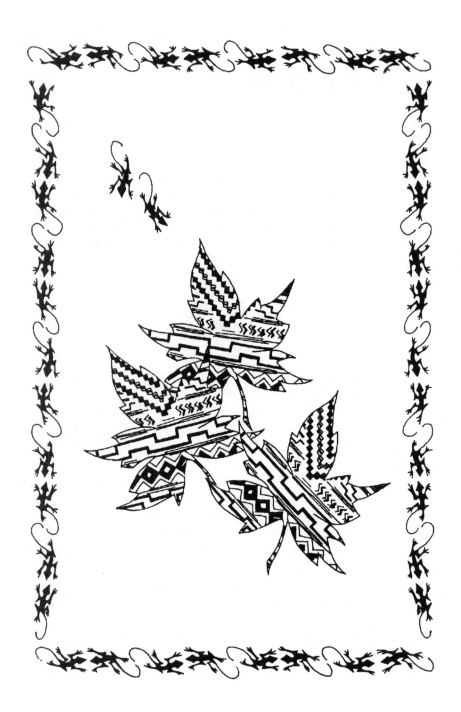

8

Love the Truth

> *"Such is the importance of our honor and our word that in the early days, lying was a capital offense. Because we believed that the deliberate liar is capable of committing any crime behind the screen of cowardly untruth and double dealing, the destroyer of mutual confidence was summarily put to death, that the evil might go no further."*
>
> Ohiyesa (Sioux)
> *The Soul of an Indian*

I walk in beauty. The opening stanza of my favorite Navajo chant reminds me of the beauty, the medicine, that surrounds all of us throughout each day. As we set our feet along this path of beauty, we need to remember that the next mandate of our journey song is to Love the Truth. Each step, each stanza of our song, is to help us grow spiritually and thereby achieve an infinite, harmonious existence with Great Spirit.

Trusting in Great Spirit and understanding that there is a Cosmic Plan for our life is the first vital step on our spiritual journey. Next, we must learn to Love the Truth, for truth will serve as a beacon in the night as we stumble along the path of life. As long as we keep this beacon in view, we can make many wrong turns and yet still arrive safely at our destination—a reunion with Great Spirit. Most of us have found that spiritual growth is not linear but is more a case of two steps forward and one step back. This is why the beacon of truth is so very important in helping us find our way.

In the previous chapters I discussed the nature of reality at some length by incorporating the concepts of modern physics. With this knowledge, we now understand that matter and energy are interchangeable;

and that they consist of quanta, or packets, that are vibrating at different frequencies. Our bodies are nothing more than amalgamations of these quanta, also vibrating at various frequencies. This vibrating energy permeates the most minute regions of the universe—quarks and s-strings—and extends to the farthest depths of the cosmos, including quasars and galaxies. When we performed the strength test, we saw how the mere presence of a color could cause radical changes in our bodies without our conscious awareness. Energy from color therefore gives some indication of the way that the energies of the universe impact us.

The pulsing energy of our universe creates a constant state of transformation and change. Energy vibrating at differing frequencies and emanating from the outermost reaches of the universe is interacting continually with our bodies and spirits. However, just as we fail to sense the interaction of the energy of color upon our bodies, so too do we fail to sense the interaction of the energy of the cosmos upon us. Because we can neither sense this energy nor quantify it does not make it any less valid.

Manifestations of this energy are numerous. They include the remarkable accuracy of astrology (excluding the daily horoscope); the fascinating correlation of numerology to the various types of energy; and the manifestations of ghosts and other spiritual phenomena. There are masses of evidence attesting to the reality of these phenomena. Science simply has not perfected a method for validating them, which does not mean that they are not real. It is a serious shortcoming of the scientific community to deny the validity of a manifestation simply because current methods of research cannot document it.

Now, let me return to a discussion of the energy or vibration of Truth. Truth is an attribute of Great Spirit, and therefore resonates with the same infinite, harmonious vibration. As we discovered earlier, Great Spirit is Omnipresent—He/She is present throughout the universe. Therefore, the vibration of Truth is also Omnipresent—the entire universe contains its energy. When the truth is spoken, written, or acted upon, it resonates throughout the universe. When truth is manifested to an individual, it will resonate within that individual.

Philosophers have grappled with the nature of truth from the beginning of time. Many schools of thought teach that truth can be attained through reason alone. Other schools of thought teach that truth is understood by an intuitive process, and reason has nothing to do with its discernment. Still other philosophers argue that there is no ultimate truth; it is simply defined by each unique situation—the end justifies the means.

I propose that the first two schools of thought (truth found by reason and intuition) are correct, but the last (that there is no ultimate truth) is antithetical to Great Spirit's harmonious energy.

Truth is among the attributes of Great Spirit, so as we continue along our spiritual journey we are said to be seeking the truth. As I noted earlier, knowledge of Great Spirit and spiritual growth come only with continual hard work. Similarly, all other knowledge comes from hard work; therefore, the philosophical school that maintains that truth can be found through reason is correct, for reasoning requires diligent thought.

However, reason alone cannot totally discern truth. Great Spirit is infinite and Truth is therefore also infinite. Since truth is infinite, no one individual can possess total truth. There can be only one Great Spirit, and the possession of total truth is an attribute of only Great Spirit. Nevertheless, each of us can gain a limited understanding of total truth. We must remember to value every human being as a window to Great Spirit. We have much to learn from one another if we are only open and receptive.

The second means of acquiring truth, intuition, comes from the resonance that truth creates within each individual. There are so many facets of truth that it often becomes quite confusing for one who is seeking the truth. In order to understand this concept, try an experiment with several of your friends. Stage an event, such as having a friend or a child run through the group carrying an object. Then ask everyone present to describe what has just transpired. The descriptions will be as varied as your guests, yet each of them has just witnessed the same truth (event). All truth is multifaceted, and each of us retains a different segment or viewpoint.

Truth is even more difficult to discern when there are half-truths involved. Half-truths complicate discernment through reason and intuition because they convey some segment of the whole truth. Therefore, these half-truths also have vibrations similar to the truth itself. For this reason, half-truths are more insidious than lies and do far more damage.

I am only a two-legged, but it seems to me that the school of thought that proposes truth as unique to each situation is dangerous. Sometimes I feel that I might be in the minority with this opinion. I was recently present during the selection of a jury at our county courthouse. Somehow the questioning of the jurors got around to the subject of ethical behavior. The judge bluntly asked the jury if they believed that the end justified the means. A majority of the jurors raised their hands indicating that they believed this to be morally acceptable. I was astonished at this attitude toward the truth. Logically (within the context of unitheism), wrong acting does not warrant further wrong acting as a response. This becomes clear when one examines the energy waves involved.

Lies and evil deeds have a dissonant vibration to that of Great Spirit and the truth. When two dissonant waves of energy collide, they lose their power and eventually cease to exist. Therefore, when the energy of a lie or an evil deed is supplemented by the energy wave of another lie or evil deed, there is a very strong possibility that the energy waves created might be consonant with each other. In the diagram showing the effect that two consonant energy waves have upon one another (Figure 2-1), the result was exponential. The sum of one consonant energy wave plus a second consonant energy wave is not simply one plus one equals two. It is more a case of one plus one is equal to one thousand and two.

Lies and evil deeds are apt to compound the magnitude of lies and evil in the world. Most of the time, however, the energy wave of one lie or evil deed will be dissonant with the second lie or evil deed, the effect being that the two waves will simply cancel one another. It is important to keep in mind that lies and evils are always dissonant to Great Spirit's energy. For this reason, one day they will all simply cease to exist. In the interim, however, there is a danger that by acting upon the belief that the end justifies the means we may compound the presence of evil within the world.

Eagle Man writes that most American Indian tribes did not believe in a devil or demonic force prior to their contact with Christians. Indian people simply could not conceive that Great Spirit would create an evil entity. If Great Spirit is all-powerful, it is not logical or realistic that He/She would create something that was not Truth. Nowhere in nature does untruth exist. Also, within the logical context of unitheism, it is impossible for Great Spirit (who is truth, love, and goodness) to create a being (the devil) whose energy is dissonant and completely opposite. Truth does not spawn lies.

In unitheism, the purpose of human life is ultimate reunion, and therefore infinity, with Great Spirit. Then why would Great Spirit create an entity whose sole purpose is to thwart this reunion? It is my opinion that the devil is simply a creation of some human beings in order to frighten and control other human beings. I feel that by accepting the concept of a devil we actually thwart our spiritual growth because we now have a scapegoat for our evil deeds.

Love of the truth must permeate all that we are, all that we say, and all that we do. It will then guide us in our search for knowledge of Great Spirit. Just look around you and you will begin to see the pattern of the harmonious vibrations of truth. Classic literature and art throb with this vibration. It is the reason that they reverberate within the hearts of generation after generation. The harmony of truth is timeless. Its vibration within us has the power to bring a feeling of peace because we are also in harmony, through this truth, with Great Spirit.

Living in truth is serenity. There is a popular myth within our society that money or fame or power will automatically confer happiness. On the contrary, I have yet to find a rich or famous or powerful person who is happy. Happiness is ephemeral; it is not reality. Our happy moments are fleeting, and they rarely help us to grow spiritually. Serenity, however, can be ours every day of our life. When we live within the zone of serenity, we have a new perspective on the tragedies and triumphs of life and understand them within the context of spiritual growth.

Vibrations of harmony are a part of all of Great Spirit's creation, because Great Spirit is everywhere present. American Indians understand these energies and utilize them in different ways, according to each person's special gift or talent. Sitting Bull had a special medicine with horses and arranged for an extraordinary dance of his Indian ponies at a Sun Dance Ceremony. An Apache woman, Mildred Cleghorn, speaks about her uncle's similar gift in *The Book of Elders*.

> ... I had an uncle that could tame horses. I will never forget when I was visiting them out in Mescalero, New Mexico. That was at White Tail, way out in the reservation. This horse would rear up, and this fellow couldn't get control of him. The horse would just jump up and stomp. So my uncle said, "I want to show you. I'm going to make that horse behave." And sure enough, he came over there and told that fellow, "Let me have those reins." That horse's ears were perked up, and he was looking at him and snorting. My uncle just jerked the reins, talking to him the whole time. Gradually, he worked his way up to the horse. Pretty soon the horse started shaking his whole body. My uncle patted him, talking to him the whole time. He rubbed his back, down his neck, and along his legs. Finally, he led him away. That was a special gift that was given to my uncle.[1]

Whenever I think of the power of harmonious vibrations, I am reminded of my own experience involving my daughter's horse, Barbir.

I was in Virginia at the time, having a difficult time adjusting to its unbearable heat and humidity after living in the cool mountain air of Santa Fe. One day I arranged for the local vet to make a farm call to attend to our Arabian gelding, Barbir. He was a magnificent creature with a glistening white coat and a long, flowing mane and tail. He had been cut at a late age and had the well-muscled appearance of a stallion rather than of a gelding. He knew that he was of regal blood and aspect and acted accordingly. Like most Arabians, he was sensitive and gentle. And like most Arabians, he was high-strung and at times difficult to manage.

On this notably hot and humid summer day he was to have major surgery on a wound on his front leg which had not healed properly. The wound had begun to grow something called "proud flesh" and was greatly engorged with blood and false tissue. Dr. Nancy gave him a sedative while we chatted about all the local issues. We waited the appropriate time and, when the sedative failed to take effect, she gave him a second dosage, and then a third. When Barbir still showed no signs of calming down enough to allow the surgery, Dr. Nancy shook her head and said that another dose of sedative might kill him. My only option was to ship him to the nearest equestrian hospital for surgery, an expense of several thousand dollars.

At the time, I was a single mother with two children to support. I simply could not afford a two thousand dollar hospital bill for this horse. I asked Dr. Nancy if she would indulge me and try an experimental approach. Would she allow me to sing in order to calm Barbir? I love to sing, but I am the only one who loves to hear me sing. Consequently, I always save my songs for that time of day when I muck the horses' stalls. While mucking and singing, I soon discovered that each of my horses seemed to have a favorite song. Barbir was especially fond of the song "Memories" from the musical *Cats*. Whenever I sang this particular melody, he would nicker softly and nuzzle my face in obvious enjoyment. To Dr. Nancy's chagrin, Barbir promptly fell into a deep sleep when I began to sing "Memories."

I gently cradled Barbir's head in my arms and sang his song over and over while Dr. Nancy bent to her bloody work, and the perspiration ran down both our faces. After about half an hour of this she looked up at me, smiled, and said, "Celinda, I think you can stop singing now—he's really out." No sooner had I stopped singing, however, than Barbir awakened and began to rear and plunge sending droplets of blood from his leg flying in all directions. I frantically burst into song, and once again he quickly fell into a sound sleep with his head cradled in my arms.

Dr. Nancy set back to work, muttering something about this being the strangest blankety-blank thing she had ever seen. After about the thirtieth rendition of "Memories," Dr. Nancy asked if I would at least sing another song. I responded that Barbir only liked "Memories," but that I would try another melody. As soon as I did though, Barbir awakened in a frenzy of flying hooves. I quickly changed back to his song, and all was peace and quiet once more.

I sang "Memories"; Barbir slept; and Dr. Nancy operated uneventfully for the next two hours. When she finally finished, her face was ashen. She looked into my eyes, shook her head, and said through clenched teeth, "If I never hear that song again in my lifetime, it will be too soon. I've been a vet for eighteen years, and this is the strangest thing that I have ever seen!" I'm sure that to this day Dr. Nancy still talks of Barbir's unusual surgery.

As the story of Barbir illustrates, certain vibrations from sounds can evoke peace and harmony. Music is the great language of the world simply because it can transcend any spoken word. This was cleverly illustrated in the hit movie *Close Encounters of the Third Kind* where music provided the means of communications with the alien visitors.

Another graphic illustration of the harmonious vibration principal is the little black box that I use for tuning my guitar. (Unfortunately, my guitar playing is about on a par with my singing ability—ground zero.) I always found tuning my guitar to be a major annoyance because of the amount of time required. I was therefore delighted when Harold bought me a wonderful gadget that greatly simplifies this onerous job. This tuner is a small black box containing various crystals. One simply places the black box on the sounding box of the guitar and dials the appropriate string. When the string is adjusted to the correct tension, it achieves a resonance with the crystal in the little black box, and a light goes on indicating that the string is tuned. The crystal and the string have achieved a harmonious vibration.

This is much the same way that truth resonates within the hearts of human beings. We are like guitar strings that achieve the appropriate amount of tension and then resonate to the vibration of Great Spirit's Truth. It is also interesting to note the effect of consonant and dissonant vibrations on the sounding box of the guitar. By placing one's fingertips across the top of the sounding box and striking two harmonious strings, one can feel a decidedly long-lasting vibration. However, if the strings are not in harmony, the vibration will be a jolting, dissonant sensation and very short-lived.

Hopi elder, Martin Gashweseoma, is keeper of the sacred stone tablets containing his people's prophesy about the future of the earth. Gashweseoma shared the Hopi method of cultivating their sacred corn in *The Book of Elders*. His story further illustrates the use of harmonious vibrations.

> ... when we pray, fast, and meditate for this corn to grow, we make all vegetation, the grass, everything to grow, too.
>
> We were trained in our societies to pray for plant life, animals, birds, all of the foods that we receive from Mother Earth, and always with a

prayer we accept those things. When we go to the field when our plants are coming up, they are just like babies, so we go and sing to them. Sometimes in this valley you can hear them early in the mornings; you can hear them singing out there. They go to the field and talk to their plants as if they were human beings and encourage them. That's how they take care of this life out here.[2]

Another fascinating demonstration of the harmonious vibration principle can be found in the emergency radios used by our volunteer fire department. When the sheriff's department changes its secured radio channels, it issues each fireperson a new crystal for his or her emergency radio. Each of these crystals resonates at a specific frequency and therefore captures the energy from that communication frequency. There are many manifestations of this principle which have been dismissed as New Age mysticism. I have a very special crystal that I use during my meditations. When used this way, the crystal heats itself to about 110 degrees and is decidedly hot to the touch. This is not "mumbo jumbo"; it is a fact. This heated crystal verifies that meditation changes my vibration level and that these vibrations then interact with those of my wotai. Scientists have only just begun to discover the amazing powers of crystals. It will be exciting to see what the future holds as the medicine from the Great Spirit is revealed through further research and revelation.

The Catholic Church is one of the few organized religions that recognize the great healing powers of truth. Two of the church's effective instruments of truth are confession and the marital annulment process. An interesting aspect of confession is the cathartic effect that telling the truth about oneself has upon one's self-esteem and future behavior. Most psychologists would agree that the first step in changing our behavior lies in becoming aware of it.

In reciting our sins and transgressions within the safety of a confessional, we are forced to hear and say the truth about ourselves. This generally has an effect upon our future actions. Many people adamantly disagree with the idea of confessing their sins and receiving forgiveness from another human being. Logically, within the framework of unitheism, there is no need for another human being to intercede with Great Spirit for us. As I illustrated earlier, Great Spirit is everywhere and with us at every moment. Confession directly to the Great Spirit is, in itself, valid. The important point here is that we acknowledge the truth about ourselves, no matter how unsavory. Some of us require the structure of the Catholic confessional in order to do this, but others do not.

There is evidence that suggests that the use of confession (whereby we acknowledge the truth about ourselves) is effective in securing ethical behavior. A recent Congressional study of the Central Intelligence Agency (CIA) found that a disproportionate number of its employees are Catholic. This seems to imply a higher degree of truthfulness in Catholics as verified by the rigorous background and polygraph tests required for employment at the CIA. If only polygraphs were used, then it might be argued that confession is similar in nature to a polygraph test, therefore giving Catholics an unfair advantage. However, polygraphs are always augmented by data from background investigations that probably reveal any untruth.

The Catholic marital annulment process is another wise use of the truth for effecting spiritual growth. It is perhaps inevitable that many human beings will fail in the selection of a lifetime mate and that divorce will result. The Catholic Church recognizes this weakness and provides the process of annulment to explore and validate divorce. My Harold could not even think of remarrying without the blessing of his church, and this meant that I had to seek an annulment.

Although apprehensive, I spent a great deal of time soul-searching and writing up my case. Corroborating witnesses were found and their statements submitted separately. When all of this evidence was gathered, I was then summoned to a formidable meeting with six aged priests in attendance. The questions were deep and probing but seemed fair in establishing the truth. When I received my annulment, it lifted a great weight from my shoulders to find that six strangers had concurred with the soundness of my decision. I was also surprised to see how it validated my divorce in the eyes of my children and my family.

I should note, however, that it is not logically necessary for another human being to determine the spiritual legitimacy of any action. This is a matter between the individual and Great Spirit, for only Great Spirit knows total truth. There is always the danger that another human being will interpose his or her ego, make subjective judgments, or have a detrimental effect on both parties. Use of an intermediary, such as an agent of the Catholic Church, is a matter of individual choice. I only use this example in order to illustrate the healing power of speaking, and therefore acknowledging, the truth about ourselves.

Many victims of abuse also report that they find that prosecuting, or at least telling the truth about their attacker, has this same cathartic effect. American Indian warriors routinely participated in a truth ceremony after their return from battle. Each warrior stood before the council fire and recounted his actions in combat before his family, his village, and his peers.

This was not boasting but a means of setting the record straight and subjecting it to peer review. It was also a means of trauma therapy by allowing each warrior to relate the rigors of battle.

Sigmund Freud was a pioneer in discovering the beneficial effects of this "talking therapy," of telling the truth. C. G. Jung became his disciple, going beyond his "religion" of sexuality and into the realm of the collective unconscious.[3] The concept of the collective unconscious further illustrates the omnipresence of truth throughout the universe and man's ability to access this truth. It is interesting that Webster's dictionary defines truth as "the body of *real* [my emphasis] things, events, and facts." This again validates the Johari window, in that the more we know about ourselves and share with others, the more they can, in turn, trust us.

Truth and a love of the truth can have a profound effect on the state of the universe. Resonating, harmonious energy within one individual will spread like the ripples on a pond to our family, community, society, the world at large, and ultimately the universe. Through my earlier discussions of quantum mechanics and other laws of physics, I concurred with the theory that the entire universe is interconnected. A Cosmic Symbiosis exists whereby my individual actions can reverberate throughout the universe. The fate of some star billions of miles away can impact the energy fields which compose my body. Conversely, my actions and thoughts can impact the energy fields of some star billions of miles away. MITAKUYE OYASIN. We are all related.

Chapter Notes

1. S. Johnson, op. cit., p. 186–187.
2. Ibid., p. 40.
3. C. Jung, op. cit., ch. 5.

9

The Resonance of Truth

"But, as an ideal, we live and will live, not only in the splendor of our past, the poetry of our legends and art, not only in the interfusion [sic] of our blood with yours, and in our faithful adherence to the ideals of American citizenship, but in the living heart of the nation."

Ohiyesa (Sioux)
The Soul of an Indian

When we take the second step of the spiritual *Journey Song* and love the truth, we create a harmonious vibration within ourselves. The previous chapter illustrated how this vibration comes about through the resonance of our words, thoughts, and actions in harmony with Great Spirit's truth. Maslow writes that healthy "people uniformly yearn for what is good for them and for others, and then are able wholeheartedly to enjoy it, and approve of it. For such people virtue [truth] is its own reward ..."[1] The resonance of truth brings serenity, a peace and harmony within the self.

However, if we are going to find truth's resonance within ourselves, we will have to keep ourselves simple. At this point, I will digress and explore the nature of being simple, and this will in turn clarify its importance. (In later chapters I will go into greater detail on this need for simplicity.)

If you find yourself constantly seeking new material goods, status, money, or power, it usually indicates a spiritual hunger. If you are addicted to alcohol or any type of drug, this also indicates a soul that wants to be fed. These worldly things, these drugs, are only temporary panaceas for our soul and they do not bring lasting happiness or peace. We may derive a momentary satisfaction from them, but they usually tend to make spiritual growth even more difficult. They impede our growth because each of

103

them carries a strong energy field, and our own energy is vulnerable to becoming submerged by them. When there are layers and layers of swirling, conflicting and dissonant energies enveloping us, it is difficult to feel the resonance of truth.

If these trappings of worldliness insured happiness to those who possess them, we would see evidence of this happiness. However, the data seems to support the opposite conclusion. As I pointed out earlier, it is almost impossible to find a wealthy, powerful, or famous individual who is spiritually at peace. Most spend years in therapy, or seek obliteration through drugs or alcohol or deviant sexual practices.

This is not to say that anyone who aspires to success in this world is wrong. On the contrary, the very diversity of human endeavor upon the earth is a part of Great Spirit's Cosmic Plan. We human beings do not endow ourselves with intellect or talents or special skills. These are gifts from Great Spirit, and as such must be fulfilled to the best of our abilities. We therefore have a moral obligation to fully develop our special gifts. Our spiritual growth does not mandate that we withdraw from the world and live as "saints." On the contrary, the economy of the world would collapse if everyone decided to emulate the saintly Mother Teresa.

Let me say again that Great Spirit endowed each of us with a specific gift to bring into the world. This truth is evident through all of creation. Plant people, stone people, four-leggeds, and winged people all contribute to the balance of nature. Each species contributes something unique, and each human being, each two-legged, is also vested with a particular talent. When we successfully utilize our individual gifts, we will find joy in our activity. Great Spirit may have given you the gift of making people laugh, or writing brilliant computer programs, or baking mouth-watering bread, or (as a trash collector) keeping Mother Earth clean. Our endowments are as varied as our faces are. When we fulfill these talents and skills, our bodies, minds, and souls will resonate with the will of Great Spirit. This resonance brings peace, a much greater source of satisfaction than the ephemeral tinges of happiness that touch our lives now and then.

I must emphasize, however, that although there is no sin in **success**, there *is* sin in **excess**. Any dissonant layer of energy that obliterates the harmonious vibrations of Great Spirit is wrong. The sources of this disabling energy can be virtually anything from wearing too much jewelry, owning an excess of clothing, depending on mind-altering drugs, to succumbing to power. We must always strive to keep our lives simple.

The presence of Great Spirit's truth within each of us is like the stone thrown into the pond—it is the source of the ripples that eventually reach the shore. Each one of us, like the stone, is at the very center of the concentric circles that reverberate throughout the universe. When one embraces truth, one begins spiritual growth and a harmonious vibration with Great Spirit. And the ripples begin.

The most immediate impact of this transformation will be upon those closest to us, our family and loved ones. Through Cosmic Symbiosis, the great interconnectedness of the universe, we know that whatever happens to one of us also affects everyone else and the Cosmos—MITAKUYE OYASIN. Humans are of great value to one another in effecting the harmonious vibrations of the universe. In addition to nurturing and comforting one another, we are also instruments of each other's spiritual growth. One of the many ways that we assist in this growth is by serving as "mirrors" for each other.

We often go through each day totally unconscious of most of our actions. But before we can change undesirable behavior we need to become aware of it, and that is why we need a mirror. Are we over-controlling of those around us rather than allowing the will of Great Spirit to operate within their lives? Within the safety and security of the family, this can be called to our attention by a loved one.

For example, I was not aware that my daughter felt smothered whenever I tried to resolve her problems. Finally one day, in exasperation, she blurted out that she only wanted me to listen to her, not to solve everything. I was totally unaware of my behavior until she brought it to my notice. I was shocked at first, but upon reflection I saw that she was right. Also (as I told you earlier) the area where I need the most work is in trusting Great Spirit, for I am a worrier. Fortunately, my husband is conscientious in bringing this shortcoming to my attention. As these examples show, in small ways, every day, we can help one another to grow. We are one another's mirrors.

Truth is the very basis of this gift we have for each other. Without truth, these daily interactions would be a source of irritation and warfare rather than a means to growth. Alcoholism provides another example of the way that we can constructively use truth. One of the most effective tools for encouraging an alcoholic or a drug addict to acknowledge the problem and to seek help is by means of an intervention. An intervention is a method whereby several family members and friends of the addict collectively confront the individual with the problem. When such a loving confrontation takes place, it is very difficult for the addict to continue to deny his or her addiction. Once the addiction has been admitted, the behavior is acknowledged, and the steps to recovery can begin. The friends and/or the family of the addict have lovingly confronted the individual with the truth of his or her behavior and, as a result, the door to spiritual growth is opened.

During my career as an accountant and auditor I encountered a good many people who were married to their work. They had no time for family or romantic liaisons; they were totally immersed in their careers and loved what they were doing. I always had fun teasing such individuals, as they seemed to retain an eternal, youthful appearance. They very rarely had gray hair or wrinkles, further evidence of a virtually stress-free life. Being single and making good money, they were able to indulge themselves completely. In contrast, the stresses of close personal relationships do not allow this type of indulgence. Every parent's gray hair and wrinkles are evidence of the many worries and compromises inherent in the give-and-take of intimate relationships.

The next ripple of trust growing from truthfulness can be found in the business world, in the workplace. If you will take a moment and look at the Johari window (Figure 5-2) again, you will see that the more we know about ourselves and each other, then the more we trust and, therefore, the less we experience conflict. Also, if we love the truth, we will know our limitations. We will be able to properly delegate work to capable coworkers, and then we will give them an honest evaluation and proper acknowledgment of their efforts. Loving confrontation with the truth is also vital for effective communications within the workplace. Ideally, this communication must be able to flow up the chain of command as well as down the chain of command.

When a business fosters honest and open relationships among its employees, the business will find great harmony in its workforce and will find great success in the marketplace. Employees and employers must know what is broken before it can be fixed. An employee must be honestly and straightforwardly told that he or she constantly fails to complete work assignments before the person can change his or her behavior. In a similar vein, employees are obligated to notify senior management of a faulty management policy. Time and again as an auditor, I found arrogance (or ignorance) in senior managers who failed to solicit the opinions, or ignored the opinions, of their experts—the people on the line doing the work. This inevitably resulted in a fatal flaw somewhere in the business.

When a company or business embraces truth and honesty as a policy, the sense of harmony within that business is palpable. The business is working in accordance with Great Spirit's will. Had the early factories in this country been more honest in acknowledging the contributions of their employees by equitably sharing profits and providing humane working conditions, there would have been no need for labor unions. Conversely, if the labor unions had not become excessive in their demands but had made honest and equitable requests of the owners, many of these businesses would not be facing serious financial problems today. The Johari window effect would have facilitated trust on both sides of the equation.

Within American Indian communities all important meetings and ceremonies are preceded with the Peace Pipe Ceremony. This is a contractual ceremony wherein each participant agrees to be truthful by the very act of smoking the pipe. The Sioux holy man, Fools Crow, spoke eloquently of the power of the pipe ceremony.

> In our pipe ceremony, which is really very simple, the pipe is smoked and pointed stem first and horizontally in a clockwise direction to the west, north, east, and south; then down to Grandmother Earth; up to Grandfather; and finally in an almost imperceptible higher movement to Wakan-Tanka. So while we speak of six directions, there are actually seven movements of the pipe, and our God is a Trinity, consisting of *Wakan-Tanka*, Tunkashila, and the Spirits. As the Pipe Ceremony is done, the pipe first of all opens the gates to release the powers, and then becomes the very channel through which the powers flow, moving from the six directions to the one who prays, blessing the person, and then through the person and out to bless the rest of creation.
>
> Therefore we say that the pipe itself has the power to transport power, and it is sacred. *Wakan-Tanka* sent the first one with Calf Pipe Woman, but any pipe used in the same way as the original one is just as sacred and effective.[2]

The next ripple of truthfulness touches society as a whole. Where truth is allowed to flourish, so do human beings. All are in harmony with Great Spirit's will. Those societies that fail to honor the truth, and instead attempt to control all information, are generally regarded by the world community as evil. (If you will remember, the logic of unitheism defines evil as anything that is in opposition to Great Spirit's will.) The dissonance created by suppressing truth within these societies will eventually cause them to collapse. A most graphic illustration of this principal is the sudden collapse of the Soviet empire during 1991. Truth is vital to civilization, for "... the main function of a healthy culture [is] the fostering of universal self-actualization."[3] Lao Tzu provides additional teaching on this point.

> A great nation is like a great man:
> When he makes a mistake, he realizes it.
> Having realized it, he admits it.

Having admitted it, he corrects it.
He considers those who point out his faults
as his most benevolent teachers.
He thinks of his enemy
as the shadow that he himself casts.

If a nation is centered in the Tao [Great Spirit],
if it nourishes its own people
and doesn't meddle in the affairs of others,
it will be a light to all nations in the world.4

Truth is especially important in establishing trust between those who govern and those who are governed, for truth is the basis for trust. Many American politicians seem to have forgotten these basic values in recent years. It is vitally important that an electorate use a loving confrontation to remind its politicians of the importance of truth. Former President Nixon is a good case in point. History books will probably remember him for his brilliant foreign policies. Unfortunately, they will also remember Nixon because he was caught in a lie and forced to resign. He succumbed to the flawed logic that the end justifies the means and then compounded this dissonant energy when he lied to cover up his mistake.

There is a similar political lesson in the fate of former presidential candidate Gary Hart. When confronted with the truth about his extramarital affairs, he lied to the public. As a result, his political career was destroyed, not because of his adultery but because of his lying. This assessment of the situation can be validated by contrasting Hart's fate with that of his rival, Jesse Jackson. It was fairly well known that Jackson was also a womanizer. However, he never compounded his mistakes by lying to the public about his conduct. He simply avoided discussing the issue rather than lie, and as a result his political career did not suffer from the same repercussions. The lesson to be learned from both examples is that voters must feel that they can trust their elected officials. If this trust is absent, then the people will turn against their government.

Issues of trust and honesty impact the state of the world and the universe as well. Again, this conclusion is based on unitheism which proves that truth is a harmonious vibration of Great Spirit. As Lao Tzu said, a nation that is centered in the Tao (Great Spirit) will be a light to the world. The natural evolution of the cosmos is a return to the eternal, harmonious vibration of Great Spirit. As this happens, evil will simply cease to exist, strangled by its own dissonant vibrations.

barely survive, but this is just one of the consequences when we don't honor the truth that Earth is indeed our mother.

At this point, I have introduced you to the first two steps on our spiritual journey, Trusting the Great Spirit and Loving the Truth. Now, I'll share a number of stories that show the profound difference that taking these steps can make in your life. As before, I have also changed the names of the people involved in order to protect their privacy. The first story contrasts the lives of two very similar men who met with two very different fates because of their philosophies of life.

The first man is named Louis who, in spite of his many gifts, is nonetheless a tragic figure. Great Spirit gave Louis a keen intellect, a charming personality, wit, and good looks. Louis has developed these gifts to the utmost, and after receiving his Ph.D. in physics, built a brilliant career. He married a beautiful and charming woman who virtually worshipped him. Louis, however, was always arrogant about the fact that Great Spirit had given him a brilliant mind. He somehow thought that his intellect was his merit. He was contemptuous of anyone not his equal, and he perceived that virtually no one was. Like Jack (in Chapter 6) he succumbed to his intellect.

His contempt for intellectual inferiors spread like a virus through his personal life and into his professional life. He enjoyed manipulating people with lies and half-truths and considered anyone who believed these lies to be nothing but a fool. He did not trust Great Spirit and believed that only his decisions and actions were best.

Louis was at the pinnacle of his career. He had all of the material possessions that spelled success— house in Washington, D.C. and a house on the beach, a brand new Mercedes Benz, tailored clothes, and the requisite Rolex watch. He was named CEO of a major defense contracting company, and was also appointed by the President to a national panel of experts. Unfortunately, some of the major lies that Louis told now began to surface. His "Top Secret" clearance was canceled; he was fired; and he lost his presidential appointment. His marriage of twenty years also ended in a bitter divorce.

These trials would have destroyed most other men. Louis was different, however, in that he couldn't even be truthful with himself. Rather than admit his mistakes and begin the next step of his spiritual growth, he created even more lies to explain his misfortune. Louis will never be able to progress spiritually until he embraces the truth. In the meantime, he is a bitter and angry man living a very unhappy life.

In sharp contrast to Louis is an honorable and well-respected man named Joseph. He is also highly intelligent but realizes that this is a gift from Great Spirit. He has diligently developed the many talents that Great Spirit has bestowed upon him. Unlike Louis, Joseph doesn't impose his will or manipulate other people. He achieved a great deal of success during his career and retired to a beautiful home in the mountains with a breathtaking view of Pikes Peak. In his retirement, Joseph continues on his path of spiritual growth and is active in his service to the community. He was elected to public office and has been a servant of the people for the major part of his retirement. He is highly respected for the integrity which he has brought to his job. He is happily married to a woman he met and married when he was nineteen and penniless.

Whereas Louis used his talents and power to manipulate everyone around him, Joseph used his to become a true servant of the public. Louis found emptiness and bitterness, but Joseph found fulfillment. "In the arrogance of exercising power without the total self-awareness demanded by love, we are blissfully but destructively ignorant of the fact that we are playing God."[6] Louis will never find fulfillment until he embraces the truth; to begin, he must be honest with himself, at least.

I also know of two young men who exemplify the power of being honest with one's self and the despair and failure when we aren't. The first young man is an inspiration to everyone who knows him. He, like Melissa in an earlier chapter, was totally neglected by a cold and distant father. His anger also surfaced in self-destructive behavior in his teenage years. Joe became addicted to drugs and then began to sell them in order to support his addiction. Unfortunately, he was sexually molested by an older man at this time. The trauma of this experience, coupled with his drug use, put Joe into a suicidal tailspin. Life, for him, had no meaning.

Fortunately, Joe was arrested and the judge forced him to attend Alcoholics Anonymous (AA). He learned that he was not the first person to have suffered from the "unfairness" of life. Joe honestly faced his alcoholism and drug abuse and slowly cleansed his body of their destructive chemicals. Joe's love of the truth saved his life. He now counsels high school children on behalf of Alcoholics Anonymous and will receive his Ph.D. in Philosophy in a few months.

In contrast to Joe is his former roommate, a young man whom he met through Alcoholics Anonymous. Regrettably, Ted chooses to be untruthful. He, too, was forced to attend AA meetings after he was involved in a near fatal accident. But Ted remains angry at the world simply because he refuses to accept that life is not fair. He feels that only a hateful God would have given him a body chemistry that is so susceptible to alcohol. Ted equates his alcoholism with that of being a victim of Dracula—cursed to be a vampire for the remainder of his life. He is embittered by his situation, but refuses to accept any responsibility. He has a brilliant mind, is charming and quite attractive. He is destroying his life, however, by refusing to acknowledge that he is an alcoholic and cannot drink. While Joe used his alcoholism to begin his spiritual journey, Ted refuses to take even the first steps. He will lose the chance to get his college degree because he has missed too many classes. He has lost his job because he can't stay sober. He is slowly and surely destroying his life. Ted does not trust Great Spirit and will not be honest, especially with himself.

The last two people that I will tell you about are two middle-aged women with a different kind of problem. The first woman, Betty, grew up believing that money was the most important thing in life. She felt that, if she only had enough money, all of life's problems would be solved. Consequently, Betty decided that she would simply marry a rich man. She never worked outside the home and had only a high school diploma. She was a beautiful and charming young girl, however, and soon caught the eye of a well-to-do young man. He was arrogant and abusive toward her, but Betty didn't care. She planned to console herself by spending his money.

The years passed, and Betty had several children. Betty was extremely unhappy, and this was exacerbated by her husband's severe restrictions on her spending. They were quite wealthy, and this was an unnecessary limitation; but the man enjoyed the power that it gave him over Betty. He enjoyed the control that he gained with his money and coupled it with control through physical, mental, and verbal abuse. Consequently, Betty's self-esteem was almost totally destroyed; still, she could not imagine living without all of that money. She lied to herself and said that it was all her fault. Someday things would be better. Her husband would need her. Every time he had an affair, she said that it only confirmed his love for her because he always came back. Now her husband is gone, and Betty is growing old. She is a complete recluse and is plagued by imaginary enemies.

Nellie is virtually the opposite of Betty. Nellie came from an affluent home and had every privilege. Nellie's father was excessively controlling, however, and ran his home like a federal prison. There were strict rules for everything, and these were enforced by terrible nightly inquisitions. Nellie was told that she was retarded and subsequently was treated as though she actually were. When she became a teenager, she ran away from home.

Fortunately, Nellie met and married a warm and loving young man. They both became involved with their church; and through her community service, Nellie has fully come to understand that she is not retarded. On the contrary, the people of the community regard her as something of a genius. Nellie is honest and forthright and disclaims her contributions to the community because she enjoys the work. She is noted for her integrity and has won the respect of everyone who knows her, including her enemies. Nellie's love of the truth and her trust in Great Spirit are transforming her life, and it is wonderful to see her blossom into her full potential. She is an invaluable asset to the community.

The Cosmic Plan for our spiritual growth includes all of the opportunities that we will ever need. If you will only take a minute and look back over the events of your life, you will begin to see its pattern. It is a wonderful mosaic of people and events, dreams and intuitions. We do, indeed, walk in beauty. We are always given choices, for free will is the means by which we grow. Each of our failures is actually an opportunity, but we must be willing to be completely honest with ourselves in order to use failure (opportunity) constructively. We must assiduously practice honesty and truthfulness every moment of every day of our lives. And finally, we must trust in Great Spirit.

Trust Great Spirit, Trust Great Spirit.

MITAKUYE OYASIN!

Love the Truth and by it live.

MITAKUYE OYASIN!

Chapter Notes

1. A. Maslow, *Toward a Psychology of Being,* New York: Von Nostrand Reinhold, 1968, p. 159.
2. T. Mails, *Fools Crow,* Lincoln, Neb.: University of Nebraska Press, 1979, p. 58.
3. A. Maslow, op. cit., p. 159.
4. Lao Tzu, op. cit., ch. 61.
5. S. Johnson, op. cit., p. 48.
6. M. Peck, op. cit., p. 154.

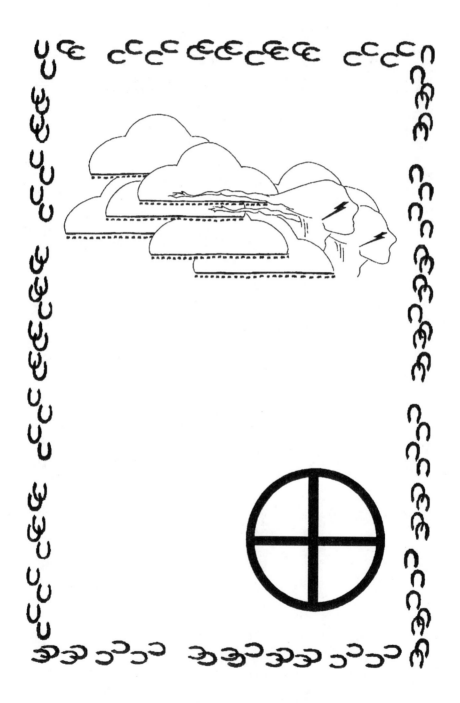

are not separate from our instruments. We are One. Great Spirit's music is innate in each of us. If even one of us is destroyed, then the Cosmos is diminished. If an instrument is damaged or destroyed, then the Cosmos is diminished. Our final symphony, though beautiful, will not have achieved its full potential. This is Cosmic Symbiosis. We are all One. MITAKUYE OYASIN.

In order to hear the music within ourselves, we must strive to be simple. In order for this music of Great Spirit to vibrate through us, in order to receive His/Her Medicine, we must be still. We cannot cloud our beings with dissonant energies. Some examples of these dissonant energies are lies, hatred, a grasping for control or power, excessive money, excessive jewelry or clothes or food, excesses of the flesh, and so on. All of these things have an energy of their own, and when their energy fields interact with our personal energy field, they create a dissonance. They prevent the resonance of Great Spirit's harmony.

Great Spirit's music—His/Her ability to activate and work within and throughout the forces of the universe—has been recorded by human beings since the beginning of time. Great Spirit is not separate and apart from the laws of science. The laws of science are of Great Spirit. They are manifestations of Great Spirit and the manner in which He/She orders the universe. Science is simply the orderly and disciplined approach to discovering Great Spirit's laws of the universe—the Cosmic Plan.

The Bible is full of stories of Great Spirit's miracles, and they become even more understandable in the light of unitheism. For example, Tesla's experiment, wherein he broke the steel beam by using harmonious vibrations, gives scientific credibility to the Biblical account of Joshua's horns tumbling the walls of Jericho. The forces of nature are the forces of Great Spirit. American Indian medicine men and women have always understood this principle. They only channel these energies; Great Spirit is the source of all healing and prophecy.

Fools Crow, the great Sioux holy man, says that he discovers each appropriate healing method through ceremony and direct communication with the Great Spirit. However, he emphasizes that, "I do exactly as I am told. Because of this, and unlike many medicine men who can treat only one kind of illness, God can cure anything through me."[1] Fools Crow goes on to detail the way that he obtains this knowledge for healing from the Great Spirit.

> ... I submit always to *Wakan-Tanka's* will. This is not easy, and most people find it impossible. But I have seen the power of prayer and I have

seen God's desires fulfilled. So I pray always that God will give me the wisdom to accept his ways of doing things.

Sometimes, in our talks, the creatures just laugh at my questions, as a human being will do. Perhaps they think my questions are foolish, and that I should know better. Our conversations range over the whole of life. They cover healing, medicines, assistance, prophecies—many things. When we talk, they come and sit down by me. I have a special song that I sing. And then we visit. The birds might fly above me when we talk, or they might land. In 1972, when I was leading the Pine Ridge Sun Dance, a meadowlark came and sang and danced with us. The people saw it dancing around and singing, gracefully hopping on one foot and then the other, and stretching out its little wings like arms. Then it danced over toward the east entrance of the enclosure and flew off. The people were very happy about this. They knew it was a good sign, that the spirits were with us.

All of these animals speak to me in Lakota. If another person who believed was there with me, he too would hear them, but I would be the only one who would know what they were saying. Unbelievers will see the animals' mouths move, and will hear the sounds and the creatures laughing. But that is all.

I also have a special song that has been given to me to use when I want to talk to the winds, clouds, and thunder, to stop the rain, or to split the clouds. I pray to them with this song, and the spirits of the winds, clouds, and thunder hear me and respond in Lakota.

After my vision quest of 1965, my power to heal seemed to increase, and I have been able to heal every person I have treated. *Wakan-Tanka* has given me this power ...[2]

As I said earlier, scientific method is nothing but the disciplined discovery of Great Spirit's laws of nature. Medicine men, mystics, psychics, and philosophers have always served as pioneers for the scientific community. They are able to listen to Great Spirit's "music" that is already within them. When they touch this harmony, they are also able to touch the Cosmic harmony, the Akashic Record. "According to Theosophy the akasha [Akashic Record] is an eternal record of the vibrations of every action, thought, emotion, light, and sound."[3]

There are many phenomena in the world that reflect Great Spirit's laws, but science does not yet understand this connection. However, merely because the underlying scientific (actually, Great Spirit's) principles have not been discovered does not mean that these phenomena do not exist. Medicine men can and do talk to plants and animals and learn methods of healing. Scientists are just discovering that plants do respond to the spoken word, but this is only half of the equation.

Ghosts and spirits have been encountered by too many people through the ages to be dismissed as unreal. Perhaps Einstein's mass-energy equivalency theory provides a first step in understanding their underlying scientific basis. Quantum mechanics could very well be the basis for the validity of astrology and numerology. Quantum mechanics and electrical theory might also be the scientific bases for auras and healing touch. We have so much to learn, but scientific methodology is a slow and cumbersome process. It is a bit like an elephant trying to catch a hummingbird. One would be hard-pressed to know if the elephant were able to even discern the presence of a hummingbird, much less capture one.

If civilization is to progress, we must insist that our scientists keep an open mind to all of these unexplained phenomena and remain truthful when they encounter them. When my youngest daughter was born, I had a powerful metaphysical experience that I vainly tried to share with my medical doctor. But he was not truthful. I'll share this experience with you in order to illustrate Great Spirit's powers and how they can help other human beings, if we are open to their revelation.

At the time of my daughter's birth, I had begun my spiritual journey in earnest. I had been blessed with a wonderful spiritual teacher, Eunice, several years earlier. Through my studies with Eunice, I had learned a Great Spirit-centered type of transcendental mediation. This has been one of the greatest gifts of my life, and it certainly saved my daughter's life.

I had been using an IUD (intrauterine device) for contraception for two years when I decided to become pregnant a second time. When the device was removed, it was extremely painful and caused severe hemorrhaging. Nonetheless, I became pregnant about one week later. Doctors had drugged me heavily for the birth of my first daughter, with traumatic medical effects on both of us. Therefore, I was adamant that this second pregnancy and birth would be different and that there would be no debilitating drugs.

My medical records for Melinda's birth were lost by the military, so neither my doctors nor I knew the entire medical history. However, I was determined to do everything in my power to have a healthy baby this time. I attended natural birthing (Lamaze) classes and read every book on prenatal nutrition that I could find. I carefully monitored my diet and exercised regularly. Therefore, I was shocked and terrified when my waters broke; I was only six months pregnant. My baby was three months early, and at only twenty-four weeks it was highly improbable that she would survive.

I was taken by ambulance sixty miles to the nearest town with intensive care facilities for premature babies. There, the doctors tried several chemical approaches to further induce labor and the birth, but to no avail. Then my heart began to weaken and stopped several times, so the doctors advised me that they would have to abort the baby in order to save my life.

I knew that I could not allow this to happen, but I faced a serious dilemma. I wanted my baby, but I also had to live in order to take care of my other daughter. In desperation, I asked the chief doctor to give me half an hour alone; then I would allow them to proceed with the abortion.

As soon as I was by myself, I began to meditate. I was in excruciating pain, but through meditation I was able to leave my body and the pain. I hovered just above my body, and visualized my unborn baby surrounded with white light from Great Spirit. Within twenty minutes, a **perfectly healthy**, beautiful baby girl (Jessica) was born. The doctors were confounded. A twenty-four-week-old baby could not be perfectly healthy (with the exception of a slight jaundice). I tried to explain the power of meditation, but it fell on deaf ears. Instead, they insisted that my due date had been miscalculated. I knew this wasn't true because of the IUD and the hemorrhaging prior to the baby's conception. I was amazed that these scientists would create a new truth simply because they couldn't explain what had happened.

Meditation could revolutionize the manner in which we give birth and the health of newborn babies. Nothing could be more simple or straightforward. One would think that any medical doctor would be wild with curiosity and enthusiasm, and at least want to explore the idea. Sadly, this was not the case. The entire experience wasn't even documented for future study. Is this a valid scientific approach?

I have recently discovered another incredible manifestation of the power of the Great Spirit. Again, it is an incredibly simple technique, and it has greatly helped my back. The reason that my daughters were both born prematurely is that my hips and spine have been deformed since birth. My right hip is almost two inches higher than my left and has caused a terrible zigzag in my spine in order to, literally, keep my head on straight. Football games with my brothers and midnight rides on wild mustangs over the mesas only exacerbated the problem. I have lived the last eight years in almost constant pain. Medical doctors have prescribed a steady diet of pain pills, which do alleviate the pain; but I feel that the side effects are much too risky. Several doctors recommended surgery for my neck, but I fail to understand how this would improve the condition of my hip. While I was weighing these different medical alternatives, I discovered a wonderful new method of healing that I call Tai Chi Touch Therapy.

This type of touch therapy is very simple. It is a blend of ancient Chinese and American Indian healing techniques. There is no secret mumbo-jumbo process, and it requires no expensive or complicated certification. Again, it is the essence of simplicity. Virtually anyone can become a practitioner and perform this incredible therapy within just a few minutes.

First, the practitioner performs the "introduction" by placing the first two fingers of the dominant (if right-handed, then the right; if left-handed, then the left) hand lightly on the solar plexus. This point on the body is also known in acupuncture as the heart meridian. In Laya Yoga it is called the manipurna chakra, or meridian, whereby the astral energy enters the body.

At the same time, the first two fingers of the alternate hand are simultaneously placed on the upper back, about an inch to the left of the spine where the neck joins the shoulders. The fingers of both hands are then left in place for about six seconds. It seems that this introduction serves to harmonize the body's electrical current between the recipient and the practitioner.

Both hands of the practitioner are now charged, similarly to the manner that jumper cables for an automobile become charged. Neither hand should now be allowed to touch the other, or any other material plane other than the recipient, or this charge will be dissipated.

Next, the practitioner simply uses the first two fingers of each hand and gently touches a series of points along both sides of the spine of the recipient. After treating the back, the practitioner may proceed to focus on any point of distress. The practitioner will feel a slight electrical charge (heat, tingling, or throbbing) in the fingertips at points on the patient's body where relief is needed and this healing energy transfer occurs.

I have found, however, that this energy transfer through the fingertips will be diminished if either participant is wearing any type of jewelry. This also happens if the practitioner's fingers should come into contact with anything other than the recipient's body—especially synthetics. I have found the therapy to be most effective if the practitioner and the recipient have recently showered and the practitioner's hands are freshly washed. The patient should stand during treatment, if possible, and then lie down for at least twenty minutes to allow the energy to work. A *Wotai*, or Indian spirit stone, can be used to complement the healing process by simply placing it on the epicenter of pain for at least twenty minutes.

Another relatively new and exciting approach to holistic healing, Behavioral Kinesiology,[4] expands on a logic similar to that of Tai Chi Touch Therapy. In his fascinating book on the subject, Dr. John Diamond leads the reader through a series of simple self-tests which illustrate the vital role of the thymus gland. These tests are somewhat similar to the color impact test detailed in an earlier chapter. In his book Dr. Diamond explains his theory of the thymus as the Life Energy or the Breath of Life. "The thymus gland lies just beneath the upper part of the breastbone in the middle of the chest ... it is the 'school and factory' for lymphocytes—the white blood cells responsible for the immunological reactions in the body."[5]

American Indians have long subscribed to the Breath of Life theory. Virtually all Indian artwork will include this "Breath" as an integral part of the design. American Indians have long understood the importance of the thymus gland, too. Historic photos show these people with their medicine bags tied around their necks. The medicine bag is lying right on the thymus gland. This medicine bag was unique to each individual, usually containing a wotai, (a spirit stone like my crystal), and a part of the umbilical cord. It might also contain a bit of hair from their horse, or other items of strong "medicine."

Dr. Diamond's strength tests and the related hypotheses provide a fascinating illustration of the premise that body, mind, and spirit are one and that the attributes of spiritual growth actually strengthen our Life Energy. His scientific work supports the logical premise of unitheism, that All is One. Dr. Diamond also documents the impact of the physical environment (including other humans) on weakening the thymus gland.[6] In tests that can be self-administered, Dr. Johnson shows that even a frown on another's face can weaken the thymus, while a smile can strengthen it. The evidence of Cosmic Symbiosis, of unitheism, is in the reaction of our own bodies to every facet of our environment.

American Indians have historically understood the properties of this medicine. Symbols are understood to carry an energy similar to the object that they depict. I am of the Eagle Clan, for example, so when I wear a symbol of the Eagle those energies will be present. There is medicine in the symbol itself. I find that I feel a perceptible rise in energy when I wear particular symbols. For example, whenever I have an important meeting of any sort, I always try to wear a turtle image—the symbol for Mother Earth. Another piece of my medicine-wear is a lovely hand-carved fetish necklace that includes images of a multitude of animals. I call it my MITAKUYE OYASIN necklace, carrying the energies of all my relations and reminding me that We are One. I try to wear only clothing that comes directly from

Mother Earth (cottons, wools, and silks) and is adorned with the medicine of different American Indian symbols. I can literally feel the energy that these things lend to my own energy field.

In contrast to these medicine items, it is interesting to note the negative impact of almost all man-made materials on our Life Energy. However, these vibrations can be returned to harmony quite simply. American Indian ceremonies always use sage or the smoke from sage (or sweet grass) to cleanse or harmonize vibrations. In their traditions, sage and sweet grass are sacred—they have a high vibration. Dr. Diamond's thymus tests can be easily used to document the change in vibrations, or strength, when sage or sweet grass is used in this manner. These tests provide further evidence for the need of simplicity in our lives. When we refrain from submerging our energy field with dissonant energies, we can keep our vibrations in harmony with Great Spirit. When we surround ourselves with a high vibration directly from Mother Earth, as we do when we smudge with sage or sweet grass, then we can begin the return of our bodies to harmony with Great Spirit.

In addition to Dr. Diamond's work, there is other scientific evidence documenting the dissonant vibrations created when human beings alter Great Spirit's creation too much. Michael Shallis details a number of interesting case studies concerning these negative physiological impacts from modern technology in his fascinating book, *The Electric Connection.*[7]

He tells a story of a woman called Norma who experienced violent shocks whenever she approached her record player and who collapsed whenever near her stove and refrigerator. Light bulbs would "pop" and burn out whenever she came near. In a similar vein, he tells of the case of Sheila who is an abnormal conductor of static electricity—two-inch long sparks flash from her fingers! She has to be careful not to pet her dog for fear of hurting him. Sheila also destroys every electric appliance that she touches. She even blew out her electric meter one day. My own experience corroborates these stories, for I am unable to wear any type of watch. My electrical field makes watches go totally haywire, and I usually interfere with the reception of my radio or television.

Shallis (an astrophysicist at Oxford University) takes great pains to substantiate the basic electrical nature of the human body as a means of explaining these phenomena. He summarizes his evidence, stating that "Living things display a whole range of electromagnetic effects as part of their life-sustaining processes. We are all electrically active creatures ... ."[8] Other corroborating evidence of the body's basic electrical nature is contained in the phenomena of auras, life fields, and Kirlian photography.

In the 1940s and 1950s two scientists (E. J. Lund of the University of Texas, and Harold Saxton Burr, Professor of Anatomy at Yale University) independently discovered overall body [electrical] fields in all living organisms. (It is interesting to note the synchronicity of these discoveries—when Great Spirit's Cosmic Plan is timed for an event, related events will occur simultaneously.) These overall body fields are called bioelectric or electrodynamic. As Burr continued his research, he further theorized that the pattern or organization of a living thing is established by its electrodynamic field. "This electrical field," he stated, "will be a characteristic of a particular living thing; it determines its growth and pattern and maintains the pattern and structure of the organism during its life." Burr named these L-fields or "fields of life."

Burr found that an electrical axis existed as every organism's most basic element, and that this electrical axis later became the central nervous system and bodily structure of the organism.

> The organization of a living thing, its pattern, is established by an electrodynamic field, which determines the arrangement of the components of the organism and is determined by them. This electrical field ... will be a characteristic of a particular living thing; it determines its growth and pattern and maintains the pattern and structure of the organism during its life.[9]

As a result of this research, scientists in the 1970s developed several techniques for using electrical stimulation to aid in bone healing. However, the size of the electric current used in these methods is considerably greater than that found in the bone naturally. This healing by electrical stimulation is probably based on the same principles that make Tai Chi Touch Therapy so incredibly effective. Hundreds of patients have benefited from these pioneering healing methods, but many doctors still feel them too controversial to be considered.

There is also an exciting new healing aspect of electricity being tested on laboratory animals. Scientists found that salamanders, who can regrow a lost limb, produce a negative electrical charge at the growth point. An electrical action of the nerve cells in the damaged limb appears to be responsible for stimulating this regrowth. (In Tai Chi Touch Therapy, it is generally the fingers of the left hand, or the negatively charged fingers, where the electrical "tingling" is felt when touched to a healing point.) Scientists successfully applied this theory by implanting a "small electrical stimulator into the stump end of the amputated leg of a rat." The rat actually regrew its leg.[10]

In similar experiments with salamanders, scientists found some interesting electrical properties. The unfertilized salamander egg exhibits a distinct voltage axis with the most positive part of the field marked by a distinct spot on the egg. This positive point later develops into the heart of the salamander. (Remember, in the earlier paragraphs on Tai Chi Touch Therapy the initial bioelectrical charge was made by placing the fingers on the recipient's heart meridian.) "It is as if the future possible form of an embryonic animal is already mapped out in the unfertilized egg ... As the salamander grows, the electrical axis extends down its backbone, accompanied by an electrical symmetry either side of its spinal cord."[11]

There are two other areas of evidence that support the theory of a preexisting design for life-forms. The first is the theory of morphogenetic fields postulated by Dr. Rupert Sheldrake in 1981, and the second is something called the phantom leaf effect.

Dr. Sheldrake proposed that there must be special fields in an organism that contain a blueprint for form, guiding growth, maintaining pattern, and representing the potential of the adult organism.[12] These morphogenetic fields are similar to the concept of the L-fields just discussed and bear a strong resemblance to the Buddhist teaching of reality being a manifestation of the mind of Buddha and the theories of Plato on God's pattern for universal forms. This also supports the hypothesis of unitheism in that Great Spirit is Omnipresent and works through the forces of nature.

The second of these scientific phenomena (that support the theory of a preexisting design for life forms) is the phantom leaf effect. Kirlian photography is a technique for photographing the electrodynamic field around living objects. Researchers using Kirlian photography are able to produce a photograph that outlines an entire leaf, even after a part of the leaf is amputated. This was labeled the phantom leaf effect. Kirlian photography is still a highly controversial scientific tool, with some scientists arguing that the results simply illustrate the discharge of electricity from an object.[13] Even if this is the case, scientists still do not truly know what electricity is. They understand some of its properties and many of the ways that it can be manipulated, but its essence remains a mystery. In either case, Kirlian photography seems to support the theory of L-fields or morphogenetic fields (fields of energy that allow self-regeneration).

Another interesting application of Kirlian photography is its ability to capture on film what is thought to be the human aura. It is postulated that the aura is "an envelope of vital energy, which apparently radiates from everything in nature: minerals, plants, animals, and humans."[14] Scientists have not yet been able to explain the existence of auras. They argue that the body's magnetic field is far too weak to emit the type of light in the auras recorded by Kirlian photography. However, this very same argument lends further support to the theory of Great Spirit's Omnipresence. Eastern mystics argue that our physical body is enveloped in an outer shell of Perfect Energy (Chi), also called the astral or etheric body.

This shell represents the potential of our being when we bring ourselves into complete harmony with Great Spirit. Ordinarily, our bodies vibrate at a lower frequency due to the dissonant choices that we make when we exercise free will. However, both our physical and astral bodies have the potential to resonate at the same high frequency when we grow spiritually. This is the same astral energy, or Chi, that flows into the chakra at the solar plexus when you charge up your fingertips in Tai Chi Touch Therapy.

A noted London electrotherapist, Dr. Walter J. Kilner, developed a method for viewing auras shortly before World War I. His method used an apparatus containing a coal-tar dye called dicyanin which enabled him to view the body's ultraviolet light. Using this technology, Kilner developed a method of diagnosing illness based on an analysis of the aura's color and size. He published his research in *The Human Aura* in 1911 and again in 1920.[15]

Once again, most scientists deny the evidence and cannot explain or acknowledge the existence of auras. This failure is symptomatic of the relationship between science and the spiritual or occult. The reality of the occult (or hidden) phenomena of Great Spirit's universe exists in spite of scientific disavowal. This lack of scientific "discovery" does not preclude the validity of the occult any more than the lack of European discovery precluded the existence of our American continent.

Occult phenomena are not evil, they simply are not yet fully discovered nor understood. As I demonstrated earlier, evil exists when human will asserts itself in opposition to the will of Great Spirit. When this happens, even a supposed good becomes evil. Religion that assists an individual in spiritual growth, and therefore in living in harmony with Great Spirit's will, is good and of Great Spirit. Religion that seeks only to control others according to human will—such as was seen in the Spanish Inquisition, the mass suicide of Reverend Jones' followers, the excesses of Muslim extremism, or even the profligate, self-indulgent televangelists of the 1980s—is evil.

Use of crystals, or of any of the occult phenomena, to achieve a harmony with Great Spirit is good. Use of crystals, or of any of the occult phenomena, to gain material goods or control over others is evil because it seeks the imposition of the individual's will and not the harmony of Great Spirit's will.

American Indian medicine men and women clearly understand this principle. They are very clear that they may not heal any patient unless that patient first requests their help. Fools Crow explains that "Everything ... is here on earth for a purpose, even the people who are ill. So when a person is ill, Grandfather shows me in my vision what medicine he has placed on earth to cure that illness."[16] Fools Crow goes on to explain why he was unable to heal his own wife when she was stricken with pneumonia.

> You have also mentioned that at the time of our last talk together in Rapid City, Kate was a patient at the Indian hospital. She was being treated for pneumonia and had been in bed for ten days or so before we visited her. She was doing quite well though, and was expecting to go home in another week. You want to know why I had not healed her if I can indeed heal any illness? The answer is that I often know when people are becoming ill, and I knew it was happening to Kate. But she didn't bring me a filled pipe or tobacco of any kind and ask for my help, so I just couldn't help her! I must remain true to my rules. I cannot, even for those I dearly love, violate procedures that *Wakan-Tanka* has directed me to follow as a holy man.[17]

Fools Crow's relationship with Great Spirit is the essence of simplicity. He has no intermediary between himself and the Creator, and his communications with the Creator are clear and straightforward. His healing techniques are just as uncomplicated; it is the plants, animals, and other forces of nature that speak to him and teach him their medicine. This is the power of simplicity, for Great Spirit is everywhere and immediately accessible to each of us as we desire. When we keep ourselves simple—that is, when we are free from pretense and ego, when we are straightforward in our communications, and when we avoid layering our bodies with dissonant energy—we then allow the power of Great Spirit to flow through us. This is the reason that simplicity is so exceedingly powerful.

Simplicity allows for the manifestation of Great Spirit throughout the universe. In order to clarify this concept a bit further, I will explore two additional phenomena, astrology and numerology, in the next chapter.

Chapter Notes

1. T. E. Mails, *Fools Crow,* Lincoln, Nebraska: University of Nebraska, 1979, p. 93.
2. Ibid., p. 184.
3. R. E. Guiley, *Harper's Encyclopedia of Mystical and Paranormal Experience,* San Francisco: Harper, 1991, pp. 3–5.
4. J. Diamond, M.D., *Your Body Doesn't Lie,* New York: Warner Books, 1983.
5. Ibid., p. 38.
6. Ibid., ch. 8.
7. M. Shallis, op. cit., ch. 1.
8. Ibid., p. 131.
9. Ibid., p. 120–121.
10. Ibid., pp. 54–56.
11. Ibid., p. 123.
12. Ibid., p. 246.
13. R. E. Guiley, op. cit., pp. 313–315.
14. Ibid., p. 40.
15. Ibid., p. 41.
16. T. E. Mails, op. cit., p. 94.
17. Ibid., p. 206.

The Nature of Simplicity

"The attitude of the American Indian toward the Eternal, the Great Mystery that surrounds and embraces us, is as simple as it is exalted. To us it is the supreme conception, bringing with it the fullest measure of joy and satisfaction possible in this life."

Ohiyesa (Sioux)
The Soul of an Indian

There are unlimited manifestations of Great Spirit's omnipresence in the universe. However, I will limit this discussion to only two phenomena, astrology and numerology, in order to clarify the meaning of simplicity within the logic of unitheism.

Due to daily newspaper publication of individual horoscopes there is a great deal of misunderstanding and misinformation concerning astrology. Trying to discern the Cosmic Pattern for our own lives based on a few sentences of general information in the newspaper is very much like making a major investment based only on a corporation's daily stock quote. It is usually destined for failure because it is not a valid representation of the entire issue.

Astrological energy forces can logically be explained by the theories of quantum mechanics. As illustrated earlier, the energies that pervade the universe are constantly interacting with our bodies. Nonetheless, the extent of the influence of these energies is not yet completely understood by scientists. Fortunately, the science of astrology (first documented over 5,000 years ago) provides one of the exceptions, although it is not generally accepted by mainstream scientists. Astrology can be easily and consistently utilized by any individual—one of the scientific criteria for validating any phenomenon. Usually, extensive mathematical calculations (based on the time and place of birth and this relationship to the exact position of sun, moon, and planets) are required in order to cast a horoscope. Luckily, there are a number of new astrology books that have these computations embedded in easy-to-use charts. Once the positions of the sun, moon, and planets are determined, an individual's horoscope reveals childhood family composition, major emotional traumas, and most of the milestones throughout life—all of which can be easily substantiated by the actual past events.

Astrology is "an understanding that the entire Universe is one gigantic whole in which all parts exist in a totally interdependent relationship with each other."[1] Central to the theory of astrology is the zodiac which represents the path of the Sun relative to the earth's horizon. Within this imaginary, narrow belt line lie the orbits of all the planets in our solar system, with the exception of Pluto. Ancient astronomers named the twelve different constellations of stars within this belt after various real and mythical animals, and these constitute the twelve astrological signs. The very word zodiac is derived from the Greek word *zodiakos* which means "circle of animals."

In addition to the twelve signs of the zodiac, Babylonian astrologers also divided the horoscope into twelve areas to represent the component parts of life; and these are referred to as houses. This division also represents the ancient Greek philosophical concept of human beings as a microcosm of the universe, resonating with the same energies. This Hermetic Theory (as it is called) acknowledges the interconnectedness of the universe. Within the context of astrology then, various energies of the universe emanate from the planets as they pass through the twelve constellations and the twelve houses of the zodiac. Every area on earth resonates with this mixture of planet, constellation, and house as the planets follow their orbits. Different areas of earth will resonate with a strength of energy correlating to their proximity to any of these celestial configurations. Ultimately, this resonance is conferred to the human beings born in that location and at that time.

An astrologer casts an individual's natal chart by noting the position, at the time of birth, of the sun, the moon, and each of the planets (creating a map of the Zodiac) in relationship to each of twelve houses. Each of these houses contains the energy impulsion which governs a specific area of the individual's life. For example, if the planet Saturn is cast in the Second House at the time of birth, the individual may have a very real fear of poverty and act accordingly. Astrologers reach this conclusion because Saturn projects an energy of responsibility and hard work. Saturn also imparts an energy that strengthens character through trial and difficulty. Through the pattern of placing Saturn in the Second House (which governs our attitude toward money and possessions), astrologers conclude that this individual's hard work will probably be a reaction to early poverty. This same logic is applied to each of the planets and each of the houses within an individual's horoscope.

I once worked with an astrologer who became quite sullen and snarly when questioned about the chart that he had just cast. He was not spiritually centered and had come to regard astrology as predestination. Unfortunately, this man felt that our entire lives are cast in stone by the gods prior to birth, and that we have no control. Astrology is **not** predestination. It is simply a method of ascertaining what is contained in the package of energies that were given to us at birth in order to effect our spiritual growth. As I have shown with the logic of unitheism, we are a part of Great Spirit prior to our birth into our physical body. While in this state of Oneness, we participated in deciding what energies, what package of attributes, would help us to achieve spiritual growth in this life. As I have shown earlier, the logic of unitheism mandates free will, not predestination. If we subscribe to the theory of predestination, then we would have to conclude that human beings are simply puppets of Great Spirit, and this is simply not logical.

Astrology is not a god and not a religion. It is simply a manifestation of the order of Great Spirit's universe and a tool to be used in gaining spiritual growth. Casting one's chart can be invaluable in gaining an understanding of the self and therefore a healthy self-acceptance. These attributes are critical to the work of spiritual growth. Astrology can also be invaluable in discerning our life's work. When we have entered upon a career path that is in harmony with the energies of our natal chart, then we will be able to maximize our spiritual growth. It is possible to struggle and ultimately achieve some measure of success apart from the direction of our natal chart. However, this progress is similar to the headway that we make when we paddle our canoe upstream against the current. We will have much greater satisfaction and success by heading our canoe downstream, and going with the strong current of energies that were present at the moment of our birth. Miracles are possible when we "go with the flow."

If one succumbs to astrology, and relies on it to govern every facet of one's life, then one is no longer living in harmony with Great Spirit's will. The very act of succumbing makes a god of astrology. But astrology is not a god, it is only a manifestation of Great Spirit. It is a tool that provides further proof of Great Spirit's omnipresence.

Numerology is a comparable manifestation of the order of Great Spirit's universe. The underlying principles of numerology are similar to those of astrology. Again, the logical basis for its validity is quantum mechanics—the interconnected waves of energy throughout the universe. According to numerology, the numbers one through nine vibrate with different intensities. The rate of this vibration carries the energy of differing attributes. Each letter of the alphabet also corresponds to one of eight numbers. The letters of a name, translated to these numbers, are then added to one another and reduced to the numbers one through nine in order to analyze the vibration and its attributes.

There are several different tables for numerology; however, it has been my experience that the ancient Chaldean-Hebrew Kabala table is the most valid. The table in Figure 11-1 comes from *Linda Goodman's Star Signs* which is a collection of most of the phenomena usually associated with New Age religious thought.[2]

Chaldean-Hebrew Kabala Numerical Alphabet			
A - 1	H - 5	O - 7	V - 6
B - 2	I - 1	P - 8	W - 6
C - 3	J - 1	Q - 1	X - 5
D - 4	K - 2	R - 2	Y - 1
E - 5	L - 3	S - 3	Z - 7
F - 8	M - 4	T - 4	
G - 3	N - 5	U - 6	

Figure 11-1

The chapters of *Journey Song* provide an interesting illustration of how the energies of the universe conform to Great Spirit's Cosmic Plan, even when we are not conscious of their impact. Chapter 1 of this book deals with unitheism, the idea that we are all created by Great Spirit and are a part of Great Spirit and one another in a harmonious, infinite vibration (All is One). Interestingly, the number one vibrates to the energies of creativity, protection, and benevolence, and so Chapter 1 vibrates with the energy that is its theme. Chapter 3 deals with spiritual growth, and the number three vibrates with the energies of overcoming adversity for spiritual growth. Chapter 7 illustrates different ways that we can make medicine with Great Spirit, and the number seven vibrates with spiritual leadership. All of the chapters of this book fall into this pattern, each vibrating with the same energy that reflects its theme. And this is true of all books. A random sampling will illustrate that a chapter number invariably vibrates with the number appropriate to its central theme. It's also interesting to note that the title of any book will invariably vibrate with the number that correlates to the theme of that particular book. The validity of numerology is not limited to books. The truth of this phenomena pervades the universe in any pattern of letters and/or numbers that human beings can devise.

Numerology is not a god; it is a tool that reflects the order of Great Spirit's universe—the Cosmic Plan. Preparatory to writing this book, I compiled a database of about 500 names and titles in order to statistically analyze the tool of numerology and its implications. One of the most fascinating aspects revealed by this preliminary analysis is the importance of the polarity of each number which, then, clearly indicates the importance of free will.

No number is inherently good or evil. Although each number vibrates with a certain type of energy, there is a polarity to that energy. We may choose to channel its vibrations for good or for evil. A profound example of this principle is the fact that the names of Adolf Hitler and Abraham Lincoln both vibrate with the strong spiritual leadership energy of the number seven. Seven also confers the energy of a high-strung temperament, which both men possessed. However, one man is considered a virtual saint and the other the devil incarnate. Yet they both have names with the same vibration. The vibrating energies of seven, of spiritual leadership, can be used constructively or destructively. The choice is ours. If Hitler had chosen to use his spiritual energies for the good of mankind, he could have been one of the most beloved (instead of despised) spiritual leaders of the twentieth century.

Numerology also seems to reflect a subconscious influence on the naming procedures which we utilize. This is another manifestation of Great Spirit's energies ordering the universe even when we are not aware of their influence. Names appear to be linked to certain potentialities; they carry the resonance of the combined numbers. Bestowing a certain name causes a resonance of that potentiality, thus allowing it to manifest itself. This principle works somewhat like the strings of a guitar. The sounding box of the guitar will resonate with the vibrations of whatever string happens to have been struck. Since there are six strings and eighteen frets, there are thousands of different sounds to which the guitar can resonate.

When viewed with this new understanding, the name that someone or something is called takes on great importance. A child or a person who is verbally abused will slowly begin to resonate with the names that he/she is called, and the person's physical nature will begin to reflect the name. On the other hand, one who is addressed by a name with positive attributes will begin to resonate and reflect these attributes—as long as the potentiality is present. (I would recommend using Linda Goodman's book to compute and interpret the numerical vibrations of names and birth dates. It is the most accurate book on numerology that I have found.)

When I first began to test the theory of numerology, I changed the names of several of my animals. I theorized that although animals are sentient beings and guardian spirits, still they do not have the same free will as human beings. Therefore, their names will reflect the principles of numerology when adjusted for any attribute linked to free will. What this means then, is that an animal vibrating to the number seven can not and will not possess spiritual leadership. Spiritual leadership is an attribute of free will. Instead, the number seven in an animal will imbue the energies of sensitivity and a high-strung temperament. Man of War, perhaps the most famous racehorse of this century, bore a name that vibrates to the number seven and was possessed of a notably high-strung temperament.

My experiment in changing animal names produced some remarkable behavioral changes in our animals here at the ranch. One of our two-year-old fillies was extremely difficult to work with, and my daughter and I were having a great deal of trouble training her. Her original name was Easter, and she was terrified of just about everything. The name Easter vibrates to the number two, and carries the energies of great fear and extreme caution.

After computing the vibrations of numerous choices, we renamed this filly "Lady." Lady vibrates to the number nine, and carries the energies of courage and a high degree of trust. Trust and courage are most desirable traits in a horse and are key ingredients in successful training. Melinda and I spent several days just feeding, grooming, and talking to her while we repeated her new name "Lady" over and over. Within three days there was a radical change in her attitude and her behavior. I have since found a shortcut to instilling the resonance of a new name. This resonance will begin almost immediately when it is bestowed through use of American Indian ceremony—calling upon all the energies (or spirits) of all six directions and the Great Spirit. Sitting Bull performed a number of considerable feats with his horses during the sacred Sun Dance ceremonies. Actually, American Indians throughout the west, in the past and present, are renowned for their almost magical ability to train horses. This magic is simply a matter of invoking the energies of the directions and Great Spirit and creating a Oneness with the animal. This magic, or medicine, is available to virtually any individual who understands the underlying principles.

Great Spirit's omnipresence throughout the cosmos ensures that His/Her potent energy is available to each of us through tools such as astrology and numerology in order to help us effect our spiritual growth. These tools may not be substituted for the spiritual growth itself, but they can be very useful in helping each person to achieve ultimate harmony with Great Spirit. Unfortunately, as New Age awareness gains momentum, it is alarming to see many people succumb to these tools as gods in themselves. We cannot simply change our names and then suppose that there is no further personal responsibility or work involved in growing spiritually. Likewise, it is self-defeating to consult an astrological chart each day for guidance on all decisions. This is an abrogation of responsibility for our own lives, and it will not aid in the work of spiritual growth. Advancing along the Good Red Road requires self-discipline and work. If we rely on a daily horoscope for guidance, we lose the opportunity to develop a good sense of judgment as we exercise our free will in making difficult decisions.

The only evil that exists in the universe is that which we human beings have created through our free will; evil does not exist in the natural world. Animals kill one another only for food or safety. Two-leggeds, however, choose to commit murder out of envy, hate, greed, and lust. An earthquake is not evil; it is simply the natural movement of the earth. On the other hand, when we explode an atomic bomb it is a conscious choice to kill. As a rule, animals do not foul their own nests. We two-leggeds, however, choose to pollute our environment, thereby condemning future generations to certain death. Let me emphasize again that within the logical structure of unitheism, evil consists of thoughts, words, or deeds in dissonance with Great Spirit's will.

Unitheism and Cosmic Symbiosis pose a challenge in the responsibility that they place on the individual. Because Great Spirit is Omnipresent, all of the tools that we need to effect our spiritual growth are at our fingertips. Great Spirit is not impersonal. Great Spirit is intimately connected to each of us, and is vitally concerned with helping us to grow spiritually. Infinity will be realized only when the entire universe resonates in consonance with the Great Spirit. Dissonant energy will simply cease to exist. Unitheism, with its Cosmic Symbiosis, presents human beings with a challenge that mandates a revolutionary rethinking of our relationship to all human beings, animals, the earth, and to the Cosmos. We are all interconnected. MITAKUYE OYASIN.

When 30,000 to 40,000 children die from hunger each day, we all participate in those deaths. When another species of animal becomes extinct because of our careless stewardship of the earth, we all participate in that death, too. MITAKUYE OYASIN. American Indians were the successful stewards of this continent for at least 10,000 years before Europeans arrived. In only four centuries under our dominant society, however, the rivers, the land, and the air have all become poisoned. We are the blue man of Black Elk's vision, and our blue man is killing the earth.

In addition to the imperative for individual spiritual growth, the logical structure of unitheism also mandates a stewardship of the Cosmos. We are all placed on this earth to love and nurture one another. When one is frightened, hungry, or cold, it is virtually impossible to focus on spiritual life. Behavioral Kinesiology has several simple tests that show the profound physiological changes that just a smile or a touch can have on another person. We two-leggeds are charged with the stewardship of the animals and plants of the earth, as well as of Mother Earth and the Cosmos. All is One. I would like to emphasize again that everything on the earth and in the Cosmos is interconnected. Whenever human beings choose to vibrate in dissonance with the energy or will of Great Spirit, we face certain extinction. Not just a transformation of energy, but an inevitable, **total** cessation of all being.

In the preceding chapters, I have tried to present some of the more interesting documentation concerning the omnipresence of Great Spirit. This Energy that permeates the universe and is of Great Spirit, is called Chi by the Chinese, *prana* by the Hindus, *mana* by the Polynesians, and the Breath of Life by American Indians. The Power of Great Spirit that courses through these energies, controlling the events of the Cosmos and assisting the work of spiritual growth, is what we call Holy Spirit, Teh, or (American Indian) Medicine. This Medicine has attributes similar to those of electricity or light, but it has a speed magnitudes beyond that of light. The manifestations of this Medicine prove its speed. Logically, Great Spirit could not be all-powerful if it takes millions of light years for Him/Her to send the power surges for changing events. And in order for Great Spirit to be Great Spirit, He/She must be all-powerful and present even in the infinite reaches of the universe. Therefore, Medicine is able to travel at speeds beyond that of light.

Again, quantum mechanics has shown that all physical manifestations—all solids, liquids, and gases—consist of packets of energy. These packets or quanta are in a constant state of interaction. On the subatomic level there is no boundary between objects, and this serves to prove the interconnectedness of the universe. This brings us to the point of understanding the value of simplicity in our quest for spiritual growth. In order for our energies to achieve an infinite, harmonious vibration with Great Spirit, we must first work to bring our energies into resonance with the energy of Great Spirit. This resonance must be achieved through body, mind, and spirit. They are all One.

Simplicity as it relates to the body is reflected in our dress, our possessions, and our relationship to nature. Whenever human beings take the raw materials of the earth and rearrange the molecules, there is a high probability that the result will not be in harmony with Great Spirit's energies. Plastics, synthetics, and chemicals are just some proven examples of man-made products that usually are not consonant with the universe. They will be consonant or dissonant depending upon the energy that was present at their inception. If greed, or the profit motive, was the only energy present during their creation by human beings, then they will vibrate with a dissonant energy. It is for this reason that recycling these materials is of vital importance. The very act of recycling is an act of love for our Mother Earth, and the products of this love will be in harmony with Great Spirit.

Chemicals that human beings have manufactured are literally killing our Mother Earth, and most plastics do not biodegrade and will probably remain on this earth long after human beings have disappeared. These materials are generally produced with one thought in mind—making lots of money. It is possible, however, for these same materials to have a harmonious vibration if produced with good intentions as a focus.

The dissonance of these negative products interacts with all who are exposed to their range of energy. Try any of the thymus strength tests that Dr. Diamond details in *Your Body Doesn't Lie* using plastics or synthetics. Almost all will have a debilitating effect upon your body, and it will be immediately and dramatically apparent. Michael Shallis has done an excellent job of documenting the debilitating effects of electricity in *The Electric Connection*. And yet, we two-leggeds have made our nests in the midst of these man-made toxins. The energy that these man-made materials produce is dissonant to the energy of Great Spirit and interferes with our physical channels for spiritual growth.

Tilda Long Soldier writes of the Sioux perception of electricity in *Walking in the Sacred Manner*.

> Grandma Dora [Little Warrior] told me, "The white people are descended from the spider people. The[y] have learned to use electricity. That electricity once belonged only to the *Wakinyan* [Thunder Beings].

To do this they put up wires on poles. They send these wires all over. As electricity covers the earth, it creates a huge spider web. One day this spider web will cause a great fire. This will cause the buffalo to lose its last leg and fall to the earth. This will be the end of the world."[3]

It is the norm for modern men and women to submerge their personal energy fields with layers of scented soaps, deodorants, perfume, makeup, synthetic fabrics, and jewelry. With these layers and swirls of dissonant energies engulfing our bodies, we soon become "plastic." The true energy and essence of our physical being is almost completely masked. Sensing the dissonance, but not understanding its source, we engage in a continual acquisition of more "stuff" to layer on our bodies. We keep looking for harmony in all the wrong places. We are literally dying of consumption.

Simplicity. We don't need layers of stuff. There is nothing more attractive than a human being who radiates inner peace. We don't need huge houses filled with stuff. The stuff that fills our homes begins to possess us. Energy from all of the man-made stuff is usually dissonant with the energy of Great Spirit. These huge houses and large cars must be heated and run on fossil fuels that are killing Mother Earth both by their extraction and the pollutants they create. Simply because one has the money to buy lots of stuff does not make it ethically right to indulge in these acquisitions. We must strive to keep our physical lives as simple and as uncluttered as possible. We cannot succumb to these physical distractions without lowering the vibrations of our bodies and creating a dissonance with Great Spirit's energy. The term "succumbing to the physical" refers to any excesses of the flesh.

Simplicity of the mind means keeping the mind healthy and clean. Any mind-altering drug creates dissonance, as does visual or verbal "trash." I am constantly appalled at the number of people who pollute their minds. They would never consider eating cow pies from the pasture, but constantly put the literary or visual equivalents into their minds. Our environment is also greatly contaminated with the lingering energy of generations of bad thoughts, words, and deeds. Our television sets spew an almost non-stop flow of dissonant energy every day to millions of willing viewers. Everyone is susceptible to contamination from this energy, so it is of great importance to edit what we allow to filter into our thoughts and what we allow to take up residency in our minds. Most people would never even consider drinking spoiled milk, yet they will entertain and indulge sour thoughts all day. When any of these types of mental pollution is allowed to reside in the mind for any length of time, the dissonant vibrations that they create will soon contaminate the rest of the body and the spirit.

Simplicity of spirit means that we must strive to live a life in harmony with Great Spirit. When living in spiritual simplicity, we actively work to enhance spiritual growth through study, meditation, prayer, and actions. Our words, written and spoken, and our actions resonate with truth and love of others and of all that Great Spirit has created. All communications are clear and straightforward. There is no game playing nor are there attempts to manipulate or control others toward our own ends. We live with the simple objective of doing Great Spirit's will.

One of my favorite people, who also exemplifies the way in which to live a life of simplicity, is Marty. She and her husband have a small and delightful cabin here in the mountains. It has just enough room to accommodate their needs, and is quite beautiful in its simplicity. Rough-planked shelves line the kitchen walls with an artful display of cooking and eating utensils. Their house is passive solar, heated only by the sun and augmented by a wood-burning stove. (Wood stoves, when properly used, are better for the environment than those using any other fuel except solar energy. In addition, wood is a "harvest crop" as opposed to fossil fuels which irrevocably deplete the capital assets of the earth.) Their house is surrounded by a rich profusion of wild flowers attractively placed and carefully nurtured by Marty and her husband. Marty's life work is a loving dedication of service to others, complementing her simple manner of living.

Years ago, a charming friend of mine from Old Europe called my attention to the profligate way in which we Americans live. He and I spent many mornings in lengthy philosophical discussions over French coffee and croissants. I can still hear his thick Bulgarian accent as he warned of the dangers confronting America. He would cluck his tongue and slowly shake his head as he spoke of the wanton way Americans spend every last dime on the latest toys—expensive new cars, stereos, clothes, and homes that are far too big. He also wondered at our preference for living such sterile lives—never out-of-doors, always in front of a television. All of our shopping done at huge supermarkets. All of our family outings consisting of trips to the malls for more shopping.

His point struck home with me. I recalled what a pleasure it is to live in Europe. The wonderful smells from the bakery as one shops for, literally, the daily bread. The warmth and camaraderie of shopping for food at the open-air markets. The exhilaration of finding virtually everyone out-of-doors and walking or biking whenever the weather permits. Beautiful, centuries-old homes that resonate with the vibrations of years of human passion now pleasantly intermingled with the vibrations of Mother Earth as she inexorably works to reclaim the bricks and mortar.

There are numerous studies sponsored by the Club of Rome concerning the future of our planet. Among the alarming conclusions which they draw are those concerning the fate of the world at its present growth rate. These provide ample warning that our way of living is slowly destroying our Mother Earth. We are on the path toward the death of our planet unless we rethink and restructure our value system. It is imperative that we return to simplicity.

James Lovelock provides an insight to the fascinating interrelationship of humans with the planet earth in *The Ages of Gaia*. Lovelock hypothesizes that the earth is a living organism for "life is defined as a self-organizing system characterized by an actively sustained low entropy [the degradation of matter or energy]." He proposes that we should view the earth as Gaia, the Greek name for the Earth goddess.[4] This is similar to the American Indian convention of referring to the earth as Mother Earth, and treating her accordingly.

It is the very lack of simplicity in our lives that is destroying Mother Earth. If we—simply—adopt the idea of earth as Gaia or Mother Earth, this can be the beginning of lifesaving change. E. F. Schumacher provides a good illustration of this principle in his bestseller, *Small Is Beautiful*. Schumacher points out that good businessmen would never sanction the wholesale depletion of their capital assets. The capital assets of the earth can never be replaced, and when man has rearranged her molecules, they become toxic. We must seek to harvest and replenish and develop a new attitude about what constitutes progress and development. Schumacher writes that this new view of the world's economy must start with a change in values.

> The task of our generation, I have no doubt, is one of metaphysical reconstruction. It is not as if we had to invent anything new; at the same time, it is not good enough merely to revert to the old formulations ... We are suffering from a metaphysical disease, and the cure must therefore be metaphysical.[5]

I offer the philosophy of unitheism and Cosmic Symbiosis as the first step toward this "metaphysical reconstruction." Once we accept and live by a simple, philosophical system, which logically and cogently proves that All is One, our manner of living will change. Our entire Cosmos is interconnected, and we must resonate with the vibration of Great Spirit in order to achieve peace and infinity. Great Spirit's energies permeate the

Cosmos, including each and every individual. Through our free will we choose eternal life or death. We have only just begun to glimpse the powers which lie waiting within each of us. Within this unitheistic philosophy, Great Spirit is intimately concerned with the eternal life of each of us. Great Spirit's infinite and immediate power, or Medicine, may be easily accessed by any individual who needs help for spiritual growth. When we live simple lives, we will feel the resonance and harmony of Great Spirit.

The Composer created us and the Cosmos from His/Her own being. We are born infused with this Divine energy or life force. We only have to be still, to quiet our will, and allow this Divine harmony to well up within us and express itself through us. We cannot live our lives immersed in a cloud of dissonant energies and expect to hear the Divine harmony. We cannot expect to destroy our instruments and the stage—our bodies, other creatures, and our planet—and expect to hear the Divine symphony. All are One. MITAKUYE OYASIN. The Cosmos is One. "Be still, and know that I am God."

We've now completed the third step along the spiritual path of our journey song.

Trust Great Spirit, Trust Great Spirit.

MITAKUYE OYASIN!

Love the Truth and by it live.

MITAKUYE OYASIN!

Walk life's path with Simplicity.

MITAKUYE OYASIN!

On the next step of our *Journey Song* we will explore the importance of Patience.

Chapter Notes

1. N. Campion, op. cit., p. 6.
2. L. Goodman, op. cit., ch. 5.
3. M. St. Pierre and Tilda Long Soldier, *Walking in the Sacred Manner*, New York: Simon & Schuster, 1995, p. 49.
4. J. Lovelock, *The Ages of Gaia*, New York: Bantam, 1988, ch. 2.
5. E. F. Schumacher, *Small Is Beautiful*, New York: Harper & Row, 1973, ch. 2.

12

Patience and Letting Go of Fear

> *"The brave man, we contend, yields neither to fear nor anger,*
> *desire nor agony. He is at all times master of himself; his courage*
> *rises to the heights of chivalry, patriotism, and real heroism."*
>
> Ohiyesa (Sioux)
> *The Soul of an Indian*

Patience is the fourth discipline within our spiritual *Journey Song*. It is of vital importance for spiritual growth, as it is the antithesis of the need to control or impose our will. In earlier chapters I discussed at length the need to trust Great Spirit and to have our will in harmony with the will of Great Spirit. Patience is a manifestation of this trust in Great Spirit. It is a recognition that this is Great Spirit's universe, and every flower, tree, stone, and creature has a purpose which contributes to the Whole. Patience demands that we allow this intrinsic purpose to manifest itself, (usually) without our interference.

The power of Great Spirit, in the form of the Medicine (or Holy Spirit, or Teh, if you will), is infinite. This power can work miracles within nature as well as within our hearts. When it begins to resonate, its vibration is the harmony of the universe; and the entire universe resonates!

Each person comes into the world with a song to sing. Each of us is a note in the melody that contributes to the complete symphony. The funny "boop, boop" of the bassoon sounds absurd and superfluous when heard by itself. However, in the context of the entire symphony, these bumping notes of the bassoon add a depth of texture that enriches and completes the whole symphony.

If you work around animals for any length of time, you will inevitably come to understand the value of patience. An impatient farmer or rancher will soon starve or kill himself. Milk cows must be milked according to their schedule, not yours. If you want to train a horse to be ridden, you do not play rodeo and sit him until he's bucked out. The horse may finally allow you to sit him, but he has now been taught to buck. It is much more effective to slowly gain the horse's trust. This is done with quiet handling and generous rewarding of good behavior. In this way, your horse will come to know that you will not hurt him. He will soon come to trust you and other humans in all situations.

On the other hand, a horse that has been bucked out can never be trusted. He **will** fear his rider and obey **most** of the time. But some day, a greater fear will overtake him and he will begin to buck again—probably when you least expect it. Handling animals with patience and building love and trust is always effective—and also pleasurable.

I saw this most graphically with some horses that we boarded when I was a girl. Mr. M., who owned the horses, was a cruel man. He felt that the only way to deal with horses was to keep them in fear. He used a logging chain to lay cruel blows across their backs for the slightest infraction. My father kept these horses in a field quite a distance from our house, and it was my job to care for them. I abhorred the way Mr. M. treated his animals and did my best to compensate for his cruelty. With much love and quiet care, his horses eventually came to know and trust me. I could do virtually anything with them without a problem.

When it was time to break his Palomino mare, Wendy, to saddle, Mr. M. couldn't even get near her. I watched in alarm as his temper rose, for I knew that he would soon grab the logging chain. Although I was afraid, I nonetheless mustered enough of my fifteen-year-old courage to intervene. Somehow I found the words to convince Mr. M. that a gentle approach would make the difference. Within a matter of minutes, I had calmed Wendy down and was mounted bareback. It took only about a half hour's work before she was going quietly under saddle. It would take a great deal of time before any of the horses would overcome their fear of Mr. M. I don't know if they ever did.

Almost all people are like Mr. M.'s horses. It is their fears that make them difficult. I grew up on a ranch so I understood this fear when dealing with animals. However, it wasn't until I began to read Taylor Caldwell's novels that I realized that the same was true of human beings. I can't remember in which novel, but Caldwell flatly stated that fear was the single greatest motivator of humans. I had never heard such a proposition in any of my college psychology classes, nor anywhere else for that matter. Initially, I vehemently disagreed with Caldwell. I felt that human beings were stirred by more noble motives, but her idea centering on fear rankled in my mind. Caldwell's words had taken seed, and I spent years testing her theory against everything that I read and every person that I observed. Finally, I had to conclude that she was right. Fear is the primary motivator.

Dr. M. J. Smith writes in *Kicking the Fear Habit* that the emotion of fear is vital for the survival of the human species.

> [Fear] is innate and involuntary, genetically built into us for the survival of the species. Our original animal brain that has come down to us from our successful prehuman ancestors is often called the 'emotional' brain in laboratory slang by neuroanatomists and physiologists. It automatically controls not only our negative emotions, but also all the bodily functions and involuntary reactions that keep us alive—temperature level, digestion, gland squirts and muscle contractions, blood flow and circulation, heart rate during stressful exercise or rest, sleep and wakefulness, and so forth. ...We are built to become afraid when the situation demands it. This capacity has evolved over eons of trial and error, because the human species had a greater chance for survival during hard times if the reaction to something dangerous was automatic.[1]

Our physical world is literally a "landscape of fear." The emotion of fear is triggered by anticipation or awareness of danger. This danger may be from other human beings or from a real or perceived physical source. Noted geographer, Yi-fu Tuan, reports that the world around us possesses "almost infinite manifestations of the forces for chaos," engendering our fear. These forces are virtually omnipresent, and therefore our human response—attempting to control—is also virtually omnipresent. Tuan writes very compellingly of these fears and humans' futile attempts to conquer them in every facet of life.

> In a sense, every human construction—whether mental or material—is a component in a landscape of fear because it exists to contain chaos. Thus children's fairy tales as well as adults' legends, cosmological myths, and indeed philosophical systems are shelters built by the mind in which human beings can rest, at least temporarily, from the siege of inchoate experience and of doubt. Likewise, the material landscapes of houses, fields, and cities contain chaos. Every dwelling is a fortress built to defend its human occupants against the elements; it is a constant reminder of human vulnerability. Every cultivated field is wrested out of nature, which will encroach upon the field and destroy it but for ceaseless human effort. Generally speaking, every human-made boundary on the earth's surface—garden hedge, city wall, or radar "fence"—is an attempt

to keep inimical forces at bay. Boundaries are everywhere because threats are ubiquitous: the neighbor's dog, children with muddy shoes, strangers, the insane, alien armies, disease, wolves, wind and rain.[2]

The people around us can be one of the greatest sources for our sense of security; but they can, just as easily, be the cause for our fears. People can be openly hostile and seek to harm us. They can betray our trust or simply be indifferent to our needs.

Jeffrey Dahmer, the gruesome mass murderer, told investigators that he committed his atrocities because he was afraid of being alone. He killed, dismembered, and ate body portions in order to assuage his fears. This is an extreme example, but how many people do you personally know who will stay in destructive relationships for this very same reason. They are afraid of being alone.

In my professional life as an auditor, I worked beside numerous women who spent their entire paychecks on their wardrobes. Other women spent thousands of dollars and risked their health for cosmetic augmentation of their breasts. Most women wore (and still wear) the absurdly crippling, high-heeled shoes. Other women focused on an ostentatious display of precious jewels, and would go to any lengths to add to their collections.

Each of these behaviors is clearly spawned by a fear of not being lovable without some sort of external enhancement. Women seem to be more vulnerable to these superficial trappings, probably because of our historic status as mere chattel and second-class citizens.

When I was young and foolish, I spent agonizing hours at the beauty shop submitting to the inhuman torture of having my hair frosted. First, a beauty technician poked a steel crochet hook through a plastic cap fitted onto my head. Then she wound several strands of hair onto the end of the hook and pulled them through the minute holes so that they alone could be bleached. I was terribly tender-headed, but submitted to this torture in order to make myself attractive. I was afraid that I would not be loved if I did not look the way that the man in my life wanted me to look. This seems to be the same motive for all of the other excesses of the women that I mentioned earlier. We all are afraid that we won't be lovable unless we look a certain way. We fear that our only value is in our external packaging.

Conversely, men are faced with a similarly debilitating fear. They feel that chaos will consume the world unless they (men) go daily into battle. As Warriors of Chaos, they feel that their only value is based upon how effectively they play this role. Their badges of self-worth are their annual salary, the amount of power they wield, and the ornaments of success they possess—cars, houses, women, whatever. This value system takes no cognizance of the inherent value of the human being. This value system does not allow time for introspection, for spirituality. Within this invalid system, a man's only value is his career.

This devaluation of men and women as human beings is caused by the metaphysical illness of fear. The cure, then, must also be metaphysical. Our landscapes of fear can be diminished, like the bogeymen of the night, through a new way of thinking of ourselves and Great Spirit. We human beings must come to an understanding that the Universe is One, and that all evil comes from ourselves through misuse of our free will. There is nothing to fear when we truly trust Great Spirit. Even the most terrible evils that man can perpetrate may be opportunities for spiritual work by others. The logic of unitheism assures us that evil has a dissonant energy that will destroy itself with time.

One of the most dangerous landscapes of fear for women is the home. In intimate relationships, including marriage, the dysfunctional issue of "who is in control" arises as a manifestation of fear. One of the partners (usually the man) fears that chaos will ensue and events will be out of control unless he personally takes control. Mental, verbal, and physical violence are the tools used to impose this order. Consequently, intimate relationships pose one of the greatest dangers to women.

In order to illustrate fear and its counterpart, control (in intimate relationships), I will go back to the story of "Jack." (I introduced him in Chapter 6 as the atheistic genius whose obsessive need for control thrust him into alcoholism.) Jack feels that it is up to "superior" people like himself to ensure that the events of the world do not get totally out of hand—his hand. This compulsion to control the world extends even into the most private details of his life. He alone must set his alarm clock each night. It will not do for his wife to set it, for then it has to be redone correctly. He decides what clothes she wears each day, and whether or not she will even shower each morning. When she brushes her teeth, it must be according to his specifications. Any infractions of these edicts propels Jack into a black rage, and he becomes physically and verbally abusive. Jack made himself into an alcoholic by acting on these fears because he feels that he must be in control at all times and at all costs.

I believe that, to some degree, Jack is not as unique among men as one at first might suppose. The dramatic increase in domestic violence, as well as in crimes against women in general, reflects a pervasive sickness within our society. It is a metaphysical sickness. As women assert their rights more and more, men become more frightened that they have lost control (and

have to have it back). This downward spiral into fear must stop. The antidote to this illness is a new value system that mandates a Trust of Great
Spirit. The world is beyond everyone's control. It is Great Spirit's universe,
and He/She alone is in control.

Patience means that we will wait on Great Spirit to work through
others in accordance with His/Her time plan, not ours. There is a Cosmic
Dance of Great Spirit's energy which draws and designs the events of each
individual's life. The thrust and swirl of these energies are custom-tailored
for the spiritual growth of each individual. Life is beautiful and fascinating
when one trusts Great Spirit enough to allow these energies to take their
natural course. Great Spirit will provide all that we need for spiritual
growth. On our part, however, we must strive to be noncontrolling and
noninterfering and to focus on spiritual growth. (I will discuss civil responsibility and intervention in the chapters centered on compassion.)

At this point, I will digress and introduce another practical aspect of
patience and interpersonal relationships. There is an interesting view of
human interaction called the Dramatic Triangle. According to this view
people are drawn into daily dramas, casting themselves in one of three
roles. The first is that of victim; the second, that of persecutor; and the
third, that of rescuer. In this daily drama, any one of the three role players
may initiate the drama. For example, a victim ("Jim") may be seen lament-
ing that a persecutor ("Bob") is out to get his job. Bob sees Jim as thoroughly incompetent and feels better qualified for Jim's job. Bob also fears
that the company will not be run well if he doesn't take Jim's job for
himself.

The interesting thing about the dramatic triangle is that the roles are
dynamic and constantly changing.

Fearful of losing his job, Jim now begins to spread stories of Bob's dis-
honesty. Now, Bob is the victim and Jim is the persecutor. The boss senses
the tension between the two men. Afraid of the demoralizing effect of their
conflict on other employees, he fires them both in his role as rescuer. The
boss is now the persecutor, and Jim and Bob are both victims. Actually,
anyone drawn into the web of a dramatic triangle becomes its victim. We
cannot rescue someone else nor are we helpless victims. We are never victims unless we choose to be. We are responsible for our lives. Even if I step
off a curb and am killed by a semi-truck, it was my decision to step off the
curb. It is not the truck's fault that I did so.

Dramatic triangles have a life of their own. They are perpetual, and
they are pervasive. The only way to stop a dramatic triangle is to refuse to
participate. This requires patience. Jim would have been better served if he

A Dramatic Triangle

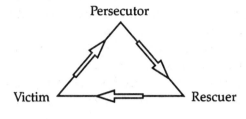

Figure 12-1

had not participated in Bob's game. Remember when we talked about consonant energy waves and the fact that when added together their sum is exponential. This is what happened to Jim and Bob. Bob initiated the dissonant energy with his envy of Jim's job. Dissonant energy is always doomed, as it is contrary to the energy of Great Spirit. But Jim unwittingly increased the volume of dissonant energies by also acting dishonorably.

If Jim had just patiently ignored Bob's illicit maneuvering, Bob's own negative energies would have created self-destruction. Jim could also have tried a loving confrontation with Bob, in private, or he could have brought the matter into the open where it could have been dealt with constructively. Unfortunately, however, there are some people who have such a volume of negative energies that the only recourse is to have as little interaction with them as possible. It is Great Spirit's work to deal with these people. To take on the burden of Great Spirit's work is to assume that we are on an equal footing with Great Spirit, an absurd proposition.

When we are presented with an opportunity to engage in a dramatic triangle, the emotional drama can be extremely seductive. It is tempting to drape ourselves in a full range of powerful emotions and make a grand entrance onto the stage of the triangle. Emotions are always valid, but it is wrong to succumb to them in such a manner. However, if we do submit, then our emotions are in control of our life; and this energy is dissonant to the energy of Great Spirit.

Emotions are teachers. Be patient and wait until the storm of their energy has subsided, and you will be able to hear the lesson that they are trying to teach you. Unfortunately, Jim's enslavement to his emotions involved him in the destructive, downward spiral of the dramatic triangle.

All of nature provides lessons from the Great Spirit if we are observant enough. Our four- footed brother, the porcupine, can teach us much about patience. Great Spirit gave him a body naturally designed for protection.

Brother Porcupine simply goes about his life minding his own business. However, when a predator attacks, Brother Porcupine simply turns his back. As the predator pounces he is filled with painful quills. The predator's actions have caused him his pain. Brother Porcupine has done nothing but be himself. Great Spirit protects all of his creatures in a similar manner. Wrong acting is dissonant energy and always comes back upon the perpetrator.

When we learn patience and mastery over our emotions, the path of spiritual growth becomes much more clear. We are often the instruments of another's spiritual growth—not every event in the world is centered on ourselves. The case of Hank and Leslie (not their real names) illustrates this principle.

Hank and Leslie are a loving couple. Hank has some emotional problems that were spawned in his childhood and never dealt with constructively. Hank always felt that his mother loved his father more than she loved him. Nonetheless, he and Leslie are a deeply devoted couple, and often leave their children unattended so that they can share time alone (ironically, repeating the same pattern his parents used).

Hank and Leslie are so in love with one another that their children feel "locked out." Actually, Hank is deeply afraid that he isn't lovable, and so he goes out of his way to prove himself worthy of Leslie's love. He is thoughtful, tender, and considerate. He feels a constant need, however, to test Leslie's love. Perhaps she really doesn't love him. Perhaps his childhood fear is true and he isn't lovable. Hank tests Leslie by blatantly flirting with other women. In this manner, Hank hopes to prove to himself how lovable he is. Sadly, this makes Leslie feel inadequate and unlovable; she then becomes jealous.

In most cases, a woman treated as Leslie is will respond in kind to Hank's provocation. (The roles for this triangle can easily be reversed, with the woman as persecutor and man as victim.) Both willingly, but unwittingly, enter upon the stage of the dramatic triangle—persecutor, victim, and rescuer. Leslie is at first the victim; if she copies Hank's behavior, she becomes the persecutor. Their marriage counselor or any close confidant will become the rescuer. All of the roles are subject to a spontaneous interchange—rescuer to persecutor, persecutor to victim, and so on. This type of situation all too often creates just another perpetual, dramatic triangle.

Everyone knows a couple like Hank and Leslie. Both partners are outrageous flirts, and social gatherings are explosively charged whenever they are present. In this case, however, Leslie had the wit to win. She acknowledged her jealousy to herself, and then patiently waited for the storm of her emotions to calm. Once calmed, Leslie lovingly confronted her husband and told him how she felt. She was open and honest about her feelings of vulnerability and made no threats or accusations. At first Hank was too frightened to acknowledge the fears assaulting him. It took several years and much patience on Leslie's part before Hank finally acknowledged and changed his behavior. Leslie's patience helped them both to grow spiritually.

Hank's problem could easily have been masked as Leslie's if she had succumbed to her jealousy. This would have had a detrimental effect on both Leslie and Hank, since the real problem was Hank's fear. Fortunately, because of Leslie's patience, the true cause of Hank's fear was eventually brought out into the open and was dealt with constructively.

Some American Indian tribes use a Talking Stick as a simple and effective method for conducting loving confrontations (similar to the one used by Leslie). A fifteen to eighteen-inch long willow stick is cut and the bark peeled off, then decorative beads and feathers are tied to one end with a leather thong. Discordant members of a family or community are brought together in a circle. The leader begins by reciting the rules for using the Talking Stick. Only the person holding the Talking Stick may speak. All others must listen and remain silent. Anyone who holds the Talking Stick must speak only constructive words and only truth. There may be no lies, no anger, no accusations. Only one issue at a time may be brought forth and explored. When it is resolved to the satisfaction of all participants, then the next issue may be addressed.

Similarly, most American Indians use the Peace Pipe as an instrument for truth in council meetings. Initially, some of the tobacco is offered to the Great Spirit in the council fire. Next, the leader invokes the six directions and the Great Spirit. After the pipe has been passed to each participant—ensuring their truthfulness before Great Spirit—discussions begin.

Loving confrontation is not always possible as a tool to resolve every situation. In most cases, however, it is the preferable tool because it presents the opportunity of spiritual growth for all persons involved. When presented with the problems (which are actually opportunities) of life, it is always best to pray or meditate about the problem situation before acting. If we approach problems in this way, then our hearts are pure and our motives are in harmony with Great Spirit.

Patience will always help us find the right path.

Chapter Notes

1. M. J. Smith, Ph.D., *Kicking the Fear Habit,* New York: Dial Press, 1977, pp. 10–11.
2. Y. F. Tuan, *Landscapes of Fear,* New York: Pantheon Books, 1979, p. 6.

deeply enough, we will usually find that fear is the true basis for negative emotions.)

The second step is to express the emotion, either verbally or in writing. This expression must be without the heat of passion, however, or the extent of the emotion will be exacerbated. Remember the effect that adding negative energies to one another will have (they grow exponentially) so simply state the facts.

The third step is to help another person or persons with the same emotional disability to overcome theirs by listening, then by sharing and, finally, by offering encouragement and support.

All of these steps allow our emotional disabilities to be vehicles for spiritual growth in ourselves and in others. A spiritual symbiosis occurs. In this way, our emotions teach us that human beings need one another in order to evolve spiritually. There has long been a spiritual tradition that holy men or women must separate themselves from the rest of humanity and live in splendid isolation. Classically, our culture presents an image of these gurus as detached from society and living on some inaccessible mountaintop. For some people this may be appropriate; it may be the song that they are meant to sing. I feel that the greater challenge, however, is to maintain a spiritual centering in the very midst of our everyday world. One spiritual person functioning in harmony with the will of Great Spirit can have a profound effect on those around him or her. The strong, harmonious vibrations from such a person reverberate throughout the environment much like the ripples in a pond.

The spiritual person selling stocks and bonds on Wall Street or hot dogs on the corner can have a profound impact on all who come in contact with them. Their serenity, their aura of peace, and the love of Great Spirit that they radiate can serve as a touchstone for all who cross their paths. They help to show others the right way to walk their path in the midst of the world's hustle and bustle. Most great modern religions do emphasize the need for this spiritual symbiosis. The vital message here is that we **must** love one another. Our symbiotic spiritual relationship with one another is the means to achieving an infinite life with Great Spirit.

This type of symbiotic relationship is actually what compelled me to begin writing *Journey Song*, although it has been a demanding exercise in patience. It took great reserves of my courage to expose myself in writing this book. I never intended to set my philosophies down on paper, even though a number of people repeatedly asked me to do so. I felt completely unworthy to undertake such a task. But then I had surgery, and my recovery proved to be a long and painful process.

I was confined to bed for several months. I was in too much pain to read or write, or do much of anything, so I just lay there. Unfortunately, my mind was not hindered by my body and nearly drove me crazy because it was so bored. I desperately looked for something, anything, to keep it busy. Then I hit upon the idea of drafting this book in my head while I was incapacitated. I mentally wrote chapter after chapter and committed them to memory, where they were locked away for several years.

When it came time for my husband to retire, I decided that I would devote myself to writing full-time. I loved my career, and it was a great challenge for me to give up my independence and financial security. My feelings changed, however, after that remarkable episode with the wolf (page 27) on the first night in our Colorado ranch house.

American Indian spirituality teaches that the wolf, or *Shuunka Manitu,* embodies the qualities of the spiritual teacher. He travels far and then returns to the pack with information on enemies, hunting conditions, and weather patterns. The spiritual correlation to these activities is that the wolf explores higher consciousness and then shares this learning and the great truths of Mother Earth with two-leggeds (humans).[1] The symbolism of the wolf's visit as I embarked on my new career had a profound spiritual effect on me. I felt as though my chosen path had been endorsed, that I must share the wisdom given to me by Great Spirit.

I now have the skull of a longhorn steer with a painting of Brother Wolf beautifully rendered on the forehead between the horns. The wolf is howling, just as my mind's eye saw him on that first night. Skulls have special meaning for American Indians, and they are often painted and used as spiritual shields because of their great medicine. My special wolf shield brings me great comfort for it reminds me that I must pass on the logic of unitheism.

As I mentioned earlier, molding ourselves to the will of Great Spirit is much like floating down a swift river instead of trying to swim upstream. If we try to swim against the currents of Great Spirit's will, we will find only frustration and exhaustion; and we will make little progress. If we float within the currents of Great Spirit's energies, however, we will have a fascinating and relaxing journey. We need to exercise patience and allow for the flow of Great Spirit's Cosmic Plan in our lives.

Great Spirit taught me this lesson time and again while I was writing this book. I found that each "interruption" to my writing was actually part of a series of events, wherein the most effective words and other vital information came to me. I learned that it was essential to meditate each day before sitting down to write. This was important in order to prevent my own ego from dominating the words and also to ensure that my words reflect truth. The pages of this book are presented as an offering. Great Spirit has given me a song to sing, and I offer this song as a gift. Patience helped me to float with the will of Great Spirit and to understand the delays and interruptions for they brought the gifts of understanding. These magical places, where Great Spirit's energy takes us, are far beyond anything that we could ever attain by ourselves while fighting the currents.

Just look around you and you will see that most people live in a frantic fight against the currents of Great Spirit's will. We thrash around, cry, and remonstrate at every unpleasant event. Our fears overwhelm us; and we fail to see that each circumstance, each happening, is a gift from Great Spirit. When we were in the spirit world, prior to birth into our physical bodies, we collaborated with Great Spirit on designing lives filled with the events and people necessary to aid our spiritual growth or to help other human beings. Therefore, if we can simply be patient and relax within the web of energies that Great Spirit created for our life, then our journey becomes beautiful and fascinating as we watch this plan unfold. Patience brings understanding and contentment.

Even the horrendous occurrences throughout history take on new meaning when viewed in this light. Descartes' Cartesian Duality fails to explain why an all-powerful God would part the Red Sea, appear in a burning bush, and personally hand Moses ten commandments, but fail to prevent the holocaust. A well-placed thunderbolt in the 1930s could have saved eleven million lives.

Within the logic of unitheism, however, even Hitler's monstrous genocide presents future generations with serious spiritual lessons on compassion. Within the logic of unitheism, his unfortunate victims knew the potentiality of their fate prior to their birth. With Great Spirit, they co-created this fate. Then they willingly entered their physical bodies as a gift in spiritual teaching for all human beings. They sacrificed their lives for the good of the generations unborn. Because of them, we now understand how important it is for us to participate in ethical politics. Because of them, we now understand how extremely dangerous apathy can be. Because of them, we now understand that dissonant ideas, such as racism, are dangerous to all human beings. Because of them, we understand the importance of love. There is no greater love than to give your life for another human being.

Descarte's God, though all-powerful, remained apart from the world and allowed this unspeakable evil to take the lives of eleven million innocent people. Conversely, unitheism's Great Spirit allowed human beings'

free will to be expressed both in the evil of Hitler and his minions and in the love and heroics of his victims and their rescuers.

Aside from major traumas, it is fascinating to simply watch Great Spirit's plan unfold within the realm of our individual lives. When we attempt a course of action and meet repeated, difficult obstacles, it usually indicates that we should abandon the project. However, when we are working within the flow of the Great Spirit's energy, everything will fall into place. We will feel the harmonious energy when the timing and the project are right. Sometimes, a project is simply undertaken at the wrong time. And sometimes, we are not ready or don't have the right information or motive to proceed. When the energies are consonant, it will all flow. Patience is the key.

This need for patience, or the open receptivity to the will of Great Spirit, is emphasized again and again in American Indian spirituality. One of the great spiritual ceremonies, the Vision Quest, illustrates this principle.

In a Vision Quest, the seeker isolates himself/herself in some remote spot on Mother Earth from one to four days and fasts while waiting for the Great Spirit to reveal a course of spiritual work. In order to be successful, however, the applicant must ensure a lack of ego and be patient. You are not in control during a Vision Quest. You must wait for Great Spirit to reveal your spiritual work, either through nature or through an actual vision. "A Vision Quest is done for the purpose of self- improvement. It is done for a deeper insight into the why of our being here."

This communion with nature helps to eliminate all self-centeredness. Eagle Man teaches that "We are not doing the Vision Quest to make ourselves feel important or to be interesting to our friends but to realize the vastness of the universe and our oneness with it." He emphasizes that "An individual can expect a strong Vision Quest, providing, of course, that ego is dispensed with and heartfelt sincerity is demonstrated during the vision-questing period."[2] In a similar vein, the Christian Bible teaches that "... In returning and rest shall ye be saved; in quietness and in confidence shall be your strength. ..."[3]

There is also a strong emphasis on this lack of ego (patience, or waiting on God's will) in training to be a spiritual leader among American Indians. Eagle Man emphasizes this aspect of spiritual leadership in *Mother Earth Spirituality.*

> Holy men and women who are schooling aspirants look for the absence of ego in their proteges. Egocentricity is considered an unwelcome trait for those who seek leadership in ceremony. One who has a

large ego, even with the counterbalancing traits of sharing and generosity, would still be considered a poor risk for the powerful position that the Holy Man or Holy Woman occupies ... Freedom from excess materialism is another prerequisite that Native American spiritual leaders look for in their aspirants.[4]

It is only logical that highly developed spiritual powers are dependent upon a freedom from ego. If we are full of ego, then we are usually intent upon controlling the people, places, and events in our lives. We are not capable of allowing the will of Great Spirit to prevail. Our egocentric energy creates a very strong energy vibration that is dissonant to the will of Great Spirit. This blockage prevents the powers of the universe, the powers of Great Spirit, from freely flowing through us. When we are filled with ego, we cannot "Be still and know that I am God."

Michael Shallis' investigation into various psychic phenomena led him to a similar conclusion. His research revealed that paranormal powers seem to be invoked, even involuntarily, when an individual is in real need or in a crisis.[5] It appears, then, that the state of emotional crisis tends to break down our ego and allow the currents of Great Spirit's power to flow through us.

Unfortunately, cults and other manipulative groups use this knowledge indiscriminately to recruit followers. Their first order of business is to destroy the ego and thereby dominate the individual. But this supplants Great Spirit's energy with a dissonant, human energy that actually thwarts spirituality. And because it is dissonant, it will be short-lived. On the other hand, openness to Great Spirit's energy creates a harmonious energy that is infinite.

Great Spirit is Omnipresent. Through the discipline of being patient we can become total vessels of Great Spirit's energies and tools of His/Her will. Eagle Man, the Oglala Sioux lawyer and holy man, attributes the success of American Indian spiritual leaders to the fact that they have "... perfected ceremonies that brought them very close to Mother Earth and the related powers. They were able to unify their being with all of *Wakan Tanka's* [Great Spirit's] creation."[6]

Most indigenous peoples possess a deep understanding of this Oneness of creation. Fortunately, some scientists are now beginning to document the technical evidence for such an understanding. Physicists have demonstrated the dynamic interchange of atomic activity throughout the universe within the laws of quantum mechanics. Einstein's famous mass-energy equivalency theory ($E = MC^2$) provides further evidence of this Oneness.

Because of this Oneness, human beings will always find spiritual renewal in communion with nature. Our natural world vibrates with the harmonious energy of Great Spirit because it is of Great Spirit. Almost everywhere that human beings have interfered and rearranged the natural order of matter, there will be a dissonant vibration. But there is no dissonant vibration within nature itself.

Evidence of our Oneness is everywhere. Recent studies have found that the human brain contains approximately seven billion microscopic magnets made of crystals of the iron mineral magnetite.7 Michael Shallis argues extensively, and convincingly, of the body's basic electrical nature and the impact of electromagnetic fields on it in the *Electric Connection*.

James Swan teaches extensively of the powers of the numerous "sacred places" throughout the earth. Swan tells us that "... sacred places [are] like electric power plants, constantly sending out energies to charge our lives, perhaps as golden spiderwebs of vitality."8 However, we must be patient and allow these healing powers of Mother Earth to flow through us. Bonding with Mother Earth requires patient interaction. Stillness. Waiting.

As the preceding pages have shown, a lack of patience is a major symptom of the metaphysical illness of our society. We seem to feel that solutions to all social problems must be immediate and must be forced. Action is our mandate. There must be a "war" on drugs, costing millions of dollars. If some famous person has suffered great personal tragedy, then we must invade their personal lives and probe every facet of the tragedy. If the earnings of a company aren't satisfactory for the quarter, then we sell the stock at a loss. We then vent our displeasure at the next board meeting and demand an immediate return for our investment. If someone has committed a crime, we want them captured and incarcerated immediately. If someone acts in a manner that displeases us, then we immediately sue them for damages. Disposable employees are hired today and fired tomorrow. If another person fails to act in accordance with our beliefs, then they must be forced to change, since our way is the only possible way.

Patience mandates that our immediate gratifications be placed on hold. Patience mandates that we wait and reflect before acting. Patience demands that we make haste slowly, thinking of the long-term, global impacts of our actions. Patience mandates that our actions be carefully considered and then performed only when they are in harmony with the will of Great Spirit.

Patience means that all decisions that impact Mother Earth be made in such a manner as to cause the least harm. Patience means that corporate decisions be based on long-term planning, not on yesterday's stock quotes. Patience clarifies that people are our most valuable assets, and requires that hiring and firing decisions be made with love and compassion and a long-range view. Patience insists that we allow Great Spirit to work through others. That we understand that Great Spirit's truth is manifest through all beings and all of nature, not just ourselves. Patience demands that we allow this intrinsic purpose to manifest itself. We've now completed the fourth step along the spiritual path of our *Journey Song*.

Trust Great Spirit, Trust Great Spirit.

MITAKUYE OYASIN!

Love the Truth and by it live.

MITAKUYE OYASIN!

Walk life's path with Simplicity.

MITAKUYE OYASIN!

Bathe yourself and others with Patience.

MITAKUYE OYASIN!

Our next steps along the Good Red Road will help us to understand and value the need for compassion.

Chapter Notes

1. E. McGaa/Eagle Man, op. cit., pp. 163–165.
2. Ibid, ch. 9.
3. Isaiah, Chapter 30, Verse 15b.
4. E. McGaa/Eagle Man, op. cit., p. 190.
5. M. Shallis, op. cit., p. 197.
6. E. McGaa/Eagle Man, op. cit., p. 45.
7. Associated Press, *Gazette Telegraph*, May 12, 1992, Colorado Springs, Colorado.
8. J. A. Swan, *Sacred Places*, Santa Fe: Bear & Co., 1990, p. 194.

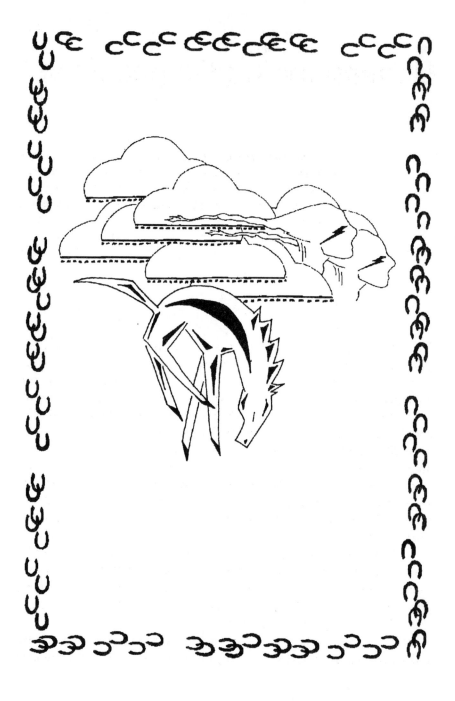

14

Understanding Compassion

"The public position of the Indian has always been entirely dependent upon our private virtue. We are never permitted to forget that we do not live to ourselves alone, but to our tribe and clan. Every child, from the first days of learning, is a public servant in training."

Ohiyesa (Sioux)
The Soul of an Indian

"Oh, Great Spirit, I ask that I may never criticize my brother until I have walked a mile in his moccasins." This popular prayer (or a similar version) is usually attributed to an unknown American Indian and has become somewhat of a cliché because of its overuse. However, this overuse is most likely the result of the great truth it contains. This prayer represents the essence of compassion—the feeling of sharing the suffering of another, coupled with the inclination to give aid or support.

Suffering is the common condition of human beings in one degree or another. The intensity and reality of our suffering ranges within the extremities of the human condition. At one end of this continuum is the individual who is unable to have his or her basic physical needs met. At the other end of the continuum is the individual who has found peace and oneness with God.

Within the James-Lange theory is the postulate that emotions are triggered by external events which then produce a bodily response.[1] Dr. Diamond (author of *Your Body Doesn't Lie*) provides numerous elementary strength tests that can be self-administered. In turn, these tests illustrate the validity of the James-Lange theory.[2]

Dr. Diamond hypothesizes that the thymus gland is quite probably the link between mind and body. This thymus gland is located in the center of the chest at the point where the second rib joins the breastbone (the sternomanubrial joint). Dr. Diamond has developed a series of simple tests which show the dramatic, instantaneous, and debilitating effects of stress and negative emotional states upon the thymus. Our thymus is of vital importance to our body because it produces lymphocytes, or white blood cells. It performs a type of immunological surveillance, producing and directing these lymphocytes to resist infections and cancer. Our thymus also controls the energy flow within our body. Dr. Diamond's tests illustrate the close relationship of our physical environment, social relationships, food, and posture upon the thymus and, therefore, upon our physical well-being.

Let me again emphasize that within the philosophy of unitheism, All is One. Great Spirit created the universe and is present throughout it. Great Spirit's universe **is** vibration, and "the universe tends to select harmonic vibrations ... from an infinite number of possible vibrations."[3] In line with this principle, scientists have also found that the "healthy human body is structured according to the laws of harmonics."[4] The human body's natural predisposition, then, is to vibrate in harmony with the vibration of Great Spirit. Great Spirit is omnipresent; therefore, body, mind, emotions and spirit are one. Dr. Diamond's work offers further logical proof of this Oneness.

Our body, our entire physiological system, is not only dependent upon what we see and feel, but also upon how we think. Our emotions are the composite of our reactions to external events and, to a large extent, our perceptions of these events.

Negative emotions (such as fear, hate, envy, or greed) serve to weaken the thymus. These emotions have an energy or vibration that is dissonant to the energy of Great Spirit. Dissonant energies cause distress, illness and, eventually, death. Dissonant energy will simply cease to exist at some point. When we entertain dissonant energies, we slowly kill ourselves through their adverse effect on the thymus. Inversely, positive emotions (such as love, trust, kindness, or courage) serve to strengthen the thymus. Positive emotions are in consonance with the energy of Great Spirit. They therefore have an eternal or infinite vibration and are life-giving. Infinity will be attained when the entire universe vibrates in harmony. Positive emotions represent a vital link in obtaining this harmonious vibration for body, mind, and spirit.

Nationally acclaimed author and psychiatrist, Gerald G. Jampolsky, underwent a personal transformation after reading *A Course in Miracles*. This book places heavy emphasis on the power of love. Based on this experience, Jampolsky authored the very popular book, *Love Is Letting Go of Fear*. A basic premise of both books is that there are only two true emotions, love and fear, and that all other emotions have their root in these.[5] In addition, fear is seen as something unreal, something manufactured by the mind. Love is seen as the antithesis of fear, and is defined as the total absence of fear.[6]

Love is the valid emotion of the two, because love is an attribute of Great Spirit and is therefore omnipresent and infinite. Only when we live a life of trust in Great Spirit are we really able to live without fear. As I said earlier, fear is an energy or vibration that is dissonant to the energy of Great Spirit. When I explored this theme in Chapter 12, I illustrated how living without fear, in harmony with the will of Great Spirit, fills us with love.

These emotions, fear and love (and their secondary manifestations), are the impetus for our spiritual growth. The *Katha Upanisad*, written approximately six hundred years before Christ was born, provides a colorful allegory for this principle. In this teaching, the self is pictured as the chariot owner with the body as the chariot. Our awareness, or higher self, is the driver with the mind as the reins and the senses (emotions) as the horses.

> Know the self as the chariot-owner (i.e. he who is carried, inactively, by it), the body as the chariot. Know awareness (buddhi) as the driver, the mind (manas) as the reins. The senses, they say are the horses, sense-objects the path they range over. The self joined to mind and senses, wise men say, is the experiencer. He who is without understanding, whose mind is ever unharnessed, his senses are out of control, as bad horses are for a charioteer.[7]

As our horses (senses and emotions) propel the chariot, they carry us to our ultimate destination, a reunion with Great Spirit. They are our spiritual teachers, for when we use them constructively, they carry us in an upward spiral. On the other hand, if we fail to use the reins of our mind to control our emotions, they can just as easily run wild and cause our death, physically and spiritually. As spiritual awareness, or spiritual growth, occurs we are better able to control and guide our horses toward complete harmony with Great Spirit.

The *Upanisad's* chariot is important in helping us understand some of the vital principles of unitheism. This chariot, our body, is the vehicle for achieving our spiritual growth. It carries us along toward our destination, for it is part of our Oneness. Without this physical vehicle, we would have a difficult (if not impossible) time achieving harmony with Great Spirit because it is our body's senses that trigger our emotions; and they in turn provide the impetus to change and grow. Our reins (the mind) control the pace and direction of the horses (senses and emotions). As we grow in awareness, as we (the driver) grow in understanding, so our skill as a driver grows. Now, as dangers and diversions present themselves along the way, our higher awareness allows us to skillfully avoid the delays and hazards that they represent.

In addition to our emotions, our body itself can be the instrument of spiritual growth. Illness and traumatic injury seem to be opportunities that we have cocreated (prior to birth) for spiritual growth. As I illustrated in the last chapter, this book itself was born while I recovered from an operation. Actually, my surgery was the result of a number of body experiences. The large tumor that was removed was caused by steroids I had taken when I broke a toe and blood poisoning set in. I didn't realize that I had blood poisoning, however, and might have died from it—if I hadn't come down with a terrible case of poison ivy and gone to the doctor for that. Ironically, this entire sequence of events is similar to the earlier story of the farmer's horse. Was my broken toe an unfortunate incident? In light of subsequent events, I don't think so. My broken toe began a chain of events that culminated in this book.

But let's return to a discussion on emotions. These "chariot horses" also present an excellent analogy for the debilitating effects of fear. Any horse that succumbs to fear, no matter how wonderful, becomes totally unmanageable and poses a serious danger to himself and to others. My beautiful, white Arabian gelding, Barbir, provides a case in point.

Barbir was an intelligent, affectionate, and sensitive animal. He went beautifully under saddle in the show ring, and of course I loved him dearly because he was one of the few beings that loved my singing. When I rode him on the trail, however, his unpredictable fears made him dangerous. I could ride him for hours without incident, but then he would inexplicably erupt beneath me. There seemed to be no logical explanation, so I jokingly blamed his erratic behavior on invisible gnomes, fairies, and displaced air molecules.

During one trail ride, we approached a particularly troublesome wooden bridge. As we began our crossing, I tightened Barbir's reins and kept a "leg on" in order to keep him under control. Experience had taught me that he would soon go ballistic. On this particular spring morning, however, we rode across the bridge without a single quiver or twitch of his body.

I was dumbfounded. Barbir **always** exploded at the bridge.

Once we were safely on the other side, my husband and daughter began to tease me about the safe crossing; and I began to giggle. It was at this point that Barbir himself suddenly realized what he had just done, and so he exploded—somewhat belatedly. Needless to say, I was not at all prepared and landed on my head on the grass beside the trail. Barbir bucked himself out within a matter of a few minutes and was soon standing beside me and gently nuzzling my face as if to say, "I'm sorry!" He was such a dear, and after I talked to him and soothed him for a few moments he stopped quivering and was fine for the rest of the ride.

Most people are like Barbir. When they have succumbed to their fears, they are a danger to themselves and to others. Humans, however, differ from animals in that they make conscious choices to embrace their fear. As we discussed in earlier paragraphs, of the two emotions, love and fear, fear is not valid because it is not of Great Spirit. Fear is a dissonant vibration, and would not exist if human beings truly trusted Great Spirit. It is a lack of this trust, and the need to impose our will, that spawns all fear.

Fear is endemic in modern society. The proof is all around you. How many people do you know who live a life of implicit trust in Great Spirit? Our human response to fear is fight, flight, or control. Look at the epidemics of violence around the world, including domestic violence. This is fear. Fear is negative energy bulging against other negative energies, and therefore growing exponentially. Look at the number of people running from the cities, running from relationships, running from themselves. This is fear.

Now look at the pervasive issues of control. Parents abusing their children verbally, emotionally, and physically. Men seeking to control women with verbal, emotional, and physical abuse. Women seeking control of their lives and succumbing to excess materialism or abusive relationships. Religions seeking control over men, women, and children through guilt and fear. People of certain ideologies seeking to impose their way of thinking upon others in order to control them. One nation seeking to control another through conquest. One company seeking to control another through hostile takeover. This is fear. If people truly trusted Great Spirit, they would not act this way. Where are the reins of the chariot driver? The horses are clearly out of control!

Dr. Jampolsky tells us that "inner peace is experienced as we learn to forgive the world and everyone in it."[8] When we harbor any of the negative energies in our relationships with others, we are harboring a negative vibration which will eventually destroy us. Dr. Diamond's thymus test will quickly show you the immediate destructive effects on the body if one simply **thinks** an unpleasant thought.

> A young male patient who had been given a diagnosis of cancer came to me for holistic therapy. In the course of the interview I asked him, "Do you hate anyone?" He said, "I loathe and detest my mother." When he test-touched his thymus, it was weak. I said, "As long as you hate your mother, this hatred will so diminish your thymus activity, your Life Energy, that you will never get completely well." He said, "I would sooner die than give up hating my mother." And that was the end of the session![9]

Dr. Diamond sadly notes that about 95 percent of all of the people he has tested have an underactive thymus gland. Just from our daily observations of human nature, we can see that this ratio extends to the population in general. The majority of people are living in fear. We can make a choice and refuse to participate in this dramatic triangle. We can detach ourselves through understanding and then forgiveness, the components of Compassion.

Understanding always precedes forgiveness. Dr. Jampolsky tells us that "Many of us become frustrated when we make the mistake of trying to love others as the first step ... some people simply seem unlovable."[10] How can it be possible to love someone like Hitler, the embodiment of evil, or the cannibalistic, mass-murderer, Jeffrey Dahmer?

As a first step, it is important to understand that Great Spirit is both omnipotent and omnipresent. Great Spirit is all powerful. No thing, no person, is beyond the power of Great Spirit. Great Spirit's work is accomplished through His/Her omnipotent and omnipresent energies—Medicine. We know that our cosmos consists of vibrations, with a constant and dynamic interchange of particles—or waves—of their energy.

Great Spirit is present within the smallest particle of energy and within the furthest reaches of the cosmos. Therefore, Great Spirit was also within Hitler and Dahmer. Although this is perhaps a difficult concept to accept, it is nonetheless quite logical in the context of Great Spirit's omnipresence. It is also a key concept in reconciling the seeming paradox of Great Spirit's omnipresence and the existence of evil, simply because all evil is a direct result of human free will. With their free will, both Hitler and Dahmer **chose** a dissonant course of action directly opposed to the harmony and love of Great Spirit.

At this point, I would also like to remind you that numerology showed that Adolph Hitler and Abraham Lincoln had names with the same vibration. Both men had the same potentialities. Hitler's free will led him to promote and "purify" the Aryan as a master race, while Lincoln's free will led him to fight for the equality of all human beings. Both men had the same potentialities. Free will made the difference.

This freely chosen dissonance changed the vibrations of Hitler's and Dahmer's bodies. Great Spirit, however, was still present. Our bodies are, in reality, ephemeral collections of billions of vibrating waves of energy. It is the self, with its free will, that can influence this sphere (our body) of vibrations. The vibrations of our body are not evil in themselves—they are of Great Spirit—but our free will can change the frequency of these vibrations from very high to very low.

At any moment, human beings can choose thoughts and actions that are consonant, or dissonant, with Great Spirit's energies. If we choose consonant energy, we can raise the frequency with which our body vibrates. The choice is ours alone. If Hitler and/or Dahmer had sought harmony with the Great Spirit, His/Her power could have transformed them instantaneously. Union with Great Spirit, however, requires a prolonged, harmonious vibration. Many philosophers and mystics place this time period at approximately two years. This seems logical, as it takes time to establish complete harmonic resonance. When we begin this resonance, however, our lives will be transformed. We will attract other harmonious people and events into our pool of good energy. We will radiate peace and love, and these energies will be magnetically drawn to us in return. We will walk in beauty.

This prolonged time period for transformation is also logically compatible with the concept of reincarnation. Conversion of our negative, or dissonant, vibrations to positive ones will probably take many lifetimes. A degree of permanency must be established, and reincarnation would serve this purpose. The theory of our soul entering successive bodies seems especially logical when coupled with Einstein's mass-energy equivalency theory, $E = MC^2$. The physical matter that constitutes our body, coupled with the energy of our spirit, could simply take on another form or even become a disembodied energy field. I am only a two-legged, however, and my hypothesis could be wrong. Only Great Spirit knows the complete truth.

Any person, at any time, can utilize free will and begin a transformation of dissonant, anti-godlike energies toward energies that are in harmony with Great Spirit. This process can be expedited by utilizing different types of Medicine. No human being is beyond redemption. However, this understanding precludes our judging any other person. We can only know, or guess, another's state of grace (the degree of harmonious god-like vibrations) by their actions and words, after the fact. Even then, we can't know the thoughts that they are holding at a particular moment.

Understanding precedes forgiveness. This is Compassion. Now that we understand that no one is beyond redemption, the next step in our understanding is to try to comprehend the "why" of one another's actions.

Chapter Notes

1. R. L. Gregory, editor, *The Oxford Companion to the Mind,* Oxford: Oxford University Press, 1987, pp. 219–220.
2. J. Diamond, M.D., *Your Body Doesn't Lie,* New York: Warner Books, 1979, ch. 3.
3. J. E. Berendt, *The World Is Sound,* Vermont: Destiny Books, 1991, p. 90.
4. Ibid, p. 82.
5. G. G. Jampolsky, M.D., *Love Is Letting Go of Fear,* Berkeley: Celestial Arts, 1979, pp. 2, 33–43.
6. Ibid, p. 17.
7. R. L. Gregory, op. cit., pp. 358–359.
8. G. G. Jampolsky, op. cit., p. 42.
9. J. Diamond, M.D., op. cit., p. 84.
10. G. G. Jampolsky, op.cit., p. 24.

15

Compassion, The Essence of Love

"At such feasts the parents often gave so generously to the needy that they almost impoverished themselves, thereby setting an example to the child of self-denial for the public good. In this way, children were shown that big-heartedness, generosity, courage, and self-denial are the qualifications of a public servant, and from the cradle we sought to follow this ideal."

Ohiyesa (Sioux)
The Soul of an Indian

Why would anyone choose a course of action that is dissonant to their inner being, the energy of Great Spirit within them?

In the previous chapters, I established that the root of all undesirable behavior is fear. When we encounter the manifestations of this fear in others in the form of fight, flight, or control, we must seek the root of the fear in order to gain understanding. "Why is this person so contentious?" "Why is this person being so mean?" "Why does this person behave in such a destructive manner?" Perhaps they feel that they can't control us; and, therefore, they feel endangered because their world is out of control. They are in the grip of fear.

Many years ago, I had an art gallery in Santa Fe, New Mexico. Generally, an artistic community like Santa Fe is highly Bohemian, and therefore openly accepting of alternate life styles. Santa Fe and northern New Mexico were rediscovered in the late 1800s by colonies of artists from Europe. They were enchanted by the crisp, pristine mountain air and the dramatic scenery of northern New Mexico. Once these art colonies were established in Taos and Santa Fe, it became fashionable for wealthy Eastern families to send their homosexual children there, where they were accepted without judgment, and would no longer "prove an embarrassment" to the family. These homosexuals were easily assimilated into the artistic community, where their great wealth served as a magnet for others. Through the intervening years, Santa Fe came to have a large gay and lesbian population.

In my gallery, I became friends with a number of gay people, as many of the artists that I dealt with were homosexual. You will remember that I grew up in the middle of nowhere with little social interaction, so I was completely ignorant of this aspect of human sexuality. I was curious as to why one would "choose" such a difficult lifestyle. There was no simple answer to my question, and I was to learn that the roots of homosexuality are as varied and complex as each human being. I have since learned that American Indians refer to homosexuals as "winkte" and view them as possessing special spiritual gifts.

The noted Sioux author, Ehanamani (Dr. A. C. Ross), writes that the literal translation of winkte is "to kill the woman." In understanding the meaning of this Sioux word for homosexual, Ehanamani calls upon the work of Dr. Carl Jung.

> ... Dr. Jung said that within each of us, there is an opposite. Within each man there is a female, the archetype of the anima. Each woman has a male within her, the archetype of the animus. When these archetypes penetrate consciousness, Dr. Jung related, you are no longer you; you become that archetype. In traditional times, the winkte was known as being a special person, and so the people even felt they were "wakan" (holy). Jungian psychology, then, gave me the understanding I needed to fully comprehend what was happening to an individual known as winkte. I reasoned, "Was the winkte called special or wakan because that individual had the ability to communicate with the unconscious mind?"[1]

Some of my friends told me that they hated being a homosexual, but that there was nothing that they could do because "their mothers had made them that way." I was somewhat taken aback when they almost uniformly referred to their mothers as "an over-controlling b – – – –." But through the patient explanations of these friends, I finally came to understand that fear was one of the greatest contributors in propelling them into homosexuality. They were deeply afraid of women. They were afraid of becoming "impotent," or unable to control their own lives in a duplication of their early mother-son relationships. Generally, they perceived their mothers as being domineering and over-controlling.

Now, upon meeting a strange man, I can usually tell right away whether or not he is this type of homosexual. When I first look into his eyes there will be a fleeting image of stark terror. Then he will quickly look away and refuse to make further direct eye contact. It is quite saddening to see so much fear in another's eyes. It is also interesting to note that the great scourge of homosexuality, AIDS, is a disease directly linked to the thymus gland. Dr. Diamond's research correlates the themes of hatred and fear and their deleterious effect on the ability of the thymus to fight any infection.

Of course, Great Spirit's universe is a complicated and wondrous place, and human beings reflect this diversity. Not all homosexuals become homosexuals because of an unhealthy relationship with their mothers. I met many who seem to have a genetic trait of some sort, and clearly belong in a body of the opposite sex. In their own words, "I was born this way." Scientists are just beginning to document the truth of this assertion. These individuals made no conscious choice (in this plane of awareness) in determining their homosexuality. Their sexuality is simply a part of their composite being that constitutes the vehicle for their spiritual growth. Just as we can claim no virtue for our heterosexuality, we can place no blame for homosexuality. Both are a part of Great Spirit's Cosmic Plan.

Actually, the diversity of the homosexual experience is even further complicated. Other of my gay friends told me stories of having been seduced or raped by an older man when they were in their early adolescence. This traumatic event caused incredible inner torment and confusion about their true sexual identity. These men did not choose to become homosexual either, and they still exhibited a great ambivalence and confusion about their identity even ten and twenty years later.

At the other extreme are those homosexuals who are not truly homosexuals—they are prostitutes. Typical of all hustlers, they seek to gain some financial, or other material advantage, from playing the role of a homosexual. A rich boyfriend can ensure annual trips to Europe and a fancy new sports car. These attractive young men use their physical beauty as any prostitute would. There are not many jobs available at times, and surviving financially is a difficult task. Their fear of poverty drives these men to sell their bodies. It is amusing, however, to see them quickly change to the role of Macho Man in the presence of an attractive and desirable young woman.

None of these gay men deserves hatred or cruelty because of his sexual preference. Homophobia will not "cure" him of his homosexuality. The basis for homosexuality is as varied and complicated as each individual.

(I have excluded lesbians from this discussion because I am personally acquainted with only a few.) Every human being is of Great Spirit and is deserving of our love and compassion. We must take the first step and strive for understanding, then compassion will follow, clearing the way for love.

This call to compassion and love is imperative in our society. The United States has recently seen an alarming increase in the number of unwed mothers. In 1992, Vice President Quayle created a furor for his outspoken criticism of a fictional television character, Murphy Brown, who chose to have a baby out of wedlock. Most sensible people were upset at Quayle's lack of compassion in his wholesale condemnation of unwed mothers. Quayle blamed this state of affairs on something he termed a "moral poverty."[2]

A sense of compassion would dictate that we view the problem differently. Why would a single woman choose to have a baby without benefit of a father? A whole range of possible reasons presents itself. I will explore just a few of these in search of understanding.

The first possible reason that comes to mind is the situation of a lonely young woman who fears that she is unlovable. She typically had a childhood wherein the only love that she received was conditional. If she were a good girl, if she got good grades, then her parents would love her. She never felt loved for simply being herself. Love was always a contingency. Consequently, this young woman deeply fears that perhaps the reason that she never received unconditional love was because she was simply unlovable. In order to assuage this fear, she enters into several unsuccessful relationships with young men. These only confirm her fear of being unlovable. Finally, this deep longing to be loved finds fulfillment in her giving birth to a baby. At last, the young woman has another person, the baby, who loves her unconditionally. This situation has the added advantage of placing her in control of her life and her baby's life. Her mother and father will not be able to control her actions, and she is finally able to break their bondage. It is her fears that have led her to have a baby out of wedlock.

The second situation that comes to mind, while trying to understand the reasoning of an unwed mother, is that of the welfare mother. Why would a woman have baby after baby without the benefit of a father—especially when she can barely feed and clothe herself or the children that she already has?

First of all, among many of the impoverished, is the presence of a father necessarily a benefit? Within the confines of poverty, regardless of ethnic background, drug use and physical abuse are epidemic. It is generally the women who suffer from this abuse; and, if he is abusive, the presence of a father rarely blesses a family with peace and stability. (Again, the father's abusive actions are usually the manifestations of his fears.)

Second, there is a spiral of hopelessness embedded in poverty, especially for women. They were rarely afforded the advantages of a higher education as children themselves. In the cycle of poverty, their education was sacrificed so that they could care for their siblings. As adults they only qualify for service jobs that pay minimum wage. In 1997 minimum wage was about $4.75 per hour. This means that at most these women would probably earn about $760 each month (40 hour weeks) to $1140 (60 hour weeks) each month. When I last paid for child care in the 1970s, it cost me approximately $350 each month; and these costs have steadily risen.

This leaves only about $330 to $670 for rent, utilities, and food. A marginal apartment in a marginal neighborhood costs at least $400, but more probably about $800, in most areas of the United States. Of course, if the woman works the 60 hour week, her child care expense will nearly double, if she can even find one for those extended hours. There is still the matter of transportation, clothing, and medical care. Under these circumstances, it would be very difficult not to choose welfare. When receiving welfare food and basic needs are addressed, and the woman can stay at home to ensure that good child care is provided.

Does this type of woman have any hope for a better life? She probably fears that her life is out of control. However, if she controls her reproductive process, if she controls her children, then she has at least some sense of empowerment. So she continues to have babies. Until very recently, the welfare system rewarded this type of thinking by increasing the financial benefits with each new child. These policies have now been changed in order to penalize women who continue to have babies while they are on welfare. Unfortunately, it is the children who will suffer the most from such a policy change. Policies of this type do not address the root of the problem, and the symptoms—the babies—are caught up in the endless cycle of poverty.

Hating and abusing homosexuals and unwed mothers will not make the world a better place. This hatred, and all of its negative vibrations, only serves to create more dissonant energy. Isn't this hatred itself a manifestation of our own fears? Once one comes to understand that fear is the basis for undesirable actions in others, how can one hate? Do you hate someone for being afraid? Will this make them unafraid? Will your hatred change their actions? No. But compassion and love will change our own prejudices. And when we change our attitudes, we then become part of the solution. We can help the unwed mother see that she has other choices; we can let the homosexual feel accepted in the community. Hostility and despair do not exist for long in the presence of love and compassion.

The first step in ridding ourselves of negative emotions toward others is to seek to understand. If we skip this step, and jump into the abyss of our fears, then we have devised our own doom. We must be patient, and seek to understand. Why is this person acting in such an undesirable manner? As we discovered in earlier discussions, when we examine all of the clues we will always find fear as the basis. This fear will be manifested in a million different ways, such as anger, hatred, abuse, manipulation, lies, and on and on.

The second step in ridding ourselves of these negative emotions is to visualize these undesirable traits as snakes that the difficult person is holding in an ugly old carpetbag. When we visualize difficult people in this manner (or whatever manner works best for you) then we are able to divorce the person from their actions. No matter how abhorrent a person's actions may seem to you, that person is still of Great Spirit. If we hate or revile or abuse another human being, then we are acting against Great Spirit. "I tell you the truth, whatever you did for one of the least of these brothers of mine, you did for me."[3]

The third and final step in transforming negative emotions toward difficult people into a positive force field is through spiritual visualization. This is a very simple but extremely powerful process, wherein we visualize the difficult person as having set the carpetbag of snakes aside. We then surround them with the white light (love) of Great Spirit, while saying something like "Great Spirit is Love" over and over. This visualization technique creates an energy field of unconditional love around the difficult person, and raises their vibrations through the proximity and infusion of the energy of the Great Spirit. Great Spirit is harmony, and the strength of this visualized energy of Great Spirit surrounding a difficult person will change their vibrations from dissonance to consonance. This harmony that we create is a process which scientists call entrainment.

> It is important to realize that the tendency toward harmony, immanent in music, in a way is nothing else but a reflection of the same tendency outside of music, in almost all fields. As George Leonard notes: "In 1665 the Dutch scientist Christian Huygens noticed that two pendulum clocks, mounted side by side on a wall, would swing together in precise rhythm. They would hold their mutual beat, in fact far beyond their capacity to be matched in mechanical accuracy. It was as if they 'wanted' to keep the same time."

Science has taught us that this phenomenon is universal. Two oscillators pulsating in the same field in almost identical rhythm will tend to "lock in," with the result that eventually their vibrations will become precisely synchronous. This phenomenon is referred to as "mutual phase-locking" or "entrainment." Entrainment is universal in nature. In fact, it is so ubiquitous that we hardly notice it, "as with the air we breathe," as Leonard put it. It is a physical phenomenon, but it also is more than that, because it informs us about the tendency of everything that vibrates—in other words, everything—to swing together, to lock in. It informs us about the tendency of the universe to share rhythms, that is, to vibrate in harmony.[4]

This entrainment, or aura of Great Spirit's grace, will last for just a little while, but while in effect it provides an opportunity for the difficult person to make a choice between fear and love. Many philosophers and mystics have referred to this experience as a "moment of grace." I have found it fascinating that, when this is taking place, the difficult person will usually physically manifest the spiritual agony of this internal struggle. It is totally their choice, however, whether they continue to succumb to fear or to embrace love. But now they have been given a choice.

When we deal with difficult people in this manner, we are increasing the peace and harmony of the universe. Dr. Diamond has a another simple strength test which dramatically demonstrates the efficacy of this approach. He suggests that you stand with your dominant arm straight at your side, and the other/alternate arm outstretched straight from the shoulder. Have another person press on the wrist of your outstretched arm and test its strength. Next, think angry thoughts about someone you're upset with. Now test your strength—you will be incredibly weakened! Now think of someone that you love with loving thoughts, and test your strength again. You will be incredibly strengthened! Our thoughts have profound and immediate effects upon our bodies. To hold hate or anger toward another person only serves to weaken our own life force.[5] The old wives' tale of hatred being an acid that destroys its vessel is absolutely true. American Indian tradition reinforces this need to act with love rather than hatred. Ancient teachings warn that this negative energy, or medicine, will return to you or your family bringing bad fortune.

Another impediment to compassion is self-centeredness or narcissism. Narcissus was the legendary Greek youth who saw himself reflected in a pond one day and fell in love with his reflection. Like Narcissus, many people choose to love no one else as they love themselves. Again, this reaction is generally based on fear. Unfortunately, however, there is no room in this type of person for compassion.

If some difficult person should hurt them, they feel that the only appropriate and justified response is to strike back. They always make a fiery entrance onto the stage of the dramatic triangle, as they will "take no s – – – from anyone."

If the extent of our love is rarely beyond the bounds of our extremities, then we will never go beyond dis-ease and disharmony. The body resonates to the vibrations of our thoughts and actions. The narcissistic self, therefore, vibrates with a dissonant vibration—as the self is finite, not infinite. If we are unable to go beyond the self with its limiting, dissonant vibrations, we will never pulsate with the strong harmonious vibrations of God and His/Her universe.

When we encounter difficult people in the course of our daily lives, we can effect a change in our relationship by employing love, the most powerful energy in the universe. Again, this is done by surrounding the difficult individual with the white light of love during meditation. This approach does not judge another person nor does it interfere with their free will. When we feel unconditionally loved, when we know that we are in the midst of Great Spirit's infinite love, then we can free ourselves from fear and fulfill our higher nature. This is the most beautiful gift that we can give another person, no matter how hate-filled their actions have been to us. When we focus this energy of love, we act somewhat like the lens that focuses a laser beam. The lens is only an instrument that enables the laser beam. When we focus Great Spirit's love in this way, we are only an instrument of love.

If we chose not to return love for hate, then we are dialing-in our body's "radio" to dissonant vibrations and thereby enabling further dissonance. We have created a communications link by vibrating with the same dissonant vibration. Isn't is wiser and more pleasant to sever this link by surrounding the difficult person with unconditional love? There is a reason for each and every person who enters our lives. Difficult people can teach us a great deal by their unpleasant behavior. They provide a mirror of the undesirable traits that we should avoid. Under the theory of karma, they may also have entered our life to resolve prior-life conflicts. When we give them the light of unconditional love in our meditation, then we create a harmonious energy and resolve the karmic relationship.

James A. Swan, the author of *Sacred Places*, developed an interesting table of vibrations correlated with the seven spinal chakras. (Chakras are energy centers within the body.) This table of vibrations provides convincing evidence for the limiting nature of self love. Chakras come down to us through Hindu teachings, and are thought to be whirls of energy between the spiritual world and the self. According to these teachings, there are seven basic chakras on the human body.

Our first chakra is located at the base of the spine, within the sacrum triangle, and is thought to be the seat of power and pleasure. Our second chakra is located just a few inches below the navel, and is thought to be the seat of sexual pleasure and the emotions. Our third chakra is centered at the solar plexus (or slightly to the left) and is thought to be the point of "chi" or the point where Great Spirit's pure energy enters the body.

Our fourth chakra is the point used in Dr. Diamond's strength test, and is located at the thymus gland. This chakra is the seat of love and compassion. (It is interesting that the thymus is also thought to be the life force center.) Our fifth chakra is the throat or thyroid gland. This energy center controls expression and communication. Our sixth chakra is located between our eyes, over the pituitary gland, and controls clarity of thought and the abilities of clairvoyance. Our seventh chakra, on the crown of the head, is governed by the pineal gland and is thought to control spirituality. It is the last of the chakras to be awakened during spiritual growth, and represents an integration and harmony of all of the chakras.

Swan developed a table of these seven chakras, their corresponding rates of vibration, and the musical note associated with each vibration. The first chakra, the seat of power and pleasure, has the lowest rate of vibration. Therefore, if we succumb to power and pleasure we will resonate to the lower vibrations of this first chakra. Swan calculated this vibration as the musical note "C" with a vibration of 261.1 cycles per second. In contrast, the seventh, or crown chakra, vibrates as the musical note "B" with a rate of 493 cycles per second.[6] When we act in a self-centered manner, we will resonate to the lower vibrations of the first two chakras. Inversely, if we strive to live a life of love and harmony with Great Spirit, we will vibrate to the much higher frequency of the seventh chakra.

Compassion is a vital tool in helping us to resonate at the seventh chakra, achieving a vibration in harmony with Great Spirit and the universe. (It's also interesting to note that in numerology the number seven vibrates with spiritual leadership.) Our society seems to have greatly devalued a compassionate outlook on life. Instead, there is a general tendency to label compassionate people as "bleeding hearts." Evidence of this cynicism is all around us—alienated minorities, starving and unwanted children, homeless people, and conspicuous consumption with a focus on self-indulgence. A lack of compassion is one of the major metaphysical illnesses that afflict our society.

I will try to illustrate this illness with the story of someone I'll call Charlie. He is a boy of about sixteen with a lonely and haunted look. His mother divorced his father when Charlie was about eleven, and it turned his life upside down. Charlie adored his father and wanted to live with him. This was not possible, however, because his father had a new wife and three young children and he now had no time for a troublesome teenager. His stepfather didn't understand his rebelliousness and simply felt that Charlie needed a firm hand. Charlie, however, did not perceive this as discipline because it was not preceded with love. As a result, Charlie resented his stepfather because of his rigid rules.

Charlie felt no bond for the stepfather, only fear. But his mother was deeply in love with her new husband and would do nothing to jeopardize their relationship. She was afraid of losing him. She rationalized that Charlie would soon be grown and on his own, and she still had her life to live. She let her new husband deal with Charlie as he pleased.

Charlie's fear of his new stepfather's "discipline," and his resentment of this man trying to take the place of his real father, finally erupted in an ugly scene one day. Charlie was placed in a foster home. He rebelled by dropping out of school and now seems a lonely and lost waif. He is so desperate for love and acceptance that he calls any woman who befriends him "Mom." He is completely estranged from his mother and his stepfather. You would never even know that they have a son, for they never speak of him.

Poor Charlie. The key people in his life failed to embrace a compassionate relationship with him. His mother's chief concern was fear of losing her new love. His father's concern was with his new family, not with the son he already had. His stepfather viewed Charlie as an object to be disciplined; he feared that this child was out of his control. No one saw Charlie as the lonely and frightened human being that he was. None of these people seem to view Charlie as a valuable human being. Unfortunately, the concentric circles of the key people in Charlie's life reveal the crass attitude of "me first." What kind of a man will Charlie grow up to be?

Human beings desperately need to be loved. We need one another. Our spiritual growth depends on this. Had one of these people shown compassion toward Charlie, he would be a different person from the lost and lonely soul that he is now. The children of this world, the generations unborn, are our future. They will rule the world and they will generate our economy. They will pay the taxes that will take care of us in our old age. They will be the stewards of our environment. A little compassion could ensure that our future, and theirs, remains bright.

In contrast to Charlie is a family that I will call the Smiths. Mrs. Smith had five children when she divorced and remarried Mr. Smith who also had two children. Mr. Smith also met resistance when he sought to discipline his stepchildren. After a few unsuccessful attempts, they held a family meeting where the children made it clear they were not ready for a substitute father nor his control. As a result of this discussion, the Smiths decided to use family meetings to replace one-on-one discipline situations. In these meetings all of the family members could air their concerns and fears. The Smiths have now been married for thirty years, and holidays are a happy and noisy event as children and grandchildren vie for attention. Compassion made all members of the new family feel loved and wanted and provided a new generation of healthy and happy people.

Another aspect of compassion is *synergy*. A. H. Maslow outlines this concept in his book, *The Farther Reaches of Human Nature*. He explains that the famed anthropologist, Ruth Benedict, postulated this idea in a series of speeches at Bryn Mawr College in 1941. In these lectures, she defined synergy as a "social order in which the individual by the same act and at the same time serves his own advantage and that of the group"—the actions of each are mutually reinforcing.[7]

Benedict found that societies with a high rate of synergy are those in which virtue pays. She was able to document the fact that these societies (with high synergy) are also more successful than those societies that are mean and selfish (low synergy). She found that the greater the number of individuals who prosper, the more the society as a whole prospers. To couch this in the terms of unitheism, the greater the number of people that vibrate in resonance to the energy of Great Spirit, the greater the prosperity of the society as a whole. The resonance of great numbers of peoples facilitates entrainment and also helps others to vibrate in harmony with the energy of Great Spirit.

Compassion is, after all, nothing more than love. All of these arguments that I have just presented serve to prove that love is, unquestionably, the most powerful force in the universe.

Chapter Notes

1. Dr. A. C. Ross (Ehanamani), *Mitakuye Oyasin "We are all related,"* Denver, CO: Wiconi Waste, 1996, p. 29.
2. *Gazette Telegraph,* May 22, 1992, Colorado Springs, Colorado.
3. Matthew 25:40.
4. J. E. Berendt, op. cit., pp. 116–117.
5. J. Diamond, M.D., op. cit., ch. 6.
6. J. A. Swan, op. cit., p. 113.
7. A. H. Maslow, op. cit., pp. 202–203.

16

Love, The Most Powerful Force in the Universe

"Where the other person is regarded more than the self, duty is sweeter and more inspiring, patriotism more sacred, and friendship is a pure and eternal bond."

Ohiyesa (Sioux)
The Soul of an Indian

After I sold my gallery in Santa Fe, I resumed a career as accountant and auditor. In the early 1980s, my work took me to Washington, D.C. What a wonderfully beautiful and culturally rich city. I was overawed by the art treasures at the Smithsonian Institution, and spent as much of my free time there as was possible. There were so many different museum buildings and art galleries that I was hard-pressed for time to visit them all. As I wandered the sidewalks of our nation's capital, however, I was dumbfounded by the number of people living on the streets. I couldn't believe that the most important city of a great nation like ours was inundated with so many people who had no home. Although I had been homeless several times myself as a child (once because of the flood and later because of the fire), there had been friends, family, and neighbors to take us in. We were not forced to live in the gutters as these people did.

My coworkers warned me to beware of the homeless, as they were "dangerous." Therefore, I too became fearful and blended in with the crowds of people who walked around these pitiful human beings lying huddled against the cold on the sidewalks and in the alleys. Although I felt sympathy for these people, my fear of them overrode my sense of compassion. Nonetheless, I couldn't understand why our government did nothing.

The park across the street from the White House was so full of home-less that it was virtually impossible to find an empty bench much less an empty patch of grass. As I watched street people rummaging through gar-bage cans for food, while Nancy Reagan sought funding for dinner plates that cost $8,000 each, I was reminded of pre-Revolutionary France. Marie Antoinette spent a fortune to enhance her fabulous country palace, Petit Trianon, while the peasants went without food. I felt a pervasive sense of injustice, but I also felt helpless to effect any change.

Thankfully, my cowardly attitude was reversed when Mitch Snyder, the founder of the Center for Creative Non-Violence, spoke one Sunday at the church I attended. He was unshaven and slightly disheveled, dressed in his usual pea-green Army fatigues. However, he virtually radiated love as he revealed the depth of his commitment to his fellow man. He told us first of the great wrong he committed by abandoning his wife and children in order to work with the homeless. He was a paradox, acknowledging his spiritual agony for this desertion while expounding on the needs of the homeless.

Snyder painted a picture for us of lost and helpless human beings. Hu-man beings who were denied any acknowledgment of their humanity by the people around them. He said that it was easier to go without food and a bed than to have people refuse to even look at you and acknowledge that you are a human being. He wryly noted that people will almost al-ways look at a stray homeless dog and feed it or try to pet it. But these same individuals will refuse to even look at a homeless person.

"Whatever you did for one of the least of these brothers of mine, you did for me." As I watched the people in Washington, D.C. react to the homeless, I had a difficult time discerning just which of them subscribed to the teachings of the Christ. And I was one of these people who suc-cumbed to their fear, doing nothing at all for our less fortunate brothers and sisters. But Mitch Snyder tweaked my conscience. He told us that if you are too fearful to try to help such a person, at least acknowledge that they, too, are God's children by smiling and saying "Good morning." At a bare minimum, he exhorted us to at least reaffirm their value as human be-ings.

Snyder's teachings deeply touched my heart. I knew that he was right. These were fellow human beings, no matter what their appearance. How could anyone of us be more concerned with our next new stereo system or new dress while others were suffering so terribly. Where was our sense of priorities as a nation? Even though I was still very much afraid, I decided to begin acting from love and not fear. Leaving the metro station the next morning, I made it a point to catch the eye of the first homeless person that I saw and cheerfully wished him "Good morning!" The second time I tried this it was easier, and I was not quite so afraid.

On the third day, as I got off the subway, my gaze fell upon a dejected-looking young man obviously in the throes of some great sorrow. He was dressed in ragged jeans and had nothing but a badly torn Levi jacket to protect him from the bitter January morning. A much-used backpack and a beat-up guitar case were on the pavement beside him. Smiling, I approached him with a cheery "Good morning." He timidly looked up for a moment, returned my smile somewhat vacantly, and then looked away. I knelt beside him and asked if I might share my good fortune by buying him a cup of coffee and something for breakfast. At this he bent his head and began to cry. He said that his life was hopeless, and that he was thinking of killing himself. I asked him to please reconsider—he was a valuable human being. I also told him that most of the people walking by, and so many more, cared a great deal what happened to him; but they were afraid.

I was late for work; but I bought this young man some coffee and a bite to eat, and then referred him to one of the local churches. He not only decided to live, but he also helped me to reach many of the other homeless who were able to find shelter through our efforts. The words of Mitch Snyder were like a pebble thrown into a pond. Ripples of his teaching are probably still spreading through the lives of those he touched. Mitch Snyder was a great human being. He was the conscience for our society in dealing with "the least of these brothers of mine." I am only sorry that I was unable to honor Mitch Snyder while he was living and tell him what a profound change he brought about in the way I now view the world around me. Mitch Snyder was an exceptional spiritual leader because he showed the effect that a single person's words and actions can have on the world. One person's compassion can have profound ramifications. One person's compassion can make a difference.

Many good people won't give to others because they are afraid—not only for their physical well-being, but also because others might call them a "chump" or a "bleeding heart." How can our society value appearances above concern for the life of another human being? What does it matter if one of these street people is simply a hustler? I would rather buy coffee and food for one hustler than to wonder if some desperate human being were suffering or considering death because I lacked compassion. Which is more important? Fortunately, there is a nearly foolproof way of protecting yourself while trying to help. I have found that a simple prayer before approaching such a person will protect you, give you discernment, and fortify your resolve.

Unfortunately, there is yet another facet to this dilemma. Many of us fear that the problems of people in need are beyond any worldly solution. Perhaps there is no manageable way to address the multitude of problems in the world. But my grandfather used to tell me that if everyone fed just one little bird, then there would be no starving birds in the world. For instance, let's examine the 30,000 to 40,000 children who die from hunger each day. If we multiply the lowest number (30,000) by 365, we can see that almost eleven million children die from hunger each year. Since there are approximately 250 million Americans, we would need only sixteen percent of them to make a small donation and the problem could be solved. Yes, 40 million people, donating less than one dollar a day could save these children. It takes only the price of a coke at McDonalds to feed a child enough to keep him or her alive. World hunger is not an unmanageable problem; it is simply a matter of priorities.

My husband and I have fostered many children around the world through a wonderful program called Plan International. It only costs us about $22 each month, and our contribution alone has already saved one young boy's life. Plan International has what I think is a model program for international aid. They focus on individual villages in numerous third world countries, and then they work with and through the local authorities.

Through Plan International's Child Reach Program, Harold and I foster a child in Cali, Colombia, South America. Our donation is used to provide a safe and sanitary water system for this village as a first priority. The Plan also sponsors a school where the enrolled families can send their children. A counselor works with each of these families to set personal goals, and then helps them to achieve their objectives each year. Our foster son's mother was taught to sew and now works for a cottage industry, and the family is saving to have a new roof put on their house. Our child wrote to us of being ill for a prolonged period, so we notified Plan International and they ensured that he received the special medical care that saved his life. Sponsors may not send money directly to their child, but are encouraged to correspond or visit as frequently as possible. Foster parents act as mentors rather than as fairy godmothers. Foreign values and foreign industries are not forced upon anyone. People in targeted villages are taught and encouraged to become self-sufficient. When this has been achieved, Plan International moves on to another village and begins the work again.

Plan International and Mitch Snyder are excellent models for implementing compassion on a day-to-day basis within the framework of society. Fortunately, they are not the only successful programs, but they illustrate the kind of approach that works. In a similar vein, economist E. F. Schumacher teaches that the best type of economic aid to give any developing country is intellectual aid—useful knowledge. He reports that "the gift of material goods makes people dependent, but the gift of knowledge makes them free."[1] Schumacher offers a compassionate alternative to the Club of Rome which theorized that development of third world countries would pollute our planet and completely deplete its store of natural resources. Schumacher's theoretical plan for world prosperity is similar to that already in use by Plan International.

Schumacher postulates that we must redefine progress, not as industrialization, but as a fully employed workforce. He writes that the heart of the matter "is the stark fact that world poverty is primarily a problem of two million villages, and thus a problem of two thousand million villagers."[2] Schumacher feels that the focus of aid programs should be to make people self-reliant and independent through gifts of relevant knowledge on methods of self-help.

> What makes us think we need electricity, cement, and steel before we can do anything at all? The really helpful things will not be done from the centre; they cannot be done by big organisations; but they can be done by the people themselves. If we can recover the sense that it is the most natural thing for every person born into this world to use his hands in a productive way and that it is not beyond the wit of man to make this possible, then I think the problem of unemployment [in the world] will disappear and we shall soon be asking ourselves how we can get all the work done that needs to be done.[3]

Ruth Benedict, the anthropologist whom I introduced earlier, corroborates Schumacher's theory. She has shown that the healthy and successful societies throughout history consisted of people helping one another to succeed (synergy). Our modern world is a global village because of advances in transportation and communication. If the members of our global village practice synergy (compassion) then the world will prosper. If we return to numerology for a moment, we will note that the word "prosperity" resonates with the same numerical vibration as the word "Saint." When people work together, helping one another, they create a vibration that is in harmony with Great Spirit.

American Indians have a number of traditions that exemplify this concept of synergy within their daily activities. One of their principal traditions is the ever-present invocation, MITAKUYE OYASIN, a reminder that We are all One. Eagle Man explains this concept simply and beautifully in *Mother Earth Spirituality*.

> We, the American Indian, had a way of living that enabled us to live within the great, complete beauty that only the natural environment can provide. The Indian tribes had a common value system and a commonality of religion, without religious animosity, that preserved that great beauty that the two-leggeds definitely need. Our four commandments from the Great Spirit are: (1) respect for Mother Earth, (2) respect for the Great Spirit, (3) respect for our fellow man and woman, and (4) respect for individual freedom (provided that individual freedom does not threaten the tribe or the people or Mother Earth).
>
> We who respect the great vision of Black Elk see the four sacred colors as red, yellow, black, and white. They stand for the four directions—red for the east, yellow for the south, black for the west, and white for the north ...
>
> All good things come from these sacred directions. These sacred directions, or four sacred colors, also stand for the four races of humanity; red, yellow, black, and white. We cannot be a prejudiced people, because all men and women are brothers and sisters and because we all [including four-leggeds, wingeds, stones, plants and trees] have the same mother—Mother Earth.[4]

MITAKUYE OYASIN! We are all related. This invocation is a constant reminder of the synergy that must pervade society in order to bring us into harmony with the energy of Great Spirit. Another American Indian custom which applies the concept of synergy is that of the Giveaway Ceremony.

Unfortunately, many of us are slaves to our possessions. I know of people who are afraid to leave their homes for fear that someone might steal something of value. I know of other people who have ruined their lives through indiscriminate use of credit cards to buy "stuff." Still others have sacrificed every principle and every friendship in their scramble for money so that they may buy houses and cars and material goods.

Sitting Bull derided this materialistic lifestyle, saying that "The life of white men is slavery. They are prisoners [where they live]."[5] The American Indian solution to this slavery is the Giveaway Ceremony.

The Giveaway Ceremony is generally conducted about a year after the death of a loved one. At that time, the possessions of the loved one are collected in one place, and a "bucket party" (a potluck) is held. The departed loved one is fondly remembered as his or her possessions are freely given to different friends and family members. Contrast this loving redistribution of wealth to our European tradition of writing a will that stipulates heirs to our material goods and often resulting in arbitration of the ensuing legal battles. (Ironically, in the 1890s our government outlawed the "barbaric" Giveaway Ceremony.)

In addition to commemorating death, the Giveaway Ceremony can be held on virtually any special occasion. Whenever someone receives a special honor—such as a promotion or civic award—American Indians celebrate it with a giveaway. One of my friends was just named Chief Dancer for the Colorado Pow Wow, so he and his wife held a generous Giveaway Ceremony in order to share their good fortune with their friends. Again, this differs markedly from many traditional European ceremonies and holidays where the emphasis is on **getting** as many gifts as possible. Eagle Man writes that he incorporates the giveaway blanket in many ceremonies that he conducts.

> In a number of Sweat Lodge and Vision Quest ceremonies that I have held lately, we have unfolded a giveaway blanket after the ceremony; those who have participated are free to give away possessions to the blanket. Everyone is also free to reach in and take a gift from the blanket. Any items that remain on the blanket will be exchanged, sold, or bartered for tree seedlings to plant in honor of Earth Day.[6]

When we love one another, when we have compassion, we create a resonance of Great Spirit's energy in all people and things that we touch. This harmonious energy field is incredibly powerful, whirling through our lives with us at the center, pulling in other resonant energies. This tornado of love can transform our lives and the world, creating peace and harmony throughout the universe.

Colorado's Ute Indians have a legend that teaches the value of this love and compassion. Like most of their stories, this one also revolves around Coyote.

* * *

One cold winter, Coyote and his family had nothing to eat. They noticed that the nearby camp of Crows had plenty to eat and were always happy. Coyote asked one of his people to become a puppy so that he could spy on the Crows and learn their secret.

Coyote's friend, Weasel, volunteered to become a puppy and spy. What Weasel learned was that the Crow had a special rock and, when they lifted this rock up, a buffalo came out. When the Crows went to sleep, the puppy lifted up that special rock and let all of the buffalo out except an old cow. The puppy went to Coyote and told him about the buffalo. Coyote said, "Thank you, friend!" Coyote was so excited that he could not sleep that night.

Next morning, all of Coyote's people set to work making bows and arrows from the wild currant bush. Everyone used the flint arrowheads made by Old Woodpecker—except for Coyote. He made his arrowheads out of an aspen leaf. Coyote's people got up early next morning to hunt the buffalo. They each rode on one horse and led another. Coyote's second horse was very fast running. Coyote told his people, "We all have a chance to get our own meat. We will not share what we kill."

When they came to the buffalo, Coyote on his fast horse had many chances to shoot. But when he shot the buffalo, his arrows just bent. He didn't kill a single buffalo. His wife was very upset with Coyote. "What will we eat?" she asked. One of the other hunters took pity on Coyote and his wife, and shared his buffalo meat.

Next morning, when Coyote organized the hunt he said, "We will all share our meat today." This time Coyote had fixed his arrows with the good hard flint points that Woodpecker made. When his fast horse drew up alongside a nice fat buffalo cow, Coyote was able to kill her. He killed every buffalo that he came near. He was the only one to kill any buffalo that day, but he shared all of the meat with his people.

* * *

This charming Ute tale teaches children the vagaries of fate and the importance of compassion. There are many American Indian legends along this same vein because they fully understood that life is difficult and precarious, and all of our fates are intertwined. Today's successful hunter could well be starving after the next hunt. All had to share for the survival of the people. Unfortunately, our advanced, dominant "civilization" seems to have forgotten this important lesson in love.

This concludes the fifth step along the spiritual path of our Journey Song.

Trust Great Spirit, Trust Great Spirit.

MITAKUYE OYASIN!

Love the Truth and by it live.

MITAKUYE OYASIN!

Walk life's path with Simplicity.

MITAKUYE OYASIN!

Bathe yourself and others with Patience.

Mɪᴛᴀᴋᴜʏᴇ Oʏᴀsɪɴ!

Carry only Compassion in your heart.

Mɪᴛᴀᴋᴜʏᴇ Oʏᴀsɪɴ!

In the next chapter, I will summarize the philosophy of unitheism and Cosmic Symbiosis and share a vision of how this Journey Song could redefine the world if everyone would carry it in their hearts.

Chapter Notes

1. E. F. Schumacher, *Small Is Beautiful*, New York: Harper & Row, 1973, p. 197.
2. Ibid, p. 193.
3. Ibid, p. 220.
4. E. McGaa/Eagle Man, op. cit., pp. 204, 205.
5. R. M. Utley, *The Lance and The Shield*, New York: Henry Holt & Co., 1993, p. 247.
6. E. McGaa/Eagle Man, op. cit., p. 123.

$$\equiv 17 \equiv$$

Mother Earth Spirituality

*"There are no temples or shrines among us save those of nature.
Being children of nature, we are intensely poetical. We would deem
it sacrilege to build a house for The One who may be met face to face
in the mysterious, shadowy aisles of the primeval forest, or on the
sunlit bosom of virgin prairies, upon dizzy spires and pinnacles of
naked rock, and in the vast jeweled vault of the night sky!"*

Ohiyesa (Sioux)
The Soul of an Indian

Although I grew up in New Mexico within the bosom of American Indian culture, there were still many facets of this spirituality that I did
not experience. My Indian friends taught me about the Great Spirit and
the Oneness of all things, but I did not participate in many of their ceremonies. I had difficulty reconciling this spirituality with my Catholicism,
and feared that I could be excommunicated. I did not fully understand
the wisdom and truth of American Indian teachings until later in my life
after years of trials, tribulations, misadventures, and mistakes. And when I
arrived at that point in my thinking, I also understood that spirituality and
religion are disparate actualities. Virtually all religions insist on interposing
another human being between the individual and the Great Spirit. Truth
and logic, however, demand that there be no such artificial boundaries for
the human spirit. We are all One. No two-legged should stand between
me and Great Spirit.

As I developed the hypothesis of unitheism, I tried to avoid speaking
directly about American Indian spirituality because I felt that this would
betray my Indian friends. But then the energy forces of Great Spirit carried
Eagle Man into my life; and he made it clear that it was not only all right,
but vital, to include American Indian teachings in this book. "American

203

Indians shouldn't complain about the white man if they are not willing to teach him. If we want to change the dominant society, if we want to save our Mother Earth, then we must share our spirituality." Eagle Man also insisted that I participate in as many ceremonies as possible—beginning with a Sweat Lodge—and include those experiences in this book.

I began building my first sweat lodge on a beautiful Spring day during the early part of April. It had snowed the night before but, as is typical of springtime in the Rockies, the next day dawned with a clear blue sky. Our pastures were covered with brightly-hued mountain bluebirds, scavenging the pale pink ground of Pikes Peak granite for insects. It is rare that my husband and I find the time to ride our horses just for pleasure, but this beautiful April day demanded such a ride. We had planned to conduct our Sweat Lodge Ceremony that evening, so there was plenty of time to have a little fun beforehand.

Our horses seemed as excited at the prospect of pleasure as we were. Harold had no trouble bringing them in for grooming and saddling. Our greatest difficulty, however, was in helping old Brownie (now a respectable forty-one years of age) to shed her heavy winter coat. Brownie is a dear old mare who came to us quite by accident. We learned that she and her foal were being starved, so we offered our ranch as a refuge. Brownie was barely alive at 750 pounds when she arrived—her normal weight was 1400 pounds. But that was eight years ago and all but forgotten as we set off on our favorite trail.

I always enjoy any opportunity for an outing—I spend far too many days glued to my computer, writing. My horse is Tess, a thickset, white quarter horse, about twenty years old. She came to me as a gift from friends a few years ago, complete with a few set-in-concrete idiosyncrasies. The first of these is that we must never touch her hind feet. Sessions with the horseshoer are always quite exciting, to say the least. The second of Tess's hard-and-fast rules is "never put anything in my mouth!" This includes a bit, but she never objects to being ridden with a hackamore. Ironically, both Tess and Brownie were originally from the same ranch in the South Park area. Both are wonderful cattle horses—Brownie gets so excited at the prospect of working cattle that she quivers all over. She and I both feel that playing tag with a stray cow is great fun. We try to use her sparingly, but she enjoys it so much that it's hard to leave her behind.

I personally feel that no perfume could be sweeter than the scent of a horse under saddle and on the trail. On this particular April morning we wound our way over meadows of grama grass, through groves of ponderosa pine, and along the aspen covered slopes of a clear, boulder-strewn stream. We dismounted for a lunch of cheese and apples on the banks of a small pond, where I also found plenty of fresh sage for the Sweat Lodge Ceremony.

Harold and I had spent the better part of the trail ride laying the plans for building our sweat lodge. I felt a great deal of trepidation at the beginning of the project, but our leisurely ride gave me time to sort out my thoughts and to talk it over. I realized that I was hesitant because I felt incompetent. I had seen many sweat lodges during my childhood in New Mexico. However, these were always led by a medicine man and an experienced American Indian drummer.

I didn't have a medicine man, a drummer, or even a drum. How could I perform such an important ceremony? But Eagle Man was insistent that I perform the Sweat Lodge and include the experience in these pages. When I objected, arguing that I should wait to find a Sweat Lodge among my American Indian friends, Eagle Man admonished me, saying that I must show leadership by taking the matter into my own hands.

So here I was at the end of the trail. I couldn't find any more reasons to procrastinate. Harold and I unsaddled, rubbed the horses down, and turned them into the west pasture. We then headed for the south pasture to cut the willows for our lodge. We have half a dozen two-year-old bulls in that pasture who thought that our presence guaranteed some edible treats, so they gathered around us as we selected fourteen willows for the lodge frame. We tried to cut only those willows that had a base diameter about the size of a quarter, were somewhat straight, and were at least a foot taller than my 5′ 3″ height.

When our arms were fully laden with the long, slender bundle of willows, we trekked past the ranch house and barn to the dry creek bed in the north pasture. We decided that this spot was ideal for our sweat lodge; the sandy stream bottom made digging the fire pit and the stone pit quite easy. It was also sheltered from the constant winds that whirl through our valley. My sweat lodge wasn't sheltered from the gaze of our cows, however; and we were soon the center of attention.

All of the bovine mommas and their babies meandered over and curiously inspected our project. One white-faced Angus named Oreo proved bolder than the others. She tentatively approached to within a few feet of our newly dug fire pit and feigned scratching her head on a small pine tree nearby. As soon as we turned our backs to begin digging the stone pit for the lodge itself, she lumbered up to the fire pit. She methodically sniffed the pit and then the pile of grapefruit-sized stones stacked beside it. These stones would be heated in the fire pit, then placed in the stone pit for the sweat itself.

I turned around just as Oreo finished her inspection of the rock pile and caught her disdainful gaze. She looked at me in disbelief for a few moments, clearly contemptuous of those inedible stones. She then snorted and pushed the whole pile over with her nose. Next, she addressed the fire pit, using her front hoof to push the stone lining aside. She then proceeded to paw all of the dirt back into the hole, filling it completely! Her bull calf, Cookie, soon ambled alongside his mother to help with her mischief.

I began to have an uneasy feeling that my four-legged friends were trying to tell me something. Harold disagreed, assuring me that their message was "Feed me, **now!**" So we continued building our sweat lodge after shooing the cows as far away as possible.

We rebuilt the fire pit about fifteen feet away from the stone pit. We dug it deep enough, about two feet deep, to allow for the strong winds in our area. We then lined the sides with rocks to help contain the fire. Next, I tied some baling twine around a short stick and planted it in the center of our proposed stone pit. At a distance of about four feet from the first stick, I tied a second stick to the baling twine and used this crude compass to draw a circle in the dirt. At the center of the circle was the stone pit. The outer circle would define the placement of our willow branches.

While I dug the stone pit, Harold used a hammer and a spike to drive holes on the circular line I had just drawn. He drove the spike about six inches into the ground, removed it, and inserted the sharpened end of a willow branch. We placed the willow branches at about two-foot intervals around this circle.

Once all of the willow branches had been planted in this manner, we took more baling twine and, after bending them over to meet one another, tied opposite branches together. It only took about thirty minutes before we had constructed a four-foot-high dome of willow branches with a shallow stone pit in the center. Our sweat lodge was nearly ready, and it had really been quite simple to construct. Reluctantly, we had to postpone the sweat itself because a strong wind came up. It was just as well, for the day's ride and the sweat lodge construction had left me completely exhausted.

It was several weeks before we completed the construction of our lodge and conducted our ceremony. Although sweats are traditionally held in the evening, we felt that it would be safer to hold a morning ceremony, since our winds always blow from noon until evening. Several snow storms later, we finally were blessed with a beautiful, clear morning.

This was the day for our sweat lodge. There was no wind, and only a small breeze stirred in the pines.

I began preparations for the ceremony by attempting to make a garland of sweet grass and sage for each of us. (I hadn't invited anyone else to join us; I was afraid the whole ceremony would be a disaster. I felt very uneasy about not having a medicine man preside.)

I hope that my gift to the world is as a writer because I am totally inept as a garland maker. When all of my efforts fell to the ground in crumpled heaps, I decided to use bandannas similar to those used by my Navajo friends. I rolled one of my bandannas to a one-inch thickness, and then fastened it around my temple, tucking little branches of sage around the top edge. (The sage changes the vibrations around the ears and the seventh chakra, enabling one to "hear.") I then slipped into shorts and a T-shirt, and gathered Harold's shorts, bandanna, sage, tobacco, matches, and my special crystal.

These were all packed into a basket for easy carrying, as I also had to carry a water bucket and cup. I chose a special Acoma pottery cup that was gaily decorated with eagle symbols for the ceremony.

Harold took the wheelbarrow, laden with a sixteen-by-twenty-foot tarp and several old woolen blankets. We also took a sheaf of sweet alfalfa hay to scatter on the floor of the sweat lodge along with the sage. I didn't want any more of Oreo's help with our ceremony, so we carefully tiptoed through the barn and out the back door. We then stealthily crept through the paddock and followed a roundabout route up to the site of the sweat lodge. Fortunately, we were successful; the cows didn't see us.

I was afraid that they might have returned our fragile willow dome and newly redug fire pit to Mother Earth. We were pleasantly surprised to find that they had eaten only one of the willow branches and had done nothing more than sniff around the stone pit. Nothing was trampled or torn down.

We carefully opened the tarp and spread it over our willow dome, leaving one of the sections on the west side open for use as a doorway. The tarp was large enough that we lay the excess on the ground around the dome, and secured it by laying several heavy logs on the edges. We next hung one of the wool blankets over the door, tying each of the top corners with twine. We fastened both of these pieces of twine around the dome and to each other on the back side. We next secured several other blankets over the top to help to hold in the heat during the sweat.

We placed our sweat stones (about twenty grapefruit-sized rocks) in the bottom of the fire pit, and then Harold laid the branches for a fire on top of them. As Harold started the fire, I used the tobacco to begin the ceremony. We were joined at this point by six mountain bluebirds who flew to the nearest pine tree and gave birth to a cacophony of song.

I smiled, for I knew that this was a good sign. I scattered the tobacco in a clockwise circle around the fire pit, then in a line to the sweat lodge, and finally, around the stone pit in the sweat lodge. As I scattered the tobacco, I spoke my prayer to the Great Spirit, asking Him/Her to bless our efforts and to show me the correct way to conduct the ceremony. The sweat lodge was now "open," and as Harold and I seated ourselves around the fire, a beautiful golden eagle appeared from the west and flew at treetop level, hanging for a few moments just above our heads.

I was greatly relieved and awed by the eagle's presence. It seemed that the eagle was a sign of encouragement from the spirits of the west, as the eagle symbolizes a connection to Great Spirit, within American Indian tradition.

I then lit a branch of sage in the fire and "smudged" both Harold and myself. American Indians use smudging, or bathing in the smoke from the sage, to cleanse the body's vibrations (bring them into harmony) prior to ceremony. I then entered the sweat lodge, while Harold used the shovel to carry in the first four of our heated stones.

In order to avoid carrying in cinders from the fire, he first shoveled the stones onto the gravel stream bed and then rolled them away from the cinders. As he placed them in the stone pit, we greeted the stones with "*Hau kola!*" (Hello, friend!). With this greeting, we acknowledge the Oneness of the Universe, for Spirit is present even in the stones. We are a part of the stones; and they are a part of us; and we both have the same mother as we both come from Mother Earth. Mother Earth, the stones, and human beings all came from the great One, and we are all a part of that Oneness. "*Hau kola!*" is an affirmation and acknowledgment of unitheism and its Cosmic Symbiosis.

We sat for a few moments in silence, and then I began the Sweat Lodge Ceremony while holding my special crystal. (As I mentioned earlier, I use my crystal instead of a peace pipe in deference to those American Indians who are offended by non-Indian use.) I had prepared index cards with instructions for each of the four endurances, and placed them in a plastic bag to protect against the humidity of the sweat. I based my ceremony on the instructions given by Eagle Man in his book, *Mother Earth Spirituality.*[1] I also read and reread Black Elk's story in preparation for the ceremony, trying very hard to gain a deeper understanding of the symbolism in his great vision.

Although Black Elk was only nine years old at the time of his vision, I noted with interest the other great mystical leaders who experienced a similar spiritual awakening as youths. Jesus of Nazareth was about twelve when he confounded the elders with his knowledge and questions. Both Gandhi and Martin Luther King, Jr., were also about that age when they experienced the death of a close family member and then entered fully into their spiritual work.

I also found comfort and acceptance in Black Elk's vision from the fact that the doorway to his vision's teepee (where the six grandfathers sat) was a rainbow. This rainbow seemed to symbolize that his revelation was for people of all races, the Rainbow Tribe (as American Indians call people of different colors). The theme of this rainbow plays strongly throughout Black Elk's vision.

I filled my Acoma cup with water from the bucket, and placed it before me. I then closed my eyes and raised my crystal to the west, while Harold held his crystal and bowed his head. I asked Great Spirit for guidance in conducting the ceremony; I then recounted how the First Grandfather of Black Elk's vision was from the west. This Grandfather gave a cup of water and a bow to Black Elk, instructing him that the water was "the power to make live," and that the bow symbolized the "power to destroy." Both powers were given to Black Elk, just as these same powers are given to each of us. With these gifts (the water and the bow) Black Elk was later able to kill (in his vision) the Blue Man who was the cause of the sickness and death of Mother Earth and her creatures.

Both of these powers, to make live and to destroy, were given by the First Grandfather (who was from the west). This Grandfather then transformed himself into a beautiful black stallion that became poor and sickly. The West, expressed by the color black, is the place where spirit beings live according to American Indian teachings. Therefore, the west symbolizes spiritual life. The black stallion in the vision became sickly, representing a deep spiritual malaise. The powers of life and death lie in the west, in our spiritual life. When we live in consonance with the will of Great Spirit, we will have an eternal vibration—eternal life.

As Black Elk's vision so dramatically demonstrates, this consonance extends to the way in which we interact with Mother Earth and all her beings. The Blue Man was killing the earth. As I mused on this symbol of the Blue Man, I thought of a newly born baby who will remain blue until an adequate supply of oxygen enters his bloodstream. We know that pollution of our atmosphere is one of the more serious environmental issues that we currently face. We human beings are killing the earth. We are the

Blue Man; we cannot breathe. We suffer from a serious spiritual malaise which causes us to be so self-destructive. And it is only through our spiritual life that we can use the water and the bow to destroy the Blue Man. A new understanding of the Oneness of the Universe, of unitheism, is imperative for human beings to survive. This understanding (for understanding is power)—symbolized by the herb—was offered by the Second Grandfather and it fattened the black horse and brought him back to health.

When I finished voicing this meditation, I poured the cup of water on the red-hot rocks in the pit. With this first cup of water, one of the larger quartz stones splintered into numerous pieces, about the size of my crystal *Wotai*. At this moment, I realized that these pieces were to be used as *Wotai* at the next sweat lodge, and that I was to invite as many people. I then poured three more cups of water on the stones, and began the Second Endurance with a similar oral meditation on the North.

This second meditation was preceded by the passing of a sprig of sage from myself to Harold to symbolize the herb given by the Second Grandfather. I lightly bruised the leaves in order to release the plant's pungent aroma, and then began the oral meditation. The Second Grandfather (who was from the north) promised Black Elk that "on earth a nation you shall make live, for yours shall be the power of the white giant's wing, the cleansing wing."

To American Indians, the powers of the north are symbolized by endurance, strength, cleanliness, and honesty. These are the attributes that ensure a strong, spiritual life. Truth is cleansing, for there is nothing stronger nor more lasting since it dispels the dissonance of untruth. Great Spirit is Truth, and therefore Truth is eternal. This cleansing, whiteness of truth is imperative for spiritual life. It is interesting that this sacred herb was given by the Grandfather from the north. I have always found that using sage to smudge is extremely effective in changing the vibrations of a room. It is also effective in changing my own vibrations prior to prayer or meditation.

Sage has always held a special spiritual significance for the American Indian. I would suppose that its power is in its ability to confer the consonant vibration of Mother Earth, of Great Spirit, and overpower the dissonant vibrations that we accumulate all day long.

With the conclusion of this second meditation, Harold brought in four more stones; and I poured four more cups of water to create more steam. Our little lodge was becoming quite toasty at this point, and we were both beginning to sweat. Each time that we added new stones, we greeted them with "*Hou kola!*" We then sat in quiet contemplation for a few minutes before beginning the Third Endurance.

It was the Third Grandfather, the Grandfather from the East, who presented Black Elk with the peace pipe that had a spotted eagle outstretched along its stem. The spotted eagle is considered by the American Indian to be the highest of the spiritual messengers. The spotted eagle is generally considered a great power, because it flies higher than any other bird and closer to Great Spirit, and returns to earth with the wisdom of the Great Spirit. I have watched the spotted eagles (peregrine falcons) here at our ranch prove their dominance over the much larger golden eagles, driving them from the pastures. It is no wonder then, that they are regarded as the highest of spiritual messengers.

"With this pipe," the Third Grandfather said, "you shall walk upon the earth, and whatever sickens there you shall make well." Again, the symbolism of this peace pipe with the spotted eagle represents the highest of spiritual teachings that Black Elk brought to his people. As I have shown in earlier chapters, we will have eternal life and live in perfection with Great Spirit when we have achieved consonance with His/Her will. This consonance comes from understanding, and then living, a life of harmony with the will of Great Spirit.

When this harmonious vibration has been achieved, there will be infinity. All dissonance, all evil, will simply cease to exist. Red, which represents understanding and knowledge, is the color of the east. The Third Grandfather also gave the daybreak star to Black Elk. The daybreak star, Venus, symbolizes an awakening; and with this awakening comes knowledge and wisdom.

In his book, *Conversing with the Planets*, best-selling author Anthony Aveni explains the universal importance of Venus among indigenous peoples around the world and through the centuries.

> Ancient astronomy was about trying to know the future—being able to predict well in advance where the powerful celestial forces and harbingers of things to come would be positioned well in advance—so people could get ready. This cycle of Venusian horizon appearances likely provided clever sky watchers with a precise device that had implications reaching well beyond setting the time for planting or anticipating rain. For if the time of appearance and position of Venus at the horizon vary in a regular way with the season of the year, people with such knowledge could predict exactly how long it would be before Venus would return once it had vanished, as well as where it could be seen when it did return. Knowledge is power, and, as you will see, the corpus of ancient

inscriptions, iconography, and architecture supports an abiding concern for such important detailed matters.[2]

Use of the daybreak star to symbolize knowledge and understanding becomes even more apparent when seen in this context. Venus has always been a universal harbinger of growth: of the time when the planting must be done, and the time when the life-giving rains will come.

The contrast between the Blue Man and the Red Man in Black Elk's vision also represents strong symbolism. While the Blue Man represents a polluted atmosphere and a dying Mother Earth, the Red Man is vital and healthy and was transformed into a bison, which symbolizes food and plenty. In Black Elk's idiom, the color red represents the east and symbolizes knowledge and understanding.

Thus, the importance of the Red Man (indicated by the Third Grandfather) is that human beings, and therefore Mother Earth, will find health and well-being through knowledge and understanding. It is interesting to note that American Indians have long been called the Red Man, and it is through their teachings of Mother Earth Spirituality that earth and human beings can be healed.

At the beginning of this Third Endurance, the wind began to sing in the pine trees around our sweat lodge. Moments later, some unknown bird began an incredibly beautiful song in the branches above our willow dome. I forgot to allow for Harold's individual prayer at this point, but the efficacy of the Sweat Lodge Ceremony didn't seem to be seriously impaired by my mistakes in conducting it, as I'm sure that I made many! I was entranced by the sweet, ethereal music of the wind and the birdsong; and so I sat in rapt silence before asking for more stones and beginning the Fourth Endurance.

When the Fourth Grandfather, representing the South, spoke to Black Elk, he told him that he would walk "with the powers of the four quarters [directions]. ... Behold, the living center of a nation I shall give you, and with it many you shall save." And with this, he gave him a bright red stick that had sprouted leaves at the top, and birds were singing in these leaves. The Fourth Grandfather then told Black Elk that the stick would "stand in the center of the nation's circle, a cane to walk with and a people's heart; and by your powers you shall make it blossom."

Black Elk interpreted this vision as meaning that he would have the power to help and to heal the earth and his people. Before he died, however, he instead saw the conquest of his people, their death and starvation and despair. He sadly lamented "I, to whom so great a vision was given in my youth,—you see me now a pitiful old man who has done nothing, for the nation's hoop is broken and scattered. There is no center any longer, and the sacred tree is dead." It is hard to read of this great man's sense of failure. Neihardt notes that shortly before Black Elk's death, he returned to Harney Peak where his great vision took place.

Having dressed and painted himself as he was in his great vision, he faced the west, holding the sacred pipe before him in his right hand. Then he sent forth a voice; and a thin, pathetic voice it seemed in that vast space around us:

"Hey-a-a-hey! Hey-a-a-hey! Hey-a-a-hey! Hey-a-a-hey! Grandfather, Great Spirit, once more behold me on earth and lean to hear my feeble voice. You lived first, and you are older than all need, older than all prayer. All things belong to you—the two-leggeds, the four-leggeds, the wings of the air and all green things that live. You have set the powers of the four quarters to cross each other. The good road and the road of difficulties you have made to cross; and where they cross, the place is holy. Day in and day out, forever, you are the life of things.

"Therefore I am sending a voice, Great Spirit, my Grandfather, forgetting nothing you have made, the stars of the universe and the grasses of the earth.

"You have said to me, when I was still young and could hope, that in difficulty I should send a voice four times, once for each quarter of the earth, and you would hear me.

"To-day I send a voice for a people in despair.

"You have given me a sacred pipe, and through this I should make my offering. You see it now.

"From the west, you have given me the cup of living water and the sacred bow, the power to make live and to destroy. You have given me a sacred wind and the herb from where the white giant lives—the cleansing power and the healing. The daybreak star and the pipe, you have given from the east; and from the south, the nation's sacred hoop and the tree that was to bloom. To the center of the world you have taken me and showed the goodness and the beauty and the strangeness of the greening earth, the only mother—and there the spirit shapes of things, as they should be, you have shown to me and I have seen. At the center of this sacred hoop you have said that I should make the tree to bloom.

"With tears running, O Great Spirit, Great Spirit, my Grandfather—with tears I must say now that the tree has never bloomed. A pitiful old man, you see me here, and I have fallen away and have done nothing. Here at the center of the world, where you took me when I was young and taught me; here, old, I stand, and the tree is withered, Grandfather, my Grandfather!

"Again, and maybe the last time on this earth, I recall the great vision you sent me. It may be that some little root of the sacred tree still lives. Nourish it then, that it may leaf and bloom and fill with singing birds.

Hear me, not for myself, but for my people; I am old. Hear me that they may once more go back into the sacred hoop and find the good red road, the shielding tree!"[3]

Neihardt reports that the sky was clear and blue until the conclusion of Black Elk's ceremony. Then clouds gathered round, and a scant rain began to fall accompanied by a low, muttering thunder without lightning. Raindrops mingled with the old man's tears as he stood silent, face up-lifted, at the end of his ceremony. In a little while the rain stopped and the sky cleared once again.

Before the ceremony began, Black Elk told Neihardt that something should happen. "If I have any power left, the thunder beings of the west should hear me when I send a voice, and there should be at least a little thunder and a little rain."

I felt that it was a tragedy that Black Elk didn't understand the fulfill-ment of his vision. And of course, within the logic of unitheism, this is true. Because of human frailty, his vision could not be realized within his lifetime alone. But the red stick that he planted in the center of his nation **has** taken root. Eagle Man assures me that "when Black Elk entered the spirit world, he immediately knew the great service his vision has done for the world."

Joseph Campbell, the world's foremost authority on mythology and author of *The Power of Myth*, stated that Black Elk's vision is the single best example of a transforming mythological experience. Campbell explains that this experience is the "transit through the earth to the realm of mytho-logical imagery, to God, to the seat of power."[4]

Black Elk's vision has indeed taken root among his people—just as the bright red stick with the leaves took root in the center of his nation's peo-ple—for this stick symbolized his words. And just as the cottonwood tree takes many generations to grow, so it has taken many generations for Black Elk's words to flourish. Black Elk saw that the hoop of his nation was one of many hoops, that all are part of the One. This is a lesson that the world is just beginning to learn. It is the central theme of the philosophy of unitheism. It is the very core of Mother Earth spirituality, of American Indian teachings. All are One. MITAKUYE OYASIN.

Black Elk's vision is corroborated by other American Indian spiritual leaders. An Oglala holy woman, Good Lifeways Woman, had a vision with a similar message.

Once I dreamed I was in a room like a Gymnasium; it was broad day-light. I was called to the corner of the room, where I found a peculiar light. It was in the form of a medicine wheel. From one quadrant of the wheel came a red light. It represented the Red Man. It came to me that

the Red Man's contribution to the whole [of mankind] was spiritual insight. From another quadrant came a dark light; it represented the Black
Man, and it came to me that his gift was in the expression of emotions,
expressed physically in things like music and dance. In another corner
was the white light, it represented the White Man. It came to me that the
White Man's gift was in bringing ideas into physical reality [technology].

In another quadrant was a yellow light; it represented the Yellow
Man. It came to me that his gift was in mental powers such as meditation
and the ancient wisdom that produced acupuncture. Each [color of the
sacred wheel] has a gift to share with the whole, none can exist without
the other; all people must have a balance in themselves. Neither should
one be too powerful and ignore the importance of the other, in this way
all things will be balanced.[5]

As I write these words, a golden eagle has been circling the ranch
house. Old faithful Brownie and her dark bay daughter, Lady, are grazing
near my office. The eagle is now hanging in the air over the horses and
within my line of sight as I gaze westward through the windows of the
sunroom.

Harold and I concluded our Sweat Lodge Ceremony with a short, final
prayer thanking the Great Spirit for a successful ceremony. We were both
soaking wet, and so stood before the fire for a few minutes before changing into our dry clothes. As we stood there, two golden eagles began to
spiral upward directly above our heads, until they flew so high they were
out of sight.

I sighed with relief, feeling that this was a sign that the prayers from
our ceremony were being carried upward to the Great Spirit. In my ab-
sorption with the eagles, I made another large blunder in conducting the
ceremony. I forgot to conclude with the Peace Pipe Ceremony (using a
crystal), giving thanks to the Great Spirit. Again, my error does not seem to
have diminished the ceremony. We were both filled with the peace and the
serenity engendered by our sweat lodge.

We walked back down the hillside to the ranch house in silence, savor-
ing the memory of our experience. The sense of oneness with all of Mother
Earth was pervasive, and I have not felt so totally relaxed in a great long
while. I know that I must now share the next Sweat Lodge Ceremony with
other of my friends who are also seekers. We found a nugget of gold in one
of the rocks during the First Endurance, symbolic of Black Elk's legacy.
There is a value more precious than gold in these ancient ceremonies and
their Mother Earth Spirituality, and knowledge of this value is spreading.
The stick that Black Elk planted in the center of the sacred hoop has only
begun to grow.

Chapter Notes

1. E. McGaa/Eagle Man, op. cit., ch. 8.
2. A. Aveni, *Conversing With the Planets,* New York: Times Books, 1992, ch. 2.
3. J. G. Neihardt, op. cit., pp. 232, 233.
4. J. Campbell, *The Power of Myth,* New York: Doubleday, 1988, pp. 87–89.
5. M. St. Pierre and Tilda Long Soldier, op. cit., p. 49.

Success Is A Journey,
Not A Destination

"*We recognize the spirit in all creation, and believe that we draw spiritual power from it. Our respect for the immortal part of our brothers and sisters, the animals, often leads us so far as to lay out the body of any game we catch and decorate the head with symbolic paint or feathers. We then stand before it in an attitude of prayer, holding up the pipe that contains our sacred tobacco, as a gesture that we have freed with honor the spirit of our brother or sister, whose body we were compelled to take to sustain our own life.*"

Ohiyesa (Sioux)
The Soul of an Indian

Travel in the Seventh Direction, inward toward spirituality, is the most challenging and exciting excursion that we will take in our lifetime. We achieve this spirituality, however, not as an ultimate reward, but through the knowledge we accumulate during the journey itself. "Success is a journey, not a destination."

Unitheism's logic provides the framework for understanding that we are the cocreators of the events, these educational milestones, of our lives. In reviewing this logic, you will hopefully recall that the soul, the spirit, is eternal and preexisted the body. While in this state of Oneness, our spirits assisted Great Spirit in determining the people, places, and events of the next life that would maximize spiritual growth so that we could achieve eternal harmony. Therefore, each time that we stumble in this life, each time that we feel pain, we gain knowledge and the opportunity to grow in spirit. Alan Watts notes that "... in the moment of death many

219

people undergo the curious sensation not only of accepting but of having willed everything that has happened to them. This is not willing in the imperious sense; it is the unexpected discovery of an identity between the willed and the inevitable."[1]

Unfortunately, there is a popular misconception concerning these educational milestones of life within the terminology of karma. Within this flawed context, karma is seen as a rigid, spiritual equation wherein a shortcoming (such as stealing) or a strength (such as giving) will require retribution (loss by theft) or reward (receiving many gifts) in the next life. This is an illogical line of thought for several reasons.

First, the majority of human beings retain no memory of past lives; therefore, any retribution in this current life would be counterproductive.

Second, the purpose of this life is to again achieve infinite harmony, Oneness, with Great Spirit; and this can only be done by education of the spirit (soul).

Therefore, the logical purpose of karma must be to help the individual gain knowledge and thereby change behavior. Rigid equations that require certain behavior in a prior life to generate certain events in a future life are not conducive to imparting this knowledge.

Eagle Man likes to use an analogy of computer technology to illustrate this point. "We are born ignorant, our soul is like a blank computer diskette, and our job is to fill it with as much information as possible during this life. When we have ended our life here on earth, and we meet with Great Spirit, we will have to account for what is written on our diskette."

Ehanamani (Walks Among), a Dakota Sioux Indian who works in our dominant society as Dr. A. C. Ross, writes about the traditional Indian view of reincarnation in his book *Mitakuye Oyasin*. In traditional Dakota/Lakota philosophy, this idea of rebirth is known as "kini."

> The D/Lakota story ... says when a person dies, his or her spirit goes up to the Milky Way and then south. At the south end, there's a fork in the Milky Way. Reaching this fork, the spirit is greeted by a woman. This old woman says, "What did you do on earth? Did you live for yourself—greedy, materialistic, selfish? Or did you live in balance and harmony with all things?" If you are judged as living a selfish life, or you've lived on the Black Road, the old woman pushes you off the Milky Way and you come back to earth. You're born into a new body and given another chance to grow and expand. Or if it's determined that you've lived in balance and harmony, that you've lived on the Red Road, then you're allowed to continue on the Milky Way—back to the center of the universe [Oneness with Great Spirit].[2]

We are all One. We now understand that Great Spirit is eternal, and that we are part of Great Spirit. From this infinite viewpoint, then, we cocreated the events in our lives in order to present ourselves with everything that would be needed for us to accomplish spiritual growth (reunion with Great Spirit). Mother Earth spirituality provides both the idiom and the structure for this growth.

> True and integrated progress on such an inner [spiritual] journey demands the means for accomplishing the progressive and accumulative integration of the following elements or spiritual dimensions: (1) Purification, understood in a total sense, that is, of body, soul and spirit; (2) spiritual expansion, by which an individual realizes his or her totality and relationship to all that is, and thus integration with, and realization of, the realm of the virtues; (3) identity, or final realization of unity, a state of oneness with the Ultimate Principle of All that Is.[3]

My own realization of the truth of Oneness was a slow and laborious process. In retrospect, I first came to realize that my spirit was older than my body when I was about four years old.

Shortly after my family moved to the small farm south of Albuquerque, my little brother Mark and I were playing under the old tamarack tree near the cowshed. Mark was two years younger than I and was still wearing a diaper while toddling around the barnyard.

Mother asked me to keep an eye on Mark while she hung snowy mounds of newly washed sheets and towels in the bright August sunshine. It must have been shortly after his birthday, as he was entranced by a brand new, brightly painted, musical top. On sudden impulse, I was curious to know how Mark would react if I took a rock and destroyed his toy; and so I did. Of course, Mark began to cry over the newly smashed lump of shiny metal; and that made me feel wretched. Wiping my own tears away, I ran to Mother and told her that I had been bad and needed to be punished. Turning from the clothesline, she paused a moment and searched my face with her deep-set blue eyes.

"No, you already understand that what you did was wrong. Just go apologize to your brother."

Sobbing, I hugged Mark and told him how sorry I was. He was soon distracted by a beetle desperately trying to hide beneath a log; but I spent a miserable afternoon, chastising myself for being so mean.

The thought processes, the understanding of right and wrong that my four-year-old self experienced, came from the same voice that I now hear at fifty-plus years of age. The only difference is that I have made many such mistakes and learned from most of them. These mistakes, complemented by my curiosity, have given me a broad expanse of knowledge. These mistakes and this learning have made my journey a success. It seems that we two-leggeds are lazy. When we are happy and everything is wonderful, we completely neglect to nurture our spirit. But when we suffer, we are forced to journey in the Seventh Direction in order to find comfort. Pain and suffering are the cattle prods that propel us further along the Red Road of spiritual growth.

My next step in understanding Oneness came from my desire to be involved with my brothers in everything, including the annual deer hunt. Our *Rancho Alegre*, west of Albuquerque, was remotely beautiful; but this isolation also dictated that my only companions were my brothers. Each fall the older boys spent weeks sighting in their hunting rifles and preparing for deer season. And after working side-by-side all year long, matching the boys stride for stride in everything we did, I refused to accept the exclusionary pronouncement that "girls do not hunt." As I told you in Chapter 1, I was finally allowed to join in this fall ritual after intensive lobbying. But I didn't really give you the full story.

My acceptance was conditional. Dove season came before deer season, and Johnny felt that it was an ideal proving ground for my "too-gentle" female nature. Yes, I could go deer hunting, but first I must participate in the dove hunt **and** eviscerate all of the birds we killed. No problem. Every Sunday we killed a chicken for dinner—this would be a snap. It wouldn't be much different than cleaning a hen.

Now I'm not particularly fond of chickens; roosters can be downright mean; and hens seem to make a mess everywhere you step. But mourning doves are a different matter. Their song is haunting, especially when it floats across the mesa in the sage-perfumed twilight. It is one of the few birdcalls that I ever successfully mastered, and I spent many evenings listening for their echoing song. Naturally, this year, our hunt was especially successful and we bagged over sixty birds. When we returned to the ranch, I resolved to make my brothers' favorite (dove pie) supper. I emptied the brown paper bags on the flagstone porch, and then sat next to the mountain of soft, pale gray bodies. Only the breast meat was edible, so I opened my pocket knife and set to work.

Our standard procedure on doves was to pluck the breast feathers, make a small incision at the base, then insert a finger and pull the breast free of the carcass. My six brothers eagerly stood in a small circle around me. I smiled confidently, cradled the first bird in my left hand while I made the incision, then thrust my right index finger into the chest cavity. And felt a heartbeat. My own heart stopped as I gazed at the leering faces surrounding me. I desperately wanted to scream or to cry; but I especially wanted to revive the dear, sweet bird in my hand. I knew, however, that this was not a viable option if I ever wanted to participate in "The Hunt." Still, my tumultuous emotions demanded release, so I began to laugh hysterically as though cleaning this bird was the most fun thing in the world. That October I was not left at home.

I loved animals, but I knew that we had to eat. Consequently, every killing (whether a dove or a deer) was a torturous spiritual moment for me. This all changed, however, when Nash, our Navajo friend, taught me a new spiritual outlook on my first deer hunt. That fall, he and I were hunting the same rim rock area; he was above and I was below. We were unaware of each other's presence until a buck and three doe bounded from their cover. We fired within seconds of each other, and the largest deer dropped immediately. When I arrived at "my" kill, Nash was already kneeling beside his body.

"Thank you, little Brother, for giving your life so that I may feed my family. Great Spirit, receive the soul of this brave deer."

I waited a respectful moment and then announced my presence with a question.

"Nash, why do you call him your brother?"

"He is my brother because we all have the same father and mother. Great Spirit is our father and Earth is our mother. When we die, our bodies turn to dust and feed the grass, and the grass feeds the animals, and they in turn feed us. It is very simple. We are all related."

"But why do you thank him for giving his life? He had no choice, you killed him."

"Yes, I killed him. But did you see the way that he bounded from cover, into the clearing, so that I had a clear shot? That is because his spirit chose to come into the body of a deer so that he could offer himself to feed us two-leggeds. It is a noble thing to offer your life so that others can live, no?"

Nash's simple words changed my life and whetted my appetite to know more of these American Indian teachings. When I was young, our current renaissance of American Indian thought and philosophy had not yet begun. There were no books that contained their wisdom, but through *kini*, my life was blessed with many American Indian friends who kindly taught me. Two of these most pivotal friendships occurred in high school and in college.

Puberty was an extremely difficult time for me. My mother's dying wish was that all of her children receive a Catholic education, and I have already told you about the callous words of one of these nuns after Mom's death. Coupled with this cold, hard treatment by the Sisters was my ostracism by my fellow classmates. Most children in Catholic school came from well-to-do families (who could afford the tuition) and lived in the city. My brothers and I were only able to attend due to the generosity of family friends, the Roneys, who provided us with scholarships.

My patched, secondhand clothing proclaimed a genteel poverty, and provided a ready target for harassment by my peers. I was blessed with one friend, however, who never seemed to take notice of what I wore or how poor I was. June, a Navajo Indian, accepted me without judgment and shared many of my same interests. We usually spent recess matching one another in foot races or trading stories and legends. I often sat in class mesmerized by June's gingham skirts heavily embroidered by her mother with Pueblo designs, and I wondered what it must be like to have such a nurturing relationship. June's friendship leavened my high school years with love and made them bearable. She taught me to value other human beings by what is on the inside, not the outside. She also taught me the difference that a single human being can make in another person's life.

My early life was blessed with other two-leggeds who taught me that the world is filled with many warm and loving people. As I said earlier, my first lesson in this love was from the Nanningas, the post-flood foster family for Mark and me. Years later, shortly after Mother's death, I met a lady at a coin-operated laundromat while I was washing our weekly twenty-six loads. She noted the piles of neatly folded Levi's, sorted by size, and asked about my family. As I told her our story, she became teary-eyed and explained that her husband of thirty years had just died. She said that she had been so involved in her own sorrow that she never even thought that life might be even more difficult for someone else. Over the next year, this complete stranger routinely made large batches of peanut butter cookies and delivered them out to our *Rancho Alegre*. Another patron of my father, Mary Speers, learned that I was ill one Christmas, cooked an entire banquet, and drove out to *Rancho Alegre* with it so that my brothers would have their holiday dinner.

Other examples of this beauty of spirit were our grocer, Roy Carson, and our neighbors, Suzie and Rufus Poole. Roy ran a small store on the west end of Albuquerque where my family always shopped. Unlike most businessmen, however, Roy never demanded payment. If we had the money, Roy cheerfully accepted it. If we didn't have the money, Roy cheerfully told my Dad to pay whenever and whatever he could.

Suzie and Rufus Poole befriended our family while they were building their beautiful adobe home west of Albuquerque on the palisades overlooking the Rio Grande River. In the parlance of the southwest, anyone within a ten-mile radius is considered a neighbor; but I would like to use a stronger term for the Pooles. They were more like guardian angels. They became patrons of Dad's art and established a scholarship (at the University of New Mexico) in Johnny's name after his death.

I remember building miniature roads one day when the Pooles first paid us a visit. A pale rose-colored Mercedes-Benz pulled up beside my brothers and me as we played in the sand; and Suzie asked where our father was. Dad later repeated my ingenuous announcement of the "beautiful lady and the old man" who had come to see him, and Suzie spent years repaying the compliment.

She became my mentor and "fairy" godmother, regularly surprising me with lovely gifts. Suzie had an exceptional voice and sang on Broadway in her early career. She also taught voice at the University of New Mexico and often appeared with the Albuquerque Symphony Orchestra. Unfortunately, my voice was beyond her professional abilities. She comforted me, nonetheless, and also assured me that my pubescent fencepost figure was the height of fashion and very much like that of Audrey Hepburn. She also graciously overlooked my freckled face and fine, brown hair. Thanks to Suzie, I actually thought I might be attractive and began to see myself in a different light.

Another mentor was my high school guidance counselor, Sheilah Garcia. My early life was a constant exercise in educating my father about the equality of women. He insisted that college was wasted on our "gentle sex," and would not allow me to apply for any of the scholarships that my 4.0 grade point average entitled me to. Fortunately, at the close of my senior year, Sheilah called me into her office and asked me why I wasn't going to college. When I told her my father's views on the matter (in spite of my hunger for a higher education), Sheilah set to work—beginning with a phone call to Dad. In order to continue taking care of my younger brothers, I had to live at home; but Sheilah solved that problem too. She not only obtained a scholarship for me to the University of New Mexico, but she also ensured that I had a car and gas for the hour-long drive into Albuquerque.

Si and Clare Lou Nanninga, Roy Carson, Suzie and Rufus Poole, and Sheilah Garcia all exhibited a high degree of compassion by giving what they could according to their means. Their kindness taught me to see Great Spirit in other two-legged human beings. Their acts of love are like the ripples from a stone in a pond; they keep multiplying and they have not yet reached the shore.

When I began my university studies, I was required to study psychology. At that time Freudian psychology was all that was taught. It seemed ridiculous to me that anyone could postulate that sexuality was the basis for all human behavior. My life experience had taught me differently. Personally, I had learned from my brothers that when I made their lives comfortable and happy I enriched my own life. I learned from my mentors and benefactors that human beings had a wonderful capacity for selfless love. This business of a hidden sexual agenda was absurd, as I informed my professor in many spirited discussions to no avail. I barely passed psychology and hated every moment of every class.

Freud seemed to reflect the world's view on the nature of two-legged beings, however; and I felt oddly out of sync. When I was in my late twenties, a friend of mine came to my rescue and recommended that I read Carl Jung's *Memories, Dreams, Reflections.* As already noted I voraciously read biographies, seeking the secrets of life, and initially thought that I was embarking upon just another life story. Instead, Jung opened a whole new world for me, the spirit world, and validated all of the metaphysical experiences of my life. When I read that Philemon was also his spirit guide, I knew that special energies had touched both of our lives. Here, at last, was someone else who understood and valued the spiritual dimensions of life.

My time at the university was interrupted by the birth of my two daughters followed by a divorce from their father. Raising my children without a college degree severely limited my earning power, and I resolved to get one. I had to work full time in order to pay the bills. Luckily, the College of Santa Fe had a special program for men and women like myself. Under its Open Studies program, we were given partial credit for our work experience and were also accommodated with evening and weekend classes. This time around I plugged the holes in my business administration curricula with courses in philosophy and really enjoyed myself.

Many of my fellow midlife students were from the eight northern pueblos surrounding Santa Fe, and they richly augmented my formal education. For example, at the end of one class session, discussion came to an impasse after an exhaustive examination of the conflicting teachings of two great philosophers. Even though the one scholar made a perfectly cogent argument about one aspect of life, still he was in conflict with the infallible logic of another philosopher on another facet of life. Every learned line of thought seemed to contradict every other line of thought. There was no Grand Unifying Theory of philosophy.

At last the Governor (Chief) of Taos Pueblo, Tom Lujan, decided that it was time to speak. He had been quiet through most of the debate, but now spoke in a low and dignified voice that we all strained to hear. I will try to paraphrase his words, twenty years after the fact, as well as my memory allows.

"It is all very simple. Our elders have taught us that we are all related. We are all a part of one another and part of the Great Spirit. While we are on this earth, we must walk the Good Red Road and love one another. When we have done this and we die, then we will return to the spirit world with Great Spirit."

We are all One. My mind did a great "Aha!" This is the Grand Unifying Theory of philosophy, and it took my red brothers to remind me of it and the other truths that I had learned from them as a child. In the intervening years, I have augmented these teachings with extensive research. As a result, I have compiled a bibliography of recommended readings which I have listed at the back of this book.

Two opposing truths cannot exist simultaneously. There must be an underlying fabric of logic to all truth that binds it together into one unified whole.

For example, we cannot argue that human beings are inherently good or evil because there is too much evidence to support either hypothesis. We can agree, however, that human beings have the *capacity* to be either good or evil. This indicates free will, and free will implies accountability. Simultaneously, we have verifiable evidence of certain predetermined factors in our lives evidenced through the science of astrology. Does this mean that our lives are predestined? And if so, this contradicts the concept of free will. Not necessarily. If we examine the entire issue within the unifying logic of unitheism, then we understand that we are all One. We were one with Great Spirit prior to occupying our physical body for the sake of spiritual growth. Prior to birth into this body, we participated with Great Spirit in determining the factors in our forthcoming life that would facilitate this spiritual growth. The choices we make when we are then confronted with these milestones come from our free will. This free will allows us to accept or reject opportunities to grow spiritually. Therefore, within the logic of unitheism, we can see that most of the events of our lives are predestined, but that these events enable our spiritual growth only through free will.

Another intriguing argument that presents conflicting truths is the theory of the duality of Great Spirit. A number of philosophers, including Jung, reached this conclusion as a means of explaining the existence of evil in the world in spite of the omnipotence of Great Spirit. They reasoned that the two truths—(1) evil is real and is pervasive, and (2) Great Spirit is all good and all powerful—cannot exist simultaneously. Therefore, since Great Spirit is all powerful, Great Spirit must also include good and evil. As proof for this hypothesis, adherents cite the duality prevalent within the natural world: night and day, man and woman, positive and negative, yin and yang. This line of reasoning also concludes that evil (such as the devil) is a natural, and even necessary, part of this world. A young man once told me that it was okay to lie, cheat, steal, or kill because it was part of the natural yin/yang energy of reality. He felt that he had to fulfill his nature by being bad in order that someone else could be good.

This is fatally flawed logic. Unitheism provides a better answer. Science has proven that only harmonious energy can expand upon itself exponentially. **Only** harmonious energy has the potential for infinity. Science has also proven that dissonant energy is finite; it will end. Since Great Spirit is infinite, dissonant energy cannot be one of His/Her attributes. If we closely examine the world around us, we find that dissonant energy is always the result of our human free will. It is important, however, to distinguish this dissonant energy from the inherent forces of nature. The forces of nature are not evil; they are not dissonant energy but are the natural evolution of our physical world and our universe to One Energy. Volcanoes, flooding, and violent storms are simply a part of this process. If human beings are killed in the process, it is because they themselves determined these spiritual milestones for their souls prior to birth.

This concept of self-determining the time and manner of our death came to me out of personal experience and from the testimony of people who have returned from the dead. I know that on two different occasions I was very close to death and was asked by my spirit guide if that was my wish. This process is part of the logical fabric of unitheism when we understand that we are cocreators of the events in our life, for dying is simply one final aspect of living. This, of course, is all hypothesis. Only Great Spirit knows all truth.

Great Spirit is **all** good and is entirely harmonious energy. It is human beings who bring evil into the world through free will. There is no logic in the concept that Great Spirit created a "devil." Great Spirit logically would not create an evil being. Great Spirit is all good and is completely harmonious energy which ensures His/Her infinity. If Great Spirit created evil,

He/She would then participate in evil with its limiting vibration, and therefore not be infinite.

This Biblical creature, the devil, may be simply a metaphor for the spirits of humans who have clung to their dissonant ways even after death. As for the dual energies of night and day, man and woman, positive and negative, yin and yang, I would argue that they are not so much opposite as they are complementary; each complements and completes the other.

We walk in beauty. We are surrounded by Great Spirit's love and embraced by Mother Earth who is ready to nurture all of our needs. Great Spirit has given us everything that we need to walk the Good Red Road and return to the eternal harmony of the spirit world. But we are free to choose. Sadly, we have developed a society that defines success in terms of money and fame. Both money and fame were developed by human beings and carry a dissonant energy. Logically, then, our society must redefine success. If we travel through this life, learning by our mistakes and by the events that we encounter, then every single one of us is successful. "Success is a journey, not a destination."

Chapter Notes

1. A. W. Watts, *Psychotherapy East and West*, New York: Pantheon Books, 1961, p. 151.
2. Dr. A. C. Ross (Ehanamani), *Mitakuye Oyasin "We are all related"*, Denver, CO: Wic'one Wast'e, 1996, p. 19.
3. J. E. Brown, *The Spiritual Legacy of the American Indian*, p. 113.

Journey's End

> *"Many of us believe that one may be born more than once, and there are some who claim to have full knowledge of a former incarnation. There are also those who believe in a 'twin spirit' born into another tribe or race."*
>
> Ohiyesa (Sioux)
> *The Soul of an Indian*

Life after life is a determinant reality for many traditional American Indian people who see spirits and ghosts as a natural part of this world. Mark St. Pierre and Tilda Long Soldier provide us with an analysis of this traditional spirit life in *Walking in the Sacred Manner.*[1] In this book, they detail the four distinct attributes of the soul based on interviews with numerous Sioux holy men and women.

First is *Niyan,* or the "breath of life." This is the very essence of life that Great Spirit breathes into us at the moment of birth; we draw our first breath, and our soul enters our body. Most paintings by American Indians reflect this breath of life as a type of bubble drawn within an animal or person. This *niyan* is thought to hold the corporal body together with the *wana'gi* (intelligent ghost) during life. In other words, *niyan* bonds the physical body with the soul.

Brown speaks to the issue of *niyan* in *The Spiritual Legacy of The American Indian.*

> ... In his seminal essay 'Verbal Art,' Dennis Tedlock reminds us that it is the breath that, universally identified with the essence of life itself, and proceeding from the center of a person's being nearest the heart, bears and fashions the word. Interpersonal verbal communication involves the intermingling of the being's most sacred element, thus establishing

through breath made audible the bond of sacred relationship not only between people, but with all phenomena throughout the cosmos. ...

The majority of Native American names, both personal and sacred, refer to animals, or their qualities, and also to other forms of forces of nature. Further, a person's sacred name, which is never used in every day speech, was normally obtained through prayer and sacrifice in the Vision Quest. In everyday Native American languages, words and names have sacred power; one uses them carefully, for their power affects both speaker and hearer.[2]

Sicun, or the Spirit Helper, is the second aspect of the soul. This Spirit Helper is an ally that is acquired at the moment of birth and remains throughout life. I acquired my Spirit Helper, Philemon, at birth. (As you will recall, he was the wise elder man who appeared to me in a dream shortly after my mother died.) When we die, these helpers return to the spirit world or choose to again help another mortal.

When I was young I was often comforted by Philemon, but I had no idea who he was or why he was attached to me. As I related in the last chapter, I first came across formal mention of his name when I read Carl Jung's *Memories, Dreams, Reflections* in my late twenties. Philemon was also Jung's *sicun*. I have never felt worthy of having the same Spirit Helper as the great philosopher. However, as I work on this book, it seems clear that Philemon's spiritual work is to help bring new philosophical understanding into the world. I am simply an instrument toward this end.

Nonetheless, I often wondered just who Philemon was and why he was compelled to help philosophers. Then late one night not long ago, I was reading Shakespeare's *Pericles, Prince of Tyre*, when I stumbled upon the character, Philemon. He was the associate of Cerimon, the learned healer and "master of the secrets of nature" who restored Pericles' nearly-dead wife to life. Both medicine men, Philemon and Cerimon, lived on an island in the Mediterranean and are thought to be based on a true Greek story dating from around the year A.D. 400. (If you will remember, Philemon wore a long white, Grecian-style robe when he appeared to me.) Cerimon claims that "I ever have studied physic, through which secret art, by turning o'er authorities, I have, together with my practice, made familiar to me and to my aid the blest infusions that dwell in vegetive, in metals, stones; And I can speak of the disturbances that nature works, and of her cures..." Perhaps this is just a coincidence in names, but I feel that there are too many similarities to entirely discount any connection.

Wana'gi, or ghost, is the third critical aspect of the soul. The *wana'gi* is the ghost of a living person, the intelligent soul. *Wana'gi* can make themselves visible, and will resemble their living, human form. *Wana'gi* can be malevolent or benevolent, the way they were in life. It is the *wana'gi* which the medicine man or woman calls upon as a spirit helper. It was the *wana'gi* of my brother Johnny who came to me to console me over his death. It was his *wana'gi* that helped me by forewarning me of my brother Mark's death, then Jeff's, Dad's, and Grandpa's deaths. Jackie Yellow Tail, a Crow Indian, provides further explanation.

> We call the place you go at death the 'Other-side Camps.' That's the closest translation I could come to. I don't think there is a word for 'hell' in our native language. There is no word for 'devil.' Some people call it the 'Happy Hunting Grounds,' but we Crow call it the 'Other-side Camps.' It is the next spiritual plane.
>
> When our people are dying, the people from the Other-side come to get them. They take them to be with the loved ones who have gone on before. It is a loved one, a favorite grandma or perhaps grandpa, who comes to speak with them and tell them their time is near. We consider this to be a blessing.[3]

I consider Johnny's forewarnings a blessing, too. It was a great help to me spiritually to be prepared for these losses and to cherish the final hours on earth with my loved ones.

The fourth and final attribute of the soul is called *Ton. Ton* is an innate spiritual power that makes the soul holy. *Ton* is also what American Indians call "Medicine," and what the Taoist philosophers call Chi. This is the presence of Great Spirit that pervades the universe, including our being. Only our free will creates dissonance in this energy. When we are in harmony with Great Spirit this power is unleashed and we have great Medicine.

This innate spiritual power, *Ton,* can be enhanced by our actions, creating a vortex of harmonious energy that magnetically attracts other harmonious energy in the form of people, animals, places, and events. Our *Ton* is also enhanced with harmonious symbols. Remember that harmonious energy, added to harmonious energy, has an exponential result. For example, certain American Indian symbols, such as the eagle or lightning, have Medicine (or energy enhancement). Traditionally, American Indians choose their symbols based on visions or dreams, for these indicate medicine specific to that person.

Similarly, I wear as many Mother Earth symbols (such as my concho belt) as I can because of their harmony. In American Indian legend, earth was created from vast oceans of water when a turtle gathered mud from the bottom and built an island. My conchos, styled after turtle shells, are a conscious statement of love and respect for Mother Earth.

In closing this book, I would like to share one final, very special story with you. This story centers around a *wana'gi* who inhabited our home when we first moved here.

My initial encounter with this ghost was shortly after we moved into our old Victorian ranch house. I only rarely visited our cellar, located just under the kitchen, because it made my skin crawl. On this particular morning, I was using the downstairs bathroom (just off of the kitchen and also above the cellar) when I heard a deep male voice speaking in a foreign language. Thinking that my husband was playing a trick on me, I yelled at him to stop teasing me.

Nonetheless, I heard this same voice several other times and always when I was in that particular bathroom. I never seriously thought much about these incidents until one day it occurred to me that Harold was nowhere around when I heard this strange man speaking. In fact, this phenomenon seemed to always happen just after Harold left for the Post Office to pick up our mail. In our small town, this is a major social event. Everyone comes into town around the same time, collects their letters and newspapers, and then stands around catching up on the latest gossip. My Harold is a talker, and this simple errand usually takes him several hours.

Consequently, I became a bit uneasy when I realized that Harold could not possibly be the "voice." Unfazed, however, I simply decided that I could solve this problem by never using the downstairs bathroom again. But then I heard the voice in the kitchen. It was unmistakable—a deep, resonant, male voice, speaking Italian. I spun around to see just who was talking, but there was no one there and the voice continued. I cautiously approached, trying to comprehend what was happening. It occurred to me that perhaps my radio was sending errant sound waves. I decided to investigate further, so I slowly walked around the voice, poked my finger into the empty air, and asked, "How are you doing that?"

It still didn't occur to me that this was a ghost. I always thought that the concept of ghosts was quite logical, but everything I read indicated that a cloudy human form always accompanied the voice. I saw no otherworldly form; I only heard the voice. Each time it manifested, I failed to really listen, and instead tried to analyze the "how" of it. I shared my experience with Harold alone, as I was half afraid that most people would question my sanity. I didn't dare tell our daughters. We live in a remote area, and I was sure that they would never stay at the ranch alone if they thought they had a ghost for company.

Our phantom visitor finally brought the situation to a climax all by himself. Late one night, our youngest daughter, Jessica, woke me from my sleep in near hysterics.

"Mom! Mom! I think I'm going crazy!"

I sleepily asked her why she was so upset, thinking that she had a bad dream. But she said that something had awakened her, and when she opened her eyes she saw *him*. *He* was a cloudlike form of a man, and was speaking in a very deep voice—in a foreign language. I assured Jessica that she wasn't crazy, that I had heard him but never told her because I didn't want to frighten her. I couldn't assuage her fears, so she slept in my bed for the next few weeks, too frightened to be alone.

This was the final straw. Something had to be done about our new "friend." I tried talking to him, but he wouldn't appear on request. I prayed for him, but he still insisted on talking to me, usually at the most inopportune times. I tried writing messages to him on my computer, telling him that he was dead and needed to go toward the light; but he wouldn't leave. Then an old cowboy happened to visit the ranch. He had once worked here, so I gladly gave him a tour of the ranch house and our restoration efforts. Then, I casually asked him if anyone had ever died here.

He looked away for a few moments and gravely answered. He supposed that it was all right to tell me now, since the man he promised to protect was now dead. Yes, about thirty years ago, the ranch owner had killed the foreman. He showed me the spot on the upstairs landing where the poor man was shot. They had a terrible argument and resorted to guns to settle the matter. One of the other ranch hands helped bury the body in the basement. This cowboy confided in my friend, but bound him to secrecy.

I thought it was a tragic but fascinating tale and asked him to repeat it into my tape recorder. Several months later a second old cowboy told me virtually the same story.

I still didn't know what to do about my mysterious *wana'gi*. An uneasy air had now settled over our old ranch house. Both of my daughters avoided the issue of our "guest," but they were also reluctant to stay in the house by themselves. Fortunately, a friend of mine came to visit about this time. Honey and I share many of the same philosophies and always have an excellent time when we're together. I was fairly confident that she knew I was sane, so one day I told her that we had a troublesome phantom (but gave her no other details). I knew that she had psychic gifts, and I gratefully accepted when she volunteered to try to contact him. Of her many wonderful talents, her ability to contact our *wana'gi* will always rank highest on my list.

We smudged the kitchen with sage, and Honey sat down at my laptop computer for a ghostly dialog. She took a deep breath, closed her eyes, and her fingers began to race across the keyboard. As she mentally conversed with our phantom, her fingers typed so fast that I couldn't even read the words. At the end of her session, we printed what her flying fingers had typed.

First, our ghost introduced himself as an Italian named Anatole. (I should have known he was a Latin lover—he first began talking to me when I dropped my britches!) He was extremely polite and apologized profusely for having frightened my daughter. He hadn't intended any harm; it was just that he was stuck on this side and could not go on. When he found that Jessica and I were tuned to his vibration, he had to let us know that he had been murdered and was buried in our basement. He was a devout Catholic and was sure that his soul could not progress without receiving the last rites and a proper Catholic burial.

He was murdered because he was blackmailing the owner of our ranch. When he threatened to increase the amount of the blackmail, he and the owner had their fatal argument. Now, after more than thirty years, he was ecstatic to find someone on his same vibrational level and finally be able to communicate his tragedy. When he tried to talk, however, he became highly emotional and lapsed into his native Italian. This was why I never understood what he was saying, even though I could hear him. Anatole promised to leave if only I could somehow manage to have the final sacrament of Extreme Unction given to him. He also requested a Catholic burial at our local cemetery.

Honey had truly communicated with our *wana'gi*. Before her amazing session, I told her nothing about our ghost other than the fact that he existed. What she wrote of him (and by him) corroborated and expanded on what the two old cowboys had told me. I now had positive verification. But how was I to proceed?

Early the next day I phoned the sheriff and told him the story, asking permission to exhume the body for proper burial. But the sheriff informed me that it was illegal for me to disturb a crime scene. He said that there was no statute of limitations on murder, even though the murderer was now a very old man. He requested copies of my taped interviews with the cowboys and a transcript of Anatole's story. He then took the matter to the district attorney, who instructed him to dig for the body. After a preliminary investigation of the ranch house, the sheriff found several bullet holes on the upstairs landing. I had never noticed them, even though that was the spot where the shooting supposedly took place. This was getting far more complicated than I had expected.

Arrangements were made, and soon the sheriff and two deputies were in my basement, trying to find Anatole's body. We found the gravesite, just where the cowboys had said it would be. As the men dug, I flinched each time their shovel hit a rock, feeling certain that poor Anatole's skull was being crushed. As the grave grew deeper, we found a few children's marbles and some gum wrappers. The ground had been disturbed. At approximately four feet, we struck water and the sides of the hole began to cave in. We decided to abandon the search before someone was hurt.

I was relieved and dismayed all at the same time. I hadn't really wanted to find a body, but I did want to free Anatole's spirit. Unfortunately, it seemed that he now would be our guest forever. His soul would never get to where it was supposed to be. As a last resort, I contacted a friend of ours who is a priest. I explained the situation, and he agreed to come to the ranch and give Anatole the last rites. When the ceremony ended, there was a palpable difference in the house. Everyone could feel the change. It has now been six years since Anatole received his last rites, and I have neither heard nor seen him again. I am sure that he is finally at peace.

Honey found that Anatole was not our only ghostly guest. There were three other phantoms in the barn: two little boys and one older woman. I had suspected that something was remiss for the horses' stalls were often mysteriously opened during the night. At other times Cisco would act so frightened that he refused to leave the safety of his stall. The tin plates in the trapper's cabin would inexplicably fly across the room and land in a heap behind the wood stove. Honey explained that this was the work of young Charlie trying to get my attention. It seems that he and his older brother had died in the 1880s typhoid epidemic and were buried in the cemetery. However, Charlie didn't get a nice headstone like his brother did, and he was going to stick around and raise a fuss until he did.

At first I was quite reluctant to believe that our small ranch had a ghost population that almost exceeded its living occupants. And, if this were true, why? If there were so many ghosts at our residence, what about all of the other homes and bars and brothels around the world? I find it interesting that it was not Great Spirit who had imprisoned these ghosts. They kept themselves locked into a time frame for temporal reasons: a religious ceremony, a headstone, a beloved husband. Their free will kept them from Oneness with Great Spirit.

My experience with Anatole taught me how to sense the presence of spirits, and it is distressing to find how many of them have bound themselves to this world. I feel that the answer to this problem lies in the energies revealed by astrology. Astrological ages consist of approximately 2,150 years and measure the period of time required for the vernal equinox (March 21) to pass through all 30 degrees of one sign of the zodiac. This is known as the Procession of the Equinoxes, and it is caused by the imperceptible but constant shift of the earth as it spins on its axis. Astrologers believe that we are nearing the end of the astrological Age of Pisces, symbolized by the fish and Christ's revolutionary teachings of love.

Our new millennium, the Age of Aquarius (the truth seeker), will begin shortly after the year 2000, and will impart the energy of Oneness. This energy will impel human beings to join together as one people in brotherhood and humanitarianism. Uranus, the ruling planet of Aquarius, is the seventh planet from the Sun, and is imbued with the energy of change and originality. "Uranus was the Roman sky god, the first ruler of the universe. In astrology Uranus is the planet of the future, associated with modern science, invention, electricity, humanitarian movements, and revolution. It is the planet of sudden upheaval and swift, unexpected happenings."[4]

Therefore, the Age of Aquarius will be alive with similar energies. Besides motivating the spirit of Oneness, Aquarius will rule the air waves. It is also a sign of mental energy, indicating that human beings will evolve into their mental potential—the sixth chakra. We two-leggeds began at the first, or root chakra (at the base of the spine), when we were one with the animals. We gradually evolved to our second chakra (located at the spleen), and became emotional beings; then to our third chakra (the vortex of the etheral and physical bodies at the solar plexus) when we became spiritual beings and our souls entered our bodies. At this point, we became human beings, *homo sapiens*. As the Age of Pisces began, we evolved to the heart chakra which brought the Christ's revolutionary message of love for one another. As the Age of Pisces draws to a close we have evolved into our fifth chakra (at the throat) and our ability to communicate has revolutionized the world.

Now, as we move into our sixth chakra (located on the brow, between the eyes), we will begin to realize and develop the full potential of the mind. We will come to a full understanding that we are One, and the combination of these two energies will compel us to fully evolve spiritually by helping those poor spirits who have locked themselves into this world. One of the major spiritual tasks of the Age of Aquarius will be to release ghosts from their haunts and help them proceed toward harmony with Great Spirit.

Ghosts, spirit guides, visions, miracles, pain, joy, Oneness—all of the mysteries of this life begin to fall into place when we adopt American Indian spirituality. Our Red Brothers and Sisters have shared their wisdom, and have given us direction for following the Good Red Road. For this is their gift to the world. Wounye' Waste' Win, Good Lifeways Woman, offers this final insight for our journey song.

> ... don't judge or compare your spiritual experience with somebody else's. Don't compare yourself with books; you'll always come up short. The more you follow the inner voice, that quiet voice, the more you will learn and grow in your own way.
>
> Sometimes you hear a voice, sometimes you feel or understand something. Maybe it will be a new song [of the soul]. When you hear it, feel it, there will be a deep knowingness that you can trust. When you're true to that, your understanding [of sacred things] will grow stronger.[5]

MITAKUYE OYASIN!

Chapter Notes

1. M. St. Pierre and Tilda Long Soldier, op. cit., p. 49.
2. J. E. Brown, op. cit., p. 126.
3. M. St. Pierre and Tilda Long Soldier, op. cit., p. 95.
4. J. M. Woolfolk, op. cit., p. 328.
5. M. St. Pierre and Tilda Long Soldier, op. cit., p. 209.

Spirit Rider

The Spirit Rider on the Thunder Horse who was killed in battle is taking the last phase of his journey to the spirit world. After spending the traditional four days on the burial scaffold, his spirit is set free to make the final journey.

Journey Song

Trust Great Sprit, Trust Great Spirit.

MITAKUYE OYASIN!

Love the Truth and by it live.

MITAKUYE OYASIN!

Walk life's path with Simplicity.

MITAKUYE OYASIN!

Bathe yourself and others with Patience.

MITAKUYE OYASIN!

Carry only Compassion in your heart.

MITAKUYE OYASIN!

Seek Knowledge of our Creator and enhance your spirit.

MITAKUYE OYASIN!

Bibliography

Books:

Aveni, A. *Conversing With the Planets.* New York: Times Books, 1992.

Berendt, J. E. *The World Is Sound.* Vermont: Destiny Books, 1991.

Brown, J. E. *The Spiritual Legacy of the American Indian.*

Campbell, J. *The Power of Myth.* New York: Doubleday, 1988.

Campion, N. *The Practical Astrologer.* New York: Abrams, 1987.

Diamond, J., M.D. *Your Body Doesn't Lie.* New York: Warner Books, 1979.

Gard, R., ed. *Buddhism.* New York: Braziller, 1961.

Gregory, R. L., ed. *The Oxford Companion to the Mind.* Oxford, England: Oxford University Press, 1987.

Hunt, I., and W. Draper. *Lightning In His Hand—The Life Story of Nikola Tesla.* Denver: Sage Books, 1964.

Jampolsky, G. G., M.D. *Love Is Letting Go of Fear.* Berkeley: Celestial Arts, 1979.

Johnson, S. *The Book of Elders: The Life Stories & Wisdom of Great American Indians.* San Francisco: Harper Collins, 1994.

Jung, C. G. *Memories, Dreams, Reflections.* New York: Random, 1973.

Lao Tzu. *Tao Te Ching.* New York: Harper & Row, 1988.

Luthans, F. *Organizational Behavior.* New York: McGraw Hill, 1981.

Mails, T. *Fools Crow.* Lincoln, Neb.: University of Nebraska Press, 1979.

Maslow, A. *Toward a Psychology of Being.* New York: Von Nostrand Reinhold, 1968.

McGaa, E., Eagle Man. *Mother Earth Spirituality.* San Francisco: Harper, 1990.

————. *Rainbow Tribe.* San Francisco: Harper, 1992.

————. *Native Wisdom.* Minneapolis, MN: Four Directions Publishing, 1995.

Neihardt, J. G. *Black Elk Speaks.* New York: Simon & Schuster, 1932.

Nerburn, Kent, ed. *The Soul of an Indian and Other Writings from Ohiyesa (Charles Alexander Eastman).* San Rafael, California: Classic Wisdom Collection, New World Library, 1993.

Pogrebin, L. *Family Politics.* New York: McGraw-Hill, 1983.

Ross, Dr. A. C. (Ehanamani). *Mitakuye Oyasin "We are all related."* Denver, CO: Wic'one Wast'e, 1996.

Shallis, M. *The Electric Connection.* New York: New Amsterdam, 1988.

Schumacher, E. F. *Small Is Beautiful.* New York: Harper & Row, 1973.

St. Pierre, M., and Tilda Long Soldier. *Walking in the Sacred Manner.* New York: Simon & Schuster Touchstone Books, 1995.

Swan, J. A. *Sacred Places.* Santa Fe: Bear & Co., 1990.

Utley, R. M. *The Lance and The Shield.* New York: Henry Holt & Co., 1993.

Watts, A. W. *Psychotherapy East and West.* New York: Pantheon books, 1961.

Wilcox, M. *Blue and Yellow Don't Make Green.* Cincinnati: 1989.

Woolfolk, J. M. *The Only Astrology Book You'll Ever Need.* Lanham, MD: Scarborough House, 1990.

Weatherford, J. *Indian Givers: How the Indians of the Americas Transformed the World.* New York: Ballantine Books, 1988.

Article:

Gazette Telegraph. May 12, 1992, Colorado Springs, Colorado.

Gazette Telegraph. May 22, 1992, Colorado Springs, Colorado.

Index

MAIL ORDER FORM
for the book entitled

Journey Song

A Spiritual Legacy of the American Indian

Description		Total
1 copy	$15.00 ea	
2–10 copies	$14.00 ea	
11 or more copies	$13.00 ea	
Postage (book rate)*		
1–10 copies	Add $1.50 per book	
11 or more copies	$10.00	
Handling	Add $1.50 per order	1.50
	Total:	

*Airmail Orders: Add $5.00 per book for orders outside of the U.S.A. For orders from outside North America, add $8.00 per book.

Make checks, money orders, and P.O.'s payable to:
(Sorry, no Credit Cards accepted)

Grey Wolves
P.O. Box 187
Florissant, CO   80816-0187

Internet Address: www.sunweaver.com/writers/journeysong

Mail books to:

Name: _____

Address: _____

_____

City:_____ State: _____ ZIP: _____

For wholesale orders please contact:

Grey Wolves
P.O. Box 187
Florissant, CO   80816-0187
(719) 748-3562